THE
NEW
DEAL

A FAIR DEAL FOR BLACK AMERICA?

ROBERT LIVINGSTON

SWEETSPIRE LITERATURE
—— MANAGEMENT ——

ISBN
978-1-964035-95-6 (Paperback)
978-1-964035-96-3 (eBook)

Dedication

To The New Dealers Who Changed Our World

Table of Contents

Other Books By Robert Livingston

- The Sailor And The Teacher
- Travels With Ernie
- Leaping Into The Sky
- Blue Jackets
- Fleet
- Harlem On The Western Front
- W.t. Stead And The Conspiracy Of 1910
- To Save The World
- In The Wake Of The Empress Of China
- The Forgotten Chaplain
- Axis Sally
- The Tarnished Rose
- American Stories 1940 - 1960
- The Anchor And The Journalist
- Taste The Wind
- A Dean's Life

Introduction

In the fall of 1960 I was enrolled in a graduate seminar at San Francisco State. The course focused on Franklin D. Roosevelt's New Deal. My professor, a quiet, introspective guy who had taught at Ohio State University before moving to Baghdad by the Bay, put the class of seven youthful scholars through our paces. We met one night each week from 7 to 9:30 p.m. in the newly constructed Social Science Building. I was expected to actively participate in a lively and often heated discussion of the Roosevelt Administration's efforts to deal with the calamity of the Great Depression. By the end of the semester I was well versed in the various then current interpretations of historians and economists as to the success of the New Deal.

After graduating from San Francisco State with a degree in U.S. History and as a credentialed teacher I taught many years at the high school level. Of course, I always gave special attention to the New Deal and its implications for American society. In time, however, I came to understand that my instruction was self-limiting. I gave a somewhat one-sided glimpse of the 1930's and what the New Dealers tried to accomplish. That is, my teaching reflected and assumed that the New Deal policies treated all citizens with fairness regardless of race, gender, or social-economic background. In doing so I was expressing a conventional, if not sympathetic view as put forth by historians at the time. However, for the most part those interpretations did not include, nor did they reflect the critical views of Black historians.

In time I altered my lessons to reflect a wider picture of the New Deal that included a more detailed understanding of its impact on people of color. This effort on my part gained importance during the Civil Rights Movement of the 1960's and beyond, even as my classes represented increased student diversity. This, I should make clear, was not revisionist history with an axe to grind or a political statement to make. It was simply an effort to be more inclusive and expansive based on the newest information available. Inclusive in that I was more aware of research by Black historians; expansive in I would now share a larger picture of the past with my students.

Over the years I had always wanted to write about the New Deal. After writing a number of books on other topics in retirement I finally decided to tackle the topic. I had accumulated a mass of material related to the topic. I now wanted to merge my lecture notes and bountiful research into a compelling narrative. In doing so two challenging questions lurked in the shadows awaiting scrutiny. Was systemic racism embedded in President Roosevelt's efforts to overcome the economic pain and suffering brought about by the Great Depression? More to the point was the New Deal actually a "Fair Deal" for Blacks? These questions I was determined to answer.

As often happens when revisiting the past there is sometimes no clear answer to our inquiries. In that sense history is a fickle creature, teasing as it discloses, yet always, it seems, holding back a few things for still another day. Because of this a review of the past is not always straightforward and certainly never complete Even the most objective analysis may be muddled by a multitude of facts that illuminate just short of a clear and unequivocal understanding that borders on elusive truth. And, of course, historians must always be mindful of selecting facts to justify preconceived notions or desired conclusions. That is, a trap to be avoided. Always there is the challenge to avoid superimposing our contemporary values on the past and those who came before us. In doing so we must balance subjectivity with the stern eye of objectivity. Interpretations of history must be grounded on provable historical facts. This is not always easy to do, or comforting in what is divulged. Probing the past can lead to unanticipated conclusions that are disquieting. As such, there are no guarantees when delving into the past.

In writing this book I departed from the traditional sequential approach to history, I didn't take a linear stance of the past, this first, then that, all in chronological order. Rather I envisioned a circular approach, one akin to our Solar System with planets revolving around the sun, all interconnected by physical forces. In a similar fashion the various events of the 1930's spiraled around the White House and the policies of FDR, all interconnected by the gravity of history.

A great many photographs were included in this work to provide the reader with a visual sense of the topics covered. In addition, where possible newspaper headlines were included to document the text.

In taking on this task I was cognizant of my own sympathetic views toward President Roosevelt and the programs implemented by the New Deal. Holding those preconceptions in check required a tight rein. Hopefully, this has been accomplished. That said, the historian Henry Steel Commager provided the challenge I have tried to meet.

History is a jangle of accidents, blunders, surprises and absurdities, and so is our knowledge of it, but if we are to report it at all we must impose some order upon it.

CHAPTER 1 – WORDS

Words are important to those who study history. They are the tools by which the "what," the "when," and the "where" of history can be determined, but not always the "why." We must, however, use words to create a narrative that will be useful in evaluating President Franklin D. Roosevelt's New Deal policies in the 1930s. This will be challenging since words used for partisan purposes may lead to a kaleidoscope of interpretations. This is especially true of a controversial figure such as FDR and his efforts to deal with the Great Depression. Millions of words thrown into the heavens about this Democrat in the White House are, in the end, about the exact polarizing, larger-than-life figure.

FRANKLIN D. ROOSEVELT

In William Shakespeare's *Romeo and Juliet,* this sense of imagery was brought to light when Juliet said," What's in a name? That which we call a rose By any other name would smell as sweet.

(Act II, Scene II)

Take, for example, the word patriot. What does it mean? For some, it is an unabashed love and loyalty to the nation; that is, supporting the government, whether right or wrong. Others might argue that dissent is the most critical reflection of a patriot living in a democracy. Some might claim that patriotism refers to the willingness of citizens to defend the country in times of need. For some, Roosevelt was an unholy traitor to his aristocratic class, an unpatriotic tyrant in the presidency, usurping the rights of the privileged and powerful. For Roosevelt, they had a "burning bitterness." For others, he was a defender of democracy, both in war and peace, a patriot seeking always to make a more just world for the average citizen. Though there are differences of patriotic expression, Juliet's injunction still rings true: "a rose by any other name…" is still a Roosevelt.

Words convey meanings and emotions, invoking a predisposition to respond based on our past experiences. Indeed, the political lexicon is rife with such words: liberal, conservative, radical, authoritarian, and socialist. In other words, they joined together to invoke a response and dot the political landscape: "Big spender," "Soft on crime," "Too idealistic," or "Too authoritarian." And, of course, the names of our political parties bring instant recognition and a constellation of feelings: Republican, Democrat, Progressive, or Socialist. Words are the glue that makes the tangible expression of our political thoughts possible in a diverse society linked by a common acceptance of constitutional government. And so it was with the Roosevelt Administration.

Words can enlighten or threaten, and often they can hurt, no matter what children learn.

Sticks and stones may break one's bones, but names will never hurt one.

"This adage from England presents an incomplete truth. Words can hurt. For example, he is unpatriotic. He is disloyal. He is a traitor. He is a dictator. Though he was elected four times to the White House as the leader of the Democratic Party, President Roosevelt was called all these things and. Obscene and cruel jokes were jabbed at the president and his family. Negative stories were circulated about his crippled legs and his0020bout with polio. It was said his wife gave him gonorrhea after she contracted it from a Negro. Some of the criticism was tinged with anti-Semitism. It was rumored that FDR descended from Dutch Jews and that the family name had been changed to Roosevelt. Though most Americans saw through this ugliness, it was also true that Roosevelt's name was unspeakable in many households. By way of example, some Republicans often referred to Roosevelt as merely "that man," never desiring to mention his name. At other times, he was simply FDR, stated with grimaces and snide comments that he would retire to his Hyde Park estate on the Hudson River. In contrast, millions of supporters merely hung a simple picture on a wall, a quiet reminder of a president in whom they had placed their hopes.

ON THE WALL

On a personal level, Roosevelt could shake off these cruel jabs as just political red meat to arouse opposition to his policies. He knew that politics was a sharp-elbowed endeavor. The president, however, had a disarming way to deal with unfair, even hateful criticism. He used humor to defrock his critics. On September 23, 1944, by way of example, the president spoke at a campaign dinner hosted by the International Brotherhood of Teamsters. With a smile and the microphone, the president responded to a maelstrom of vicious charges about his little dog, Fala. Conservative Republicans charged the president with spending $20 million of taxpayers' money to send an American destroyer to the Aleutian Islands to fetch his dog, who had been accidentally left on a remote island. Of course, the story was untrue, but rather than saying that straightforwardly, the president said:

These Republican leaders have not been content with attacks on me, or my wife, or on my sons. No, not content with that, they now include my little dog, Fala. Well, of course, I don't resent attacks, and my family doesn't resent attacks, but Fala does resent them.

FALA AND THE PRESIDENT

Roosevelt was excoriated as a communist, damned as a "traitor of his (wealthy) class, and hated for "disregarding property rights and violating the canons of the capitalistic marketplace." The "better-off" held a consuming dislike for the New Deal and that man in the White House, and they let him know it. In response, the president blasted the privileged naysayers as "narrow-minded agents of greed."

The president's wife was attacked unceasingly in the press and on the radio by those opposed to the New Deal and her political power as the First Lady. Westbrook Pegler, the noted conservative columnist, attacked her as a threat to America. He said:

After years of masquerading as a rather naïve but always well-meaning amateur fuss-budget, Mrs. Eleanor Roosevelt lately has been revealing herself as a cunning and indefatigable conspirator against the rights and independence of the individual American citizen and an active proponent of power government.

The president and his family needed a tough political hide to deal with the criticism that came their way. The same was true of the New Dealers in the Roosevelt Administration who assisted in formulating public policies. One accusation, however, was difficult to accept and challenging to deny: that there was a racist element to New Deal programs to thwart the havoc sewn by the Stock Market Crash in 1929 and the ensuing collapse of the economy.

In dealing with the Great Depression, many contemporary historians have accused the Roosevelt Administration's New Deal policies of being prejudicial toward Blacks based on racial distinctions prevalent in America in the 1930s. The accusation suggests a pre-judgment or an irrational attitude towards Blacks, the living legacy of "slave days." Was this an expected outcome of the president and his supporters, nearly all white? Those holding this view suggested the New Dealers were influenced by Jim Crow attitudes, not solely restricted to the post-Civil War South. Racial views, whether explicit or implicit, were deeply embedded in the president's advisors, so the argument goes. The contention, therefore, was that "institutional racism" played a prominent role in developing and implementing New Deal policies to deal with the economic collapse that shattered the prosperity of the "Roaring 20s."

WAS THE NEW DEAL GOOD FOR ALL AMERICANS?

In dealing with the New Deal, we are confronted by difficult questions. If the policies were racist, was that the result of individuals who cultivated such views, or was something more at work beyond individual bias and prejudice? Was the alleged racism already built into the various social systems of our society, in stark contrast to our cherished notion of a "color-blind society?" Were the New Deal policies regarding housing, education, healthcare, and unemployment the result of institutional racism? Did the New Deal policies complicate or even encourage already negative social patterns? In the challenging arena of politics and the messy world of representative government, were the New Dealers unable to extricate themselves from existing passions and prejudices in society? These are the questions we must deal with and the words that challenge us: prejudice, stereotyping, discrimination, and racism. According to the Roosevelt supporters, these are the words the "first family" struggled to overcome.

FRANKLIN AND ELEANOR

Words... Roosevelt used them to entice and entreat support for his New Deal policies. They were the magic that connected him to the American people, always with a message of self-support and a "we're in this together" philosophy. As he said:

Without the help of thousands of others, any one of us would die, naked and starved. Consider the bread upon our table, the clothes upon our backs, the luxuries that make life pleasant, how many men worked in sunlit fields, in dark mines, in the fierce heat of molten metal, and among the looms and wheels of countless factories, to create them for our use and enjoyment. In the final analysis, the progress of our civilization will be retarded if any large body of citizens falls behind.

On June 28, 1934, Roosevelt answered his critics in a Fireside Chat. Sitting comfortably in the Oval Office, he spoke quietly and directly to the American people about the emergency measures taken since entering office. He also challenged his severest conservative critics who accused him of usurping American liberties and moving the country toward socialism. He answered the stinging charges with words cultivated to assure his fellow citizens that this was not the case.

Have you, as an individual, paid too high a price for these gains? Plausible self-seekers and theoretical die-hards will tell you of the loss of individual liberty. Answer this question out of the facts of your own life. Have you lost any of your rights or liberty or constitutional freedom of action and choice?

He then flung a barrage of sharp words about those who sought to extinguish the New Deal for personal reasons.

In working out a great national program that seeks the primary good of the greatest number, it is true that the toes of some people are being stepped on and will be stepped on. But these toes belong to the comparative few who seek to retain or gain position or riches or both by some shortcut, which is harmful to the greater good.

Years earlier, President Theodore Roosevelt answered his critics, and by extension those of FDR, with a salvo of stirring words:

It is not the critic who counts, nor the man who points out how the strong man stumbles, or where the doer of deeds could have done them better. The credit belongs to the man who is actually in the arena, whose face is marred by dust and sweat and blood; who strives valiantly, who errs, who comes up short again and again, because there is no effort without error and shortcoming.

CHAPTER 2 –PHOTOS OF DESPAIR

A picture is worth a thousand words. You have heard the phrase more than once. Did you ever wonder how it got started? The mantle goes to Fred R. Barnard. In 1921, he wrote those words in *Printer's Ink*, an advertising trade journal. He promoted using images in advertising, primarily when used on the side of streetcars. In his view, products and services could be shown with a single image, increasing sales. His business was to induce people to buy commercial products like a new car or a better radio. He wanted to reach the viewer on a visceral level so that there was an emotional response to the ad. All this was also true of the Great Depression. The day's photographers conveyed the country's economic troubles to all Americans. Their images went beyond mere statistics and political partisanship. They captured the pain of proud men, jobless and destitute.

JOBLESS MEN SEEKING WORK

Without the plight of millions and the whole capitalistic economic system in disarray, the New Deal might never have occurred, or at least in the fashion it did. However, the fickleness of history altered the political landscape. In 1928, a good Republican conservative was elected with a host of congressional representatives to run the government. Herbert Hoover was the face of that thorough trouncing of the Democrats.

Four years later, that political world was upended. President Hoover was out. The trauma of the Great Depression had been seen in that. This was not unprecedented in American history. For example, a reversal of fortune occurred in 1856 when James Buchanan led the Democrats to victory. Four stormy years later, Abraham Lincoln entered the White House as the leader of a new political party, the Republicans. What altered the political landscape? In a word, only one thing: slavery.

Photographs taken during the Great Depression illustrated the desperation of millions of Americans. They showed fear and frustration, the pain and suffering of the 1930s, and the loss of hope experienced by those out of work and those evicted from their farms. They always showed those brutally crushed by economic forces beyond their control. It all began with a shattering headline.

The major banks and powerful investment firms in New York City were collapsing. The beating heart of capitalism, based on a free market and private sector economy, was coming apart at the seams, causing a painful, unparalleled upheaval in American society. One word described everything: *panic.* Soon, stockholders were selling their shares at discount prices before they dropped even more in value. People stormed their banks to retrieve their deposits before the institutions went belly up. Consumer confidence dwindled and then collapsed. Purchases were put off or not made. Small and large businesses began to fail as sales evaporated, leading to massive cutbacks for workers. The unemployment rate swelled like a rain barrel in a Midwest storm. Fueled by fear, panic hung in the air, toxic and ugly as the nation careened into uncharted economic conditions beyond anyone's experience. All were affected. The affluent suddenly found themselves in unaccustomed economic waters. A single picture captured that moment, soon to be replicated many times over as the depression deepened and continued unabated.

TROUBLED TIMES

Many invested in the stock market through the New York Stock Exchange. Some poured their life savings into what they considered a safe investment for their retirement years. Others seeking a quick buck and profits beyond the sweat of their brow wanted to go from rags to riches. Wealth, whether for the most affluent or the cautious little investor, disappeared before their eyes. To pay their bills, people reached into their savings or sold precious assets, anything to bring in a dollar. In time, moneyless, jobless, and hopeless, millions were forced onto the dole once charities ran dry and friends and families had little to offer. Though only 4,000,000 Americans had money invested in the stock market, and some 90% did not, the "market crash" ultimately affected almost every family somehow.

Millions of formerly employed men were unemployed, all seeking jobs to care for their families. These were always the lingering faces of the financial fiasco. Proud men now unable to care for their families... Proud men now willing to work for the lowest wages, assuming a job was available... Proud men who once believed in the American dream: work hard, play by the rules, and success will follow... Proud men now standing in the soup kitchens or receiving a doughnut and coffee from the Salvation Army... Their faces reflected the times, whether in the unemployment line or a soup kitchen.

PROUD MEN IN DISPAIR

The Farm Security Administration FSA) is hardly worth a footnote in most histories of the Great Depression—just another New Deal agency created in 1937 to deal with rural poverty. A "small but highly influential photography program" was embedded in the FSA. Over 175,000 black and white photographs were taken to chronicle American life between 1937 and 1945. It is often difficult to appreciate the suffering brought on by the collapse of the nation's economy. Dorothea Lange was on the staff of the FSA and *Life Magazine*. She was one of the first photojournalists. Her work as a documentary photographer brought home to average Americans the human tragedy of the Great Depression, disrupted lives, and a barren landscape.

LANGE ON A TRUCK | THE BRUTAL DROUGHT

The photo below became one of the most well-known images of the Great Depression. It was entitled "Migrant Woman." The woman in the photo was Florence Thompson. She was living in a migrant camp in California with her children. A woman and her children…

MIGRANT MOTHER

What were her thoughts? What future did her children have? She could not fathom what had happened on Wall Street nor conceive of how to end the unending disaster. She was one of the countless millions caught up in a Greek tragedy. Where was an American Odysseus to end her suffering? Impoverishment strode the land in cities and the countryside, sapping the strength to go on. There was little people could do. They could only endure and perhaps survive another day. The struggle was unceasing.

Years later, Lange described how the photo came about.

I saw and approached the hungry and desperate mother, as if drawn by a magnet. I do not remember how I explained my presence or my camera to her, but I do remember she asked no questions. I did ask her name or her history. She told me her age, that she was thirty-two. She said they had been living on frozen vegetables from the surrounding fields and birds that the children killed. She had just sold the tires from her car to buy food. There she sat in that lean-to-tent with her children huddled around her, and she seemed to know that my pictures might help her, and so she helped me. There was a sort of equality about it.

Lange's work and that of others gave voice to the tragedy the country was experiencing. Irony pervaded the months and years following the collapse of Wall Street. Farmers were forced to spill milk onto the ground even as children went hungry in the cities. They could not sell their milk to cover costs, so they had no choice. Pig farmers butchered their animals instead of selling them at a loss. Again, this frightful ritual occurred as millions went without a meal. And then, unable to pay their mortgages, American farmers, who urban dwellers depended on for sustenance, were evicted from their land. All suffered, the workers who could not afford a cup of coffee, and the farmers who could not make a profit. The camera recorded the tragedy.

DESTROYING MILK

Many without a job headed to California, always seeking a better life. John Steinbeck captured their migration in his masterpiece, *The Grapes of Wrath:*

Up ahead they's a thousand' lives we might live, but when it comes it'll only be one.

The desperate and the weary took to the road, taking with them in their beat-up old cars the human cargo of lost hopes, yet balanced by the possibilities of a new life out west. They were called Okies and Arkies. They had left the depleted land of the "Dust Bowl" in Arkansas and Oklahoma for California's rich orange and lemon groves in hopes of finding work. They had left behind the eviction notices and bank closures that tore the land from them, the land they had toiled, the land that bore their sweat. They left behind them the family cemetery and cherished memories. They took to the lonely "Mother Road," US Highway 66. Along the way, they were not always welcomed...

ON THE MOTHER ROAD | KEEP GOING

What began in 1929 brought two realities into stark contrast. For those with a good job, a new car beckoned for an idealized American family, alive and well in a world of safety and security, beginning with ample food on the table and a bright future. The billboard said so. For others, the plastered paper signs were a mocking reminder of what they had lost and might never regain.

THE IDEAL | THE REALITY

The two realities clashed. If you had a job, you had a buck. If not, you were penniless. American society was under stress. Something had to be done to get the country back on track.

It all began with the headlines in 1929. For almost a decade, the bold print of that late afternoon edition haunted America. It was as if the prevailing economic system had turned on its practitioners with soulless revenge. Everywhere there was a clamor for jobs. The headlines of despair chronicled the economic disaster.

The optimistic words of the President of the New York Stock Exchange howled into the night of lost hopes and futures destroyed by the "Crash" on Wall Street in 1929. On January 12, 1928, E.H. Simmons said:

I cannot help but raise a dissenting voice to statements that we live in a fool's paradise, and that prosperity in this country must necessarily diminish and recede soon.

President Hoover echoed those sentiments, saying in early 1932:

With God's help, We shall soon be within sight of the day when poverty will be banished from the nation.

PRESIDENTIAL OPTIMISM | THE AMERICAN DREAM LOST

CHAPTER 3 – DEADLY ABSTRACTIONS

It is not possible to talk about the Great Depression without explaining what depression is, at least as economists define and explain it. Economists postulate the existence of what they call the business cycle. By that, they mean the rise and fall of economic growth that occurs over time in our capitalistic system. The business cycle describes the increase or decrease in economic activity over time, or the total of all activities carried on by our society in a given period. That activity includes all consumer goods and services produced in the country. When the numbers are added up, they describe the productivity of the business cycle. That measurement is called the Gross Domestic Product or the GDP. The chart shown below visualizes the four major phases in a recurring cycle.

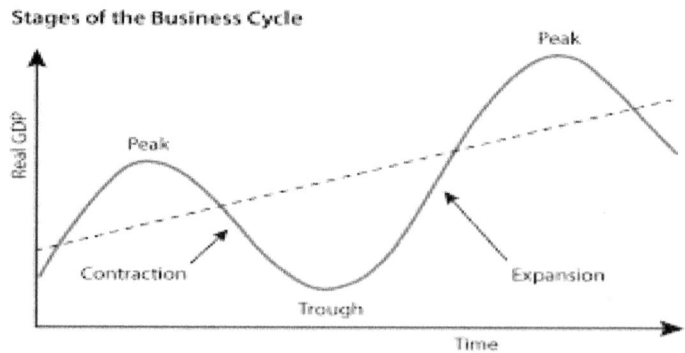

All business cycle phases can vary in length and degree since they are subject to many variables. The *Peak* refers to a period of extreme economic activity. Businesses sell products and services. Revenues and profits are substantial. In particular, the value of corporate stock is appreciated, and substantial dividends are shared with stockholders. Employees are enjoying healthy wages, permitting them to maintain a reasonably high standard of living. They can also save a few bucks or put money into investments. People can afford to buy a home and enjoy the economic blessings of value appreciation over time. The *Peak* is generally a function of economic expansion. That is, the GDP is growing. However, that growth is not preordained nor infinite in its increases. At some point, that process ebbs, leading to a contraction in the economy.

It was President Herbert Hoover's good political fortune to take office in 1928 when the economy was humming along, and prosperity seemed almost ordained. The only question facing this conservative Republican was how long the good times could continue. Most economic indicators (or signs) suggested ongoing prosperity, but again, for how long? In particular, the New York Stock Exchange continued to gain value as measured by the Dow-Jones index of representative stocks. On inauguration day, everything seemed fine. By 1932, however, the economy had tanked. The Trough had inundated the economic landscape. The country was in what economists called a depression, or the opposite of prosperity. When President Roosevelt came to power in 1932, if the right economic policies were implemented, the economy had nowhere to go but up. That was his good fortune, but what policies would lead to an expansion of the economy? That remained to be seen.

Between the *Peak* and the Trough was a process called *Contraction*. In a word, the GDP decreases. The economy does not experience growth. Business is treading water at best. The job market is bleak. The Stock Market shifts from a "bull" to a "bear" market as stocks lose value. Wages and profits also decline. Only unhappiness seems to increase. Theoretically, the economy hit rock bottom before beginning a period of expansion that reverses the economic decline, leading to a new *Peak*. The depths of the *Trough* and the expansion's strength are a function of many things and are difficult to predict in advance. Past economic history suggested that contraction would eventually lead to a new expansion cycle. This was the notion behind a "self-correcting" business cycle, which conservatives considered an article of faith. That said, how long before the correction began was always an open question, as was the strength of the economic rebound.

Two other factors are tied to the business cycle: inflation and deflation, and both are related to the economic laws of supply and demand. Rising prices characterize inflation and are necessary for expansion to take place. In basic terms, if inflation is 3% the dollar has lost 3% in value. You now need $1.03 to buy what a dollar used to purchase. Suppose you do not have the extra three cents; your dollar can only buy 97% of what it used to get. An expanding economy always carries with it some level of inflation. Why is that? People are working. They are spending dollars. Prices increase if too many dollars (demand) are chasing a limited number of items (supply). These increases only taper off when supply and demand balance or reach an equilibrium. A certain amount of inflation is necessary when the GDP expands. The economic trick is to have maximum expansion with minimal inflation. During Hoover's term of office, inflation was not a serious problem with one major exception. Demand for stock far exceeded the supply of shares available, leading to what some economists called a "bubble" based on out-of-control speculation. Shadowing the stock market was one question. What would happen if the bubble burst? What would happen if the stock market collapsed?

What is deflation? Prices are declining which sounds like a good thing. Things cost less. Consumers do not have to spend as much. By way of example, if deflation is running at 5% my dollar is now worth $1.05. It has gained in value. Alternatively, I only need 95 cents for what I used to pay a buck for. I am a nickel ahead. Again, that is nice. However, why are prices falling? One reason is that supply is greater than demand. Why is that happening? Consumption is down. Prices are falling because sales are declining. Inventories are building up. They must be liquidated. This leads to price reductions. Goods and services are discounted. Consumers take advantage of the steep discounts. A "fire sale" is taking place. Sales are temporarily up, but the profit margin has disappeared. This happens when a business goes bankrupt due to falling sales. That occurs as the business cycle moves from the *Peak* to the *Trough*. Yes, you could pay less for something, but someone probably lost a job. Think of this in terms of millions of workers as the country's industrial, financial, and agricultural economies collapsed. This process tormented President Hoover, beginning with the Stock Market Crash 1929. It was up to Roosevelt's policymakers to end what Hoover's policies could not stop, an unending spiral downward.

It is important to keep a few things in mind. First, during prosperous times, individuals and groups, even sections of the economy, are not enjoying the ride. Many would argue that American farmers were in a fix long before 1929. This was partially due to over-expansion during World War I, as farmers were encouraged to feed the world. In time, supply outstripped demand, leading to declining prices. Second, things are okay if you have a job during the worst times. Your cash was king. Conversely, things would not be OK if you were out of work in prosperous times. Third, individuals have little control over the forces affecting the economy. Individuals are mostly very dependent on government policies to ensure a strong economy. The federal government has two ways of doing this: through fiscal and monetary policies.

The federal government sets fiscal policies in terms of expenditure and tax rates. In terms of expenditures, three options are available when Washington spends public funds: (1) a balanced budget, where taxes cover expenditures and interest payments for past indebtedness; (2) a surplus budget, where tax revenue exceeds expenditures; and (3) a deficit budget, where expenditures outstrip tax revenue. These options aim to maintain a healthy economic climate over the longest period. In prosperous times, options 1 and 2 hold sway. As a traditional Republican, President Hoover supported these positions. Budget deficits were to be avoided.

The counterargument was that a contraction in the business cycle required increased government expenditure to compensate for diminished demand in the private sector. Also, lowering the tax rate would make more money available to consumers to spur demand. This was often referred to as Keynesian economics in honor of John Maynard Keynes, a British economist.

The chart below illustrates his ideas.

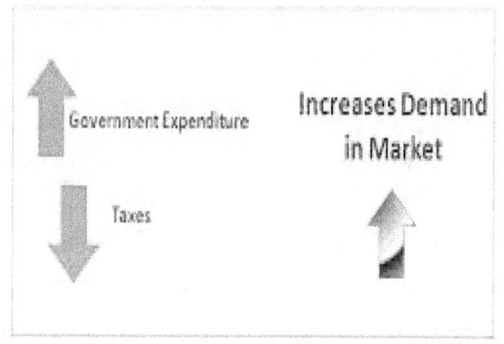

JOHN MAYNARD KEYNES

In theory, the Keynesians declared that the government should not be a bystander concerning the business cycle. During a depression, in particular, the federal government should run deficits to compensate for the lack of private sector consumption. In time, the economy would turn around, leading to a period of expansion. In other words, the GDP would be spurred to end the contraction in the business cycle. In contrast to the conservative position held by Hoover, deficit spending was eventually accepted by President Roosevelt and his policymakers as the road out of the Great Depression.

Fiscal policy is essential, as is its sibling, monetary policy, which is conducted through the Federal Reserve, America's central bank. Its policies impact the business cycle by influencing inflation and unemployment with "targeted rates" or goals. Monetary tools are designed to alter interest rates, lending, and borrowing by private sector businesses, banks, and consumers. Lowering interest rates can encourage borrowing since some factors reduce the cost of a loan. Done on a wide enough basis, this can end a contraction of the business cycle and begin a recovery. This is called expansionary monetary policy. However, to keep the economy from growing too fast and causing too much inflation, the central bank can raise interest rates, making borrowing more expensive. This is called contractionary monetary policy. The central bank is trying to keep the economic expansion under control. It does not want the economy to overheat. In doing so, the Federal Reserve intends to serve two masters simultaneously. It wants to encourage maximum employment with minimum inflation. This leads to a question: what is the sweet spot? A desirable goal is 3 - 4% GDP expansion, 3% unemployment, and 2.5% inflation.

In summary, fiscal and monetary policy aim to keep the economy growing sustainably by creating enough jobs for everyone who wants one while ensuring that inflation does not get out of control. The goal is always to avoid a recession that would lead to a severe contraction of the GDP and an economic depression. The chart that follows compares the goals of fiscal and monetary policies.

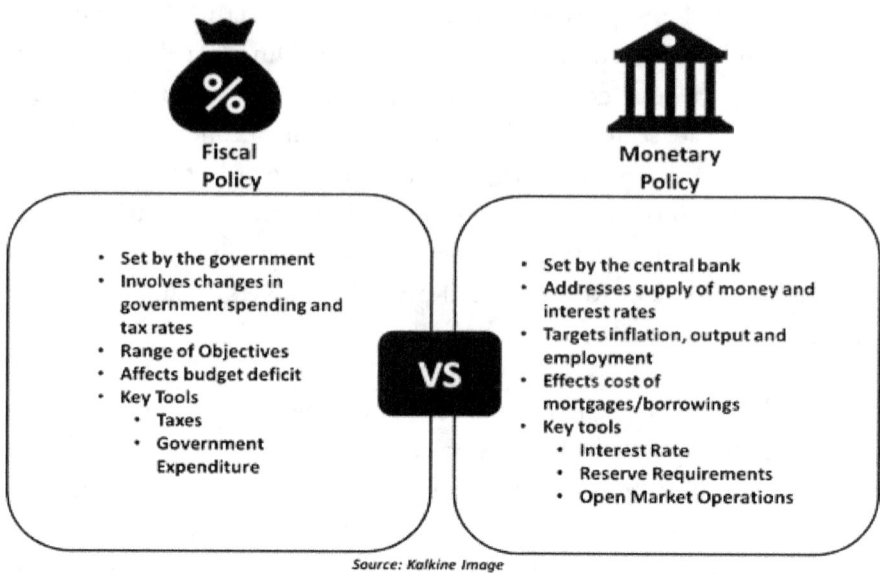

Fiscal Policy

- Set by the government
- Involves changes in government spending and tax rates
- Range of Objectives
- Affects budget deficit
- Key Tools
  - Taxes
  - Government Expenditure

VS

Monetary Policy

- Set by the central bank
- Addresses supply of money and interest rates
- Targets inflation, output and employment
- Effects cost of mortgages/borrowings
- Key tools
  - Interest Rate
  - Reserve Requirements
  - Open Market Operations

Source: Kalkine Image

According to many economists, the Hoover Administration held fast to the traditional view of the business cycle. It failed to adjust fiscal and monetary policies to stem the unprecedented economic contraction. What was that view? The government should not intervene in free markets. Instead, the "invisible hand" of individuals acting in their self-interest will lead to socially appropriate outcomes. The notion was a metaphor coined by Adam Smith, a British economist, in his seminal work, *The Wealth of Nations (1776)*. Specifically, he contended unseen forces of "self-interest" were always at work as consumers sought the lowest prices with the highest quality. Conversely, producers and providers, seeking the greatest return on their investments, would charge them the most at the least cost. Out of this "mutual self-interest," a price would be determined that optimizes sales and consumer satisfaction. The chart below shows how this works, at least in theory. Without government interference, the free market, responding to self-interest and a competitive marketplace, would ensure a free market driven by a desire for profits and valuable goods.

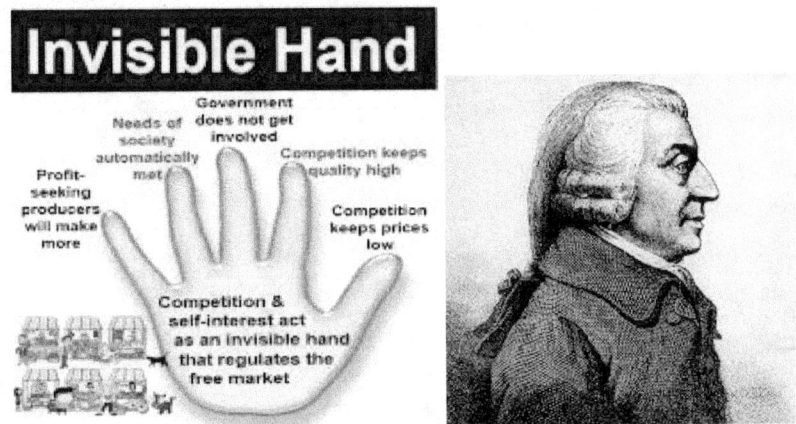

ADAM SMITH'S INVISIBLE HAND

Theoretically, the "invisible hand" would self-regulate the business cycle without government intervention. The Hoover Administration accepted this view as gospel, which the Roosevelt Administration rejected.

Adjusting fiscal and monetary policy became President Roosevelt's challenge. That would prove a difficult task. Bank failures were unprecedented, and unemployment rates defied policymakers. Beyond the bank failures were the faces of millions of depositors who lost their savings. A family was without a breadwinner for each tick upward in the unemployment rate. Beyond the statistics, millions were cast adrift by the economic collapse and the forces that brought it about. The two charts below indicate the magnitude of the problem.

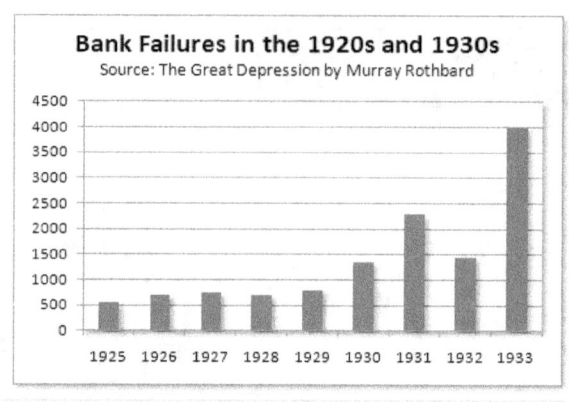

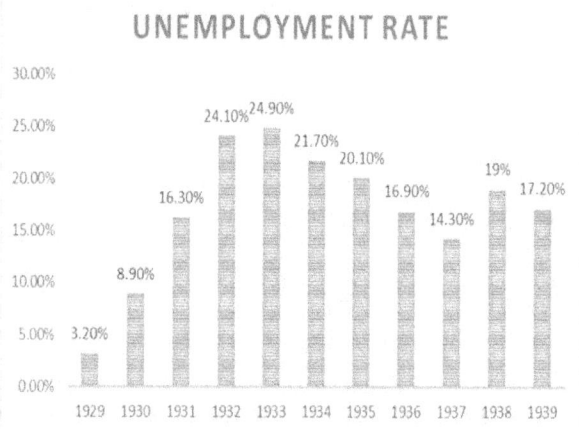

The business cycle provides a graphic and statistical understanding of the economy's ebb and flow. The New Deal would attempt to alter the economic landscape by dealing with these factors so that the economy could recover. What would this mean in practice? Monetary policy would lower interest rates and encourage borrowing. Fiscal policy would accept deficit spending to achieve economic expansion. The political trick was to get them working together toward a common goal, sustaining a consumer-based economy.

This aspirational goal would be at the heart of the New Deal and Roosevelt's efforts to implement his magical three "R's" - relief, recovery, and reform. Relief: provide shelter and food for those in need until the economy improves. Recovery: end the contraction through government-sponsored infrastructure projects on a massive scale. Reform: Though new government regulations wring out of the economic system those things led to the debacle. Doing all this proved to be a monumental task.

In 1933, some 24.9% of the total labor force was unemployed. In other words, 1 out of every four workers had no job. That amounted to 12,839,000 people. With 2 to 3 people dependent on one unemployed worker, over 36,000,000 people were without a paycheck. Between 1929 and 1933, wages fell 42.5% for those fortunate to have jobs still. The average family income dropped by 40% during the 1930s. Consumer prices fell 25%. Wholesale prices fell 32%. Deflation was surging ahead downhill. The Stock Market lost almost 90% of its value between 1929 and 1933. Nearly 11,000 banks folded. That was about 1/3rd of all banks in the country.

By any measure, income distribution was skewed in the wrong direction even before the Great Depression. The top 5% of income earners earned 33% of all money. Some 95% of workers shared 67% of the income earned. The chart below indicates the breakdown of these numbers by income. Note $2,000 in 1929 was the minimum necessary to meet the basic needs of the average American family. Over 42% of family incomes were below that threshold. This leads to two points. First, millions of Americans barely made it before the collapse of the economy. Second, the collapse slammed these folks harder than other income groups.

U.S. Family Income Distribution (1929)	
Annual Income	Percent of American Families Earning this Income
Over $10,000	2%
$5,000 - $10,000	6%
$2,000 - $5,000	32%
$1,500 - $2,000	18%
$1,000 - $1,500	21%
Under $1,000	21%

Note: In 1929, a $2000 income was considered the minimum necessary for meeting basic needs of the average US family. It marked the poverty line.

Note: In 1929, the wealthiest 5% of the US population received about 33% of the nation's personal income. In 1948, the wealthiest 5% received less than 20%. (Galbraith, *The Great Crash*, pp. 197-198.)

Altering the unequal distribution of wealth was a challenge for Hoover, as it would be for Roosevelt and every president since.

By adopting Keynesian views, the Roosevelt Administration accepted the necessity of deficit budgets and an increasing national debt. As FDR said:

No one lightly lays a burden on the income of a Nation. But this vicious tightening circle of our declining national income supply had to be broken. The bankers and the industrialists of the Nation cried aloud that private business was powerless to break it. They turned to the Government as they had the right to turn. After all else had failed, we accepted that government's final responsibility to spend money when no one else had money left to spend.

Economics has been called the "dismal science." It does not have the exact predictability or causality of physics. In formulating economic policy, economists often say, "Well, on the one hand, this may happen. However, on the other hand, this may occur." That is why, as the joke goes, presidents would prefer a "one-handed" economist. In adopting Keynes' theories, Roosevelt was mindful of the economist's famous witty observation:

It is better to be roughly right than precisely wrong.

CHAPTER 4 – HOUSE OF CARDS

The headlines revealed the awful truth: The New York Stock Exchange had crashed. No one could hide from the bold print. The dark ink splattered across the country, taking with it the fortunes of many and the hard-earned savings of millions more. Only one word described the moment: despair. It was as if the world were ending, bringing an entire population into an unexpected economic twilight zone beyond their comprehension.

PANIC IN THE STREET

For one group, however, the economic plight was nothing new. To a degree, it was the norm of their existence, what they faced each day, and had been since emancipation. Blacks were inordinately affected by the downturn. Already at the bottom of the economic ladder, they could not cope with the layoffs and increasing unemployment. An adage haunted this group: "Last to be hired, first to be fired." In prosperous times, they, as a group, got a sliver of the action. In a depression, even that slice of the economic pie was cast aside. Curiously, though the stock market debacle affected millions of American investors as the value of their stock holdings declined, Blacks were least affected in this direct manner. Why was that? Most Blacks did not have the disposable income to invest in the market. They needed every dime for mere existence. Again, as a group, they could not borrow money to join the frenzy on Wall Street. Banks and investment firms were reluctant to lend funds to them. It can be argued that Blacks were already in a depression long before the economic system went south. White Americans were catching up to this unhappy experience. Assuming that there was government assistance of some form, Blacks believed they would receive less aid than white citizens. That had been their experience, especially in the South, where Jim Crow reigned and segregation and discrimination blighted the social framework. Moreover, while whites could bring considerable political pressure on their elected representatives, Blacks did not enjoy that influence. Disenfranchisement had led to that.

The stock market had collapsed, but what exactly did that mean? Some necessary information… Assuming you have a company building an exotic new cell phone form. Sales are good. Revenues flourish. Profits abound. Sounds good, but you have a problem. You need to expand. You need a new manufacturing plant. That will be expensive. Your profits will not cover it. You need more capital than you can borrow. What can you do? You bring in some partners. Their investments help, but you require even more financial assistance over time. You need more investors, perhaps in the thousands or the millions. You decide to go public. You sell shares in your company. The shares are called common stock (see below). Shareholders are partial owners of the company based on the number of shares they control. Going public raises the needed funding for your expansion. Assuming the company is profitable, the shareholders receive a percentage of the profits based on their stock ownership. They receive dividends. Your business is now a corporation.

Your stock and other companies are listed on the New York Stock Exchange. Now the immutable law of supply and demand enters the picture. Only so many shares were initially offered to the public. Others would like to own the stock as your company expands and becomes even more profitable. If the demand for the stock is greater than the supply, the value of your share increases. In reverse, your shares would be less valuable if sellers exceeded buyers. So, what is the problem? In a word: *speculation*. The desire to own shares may far exceed the company's real value, driving the price of each share you own skyward in a buying frenzy. What is driving this? The answer is the lure of instant wealth and the belief that the value of shares would only increase. In other words, human greed… Everyone dreams of being a millionaire… Wall Street has become Easy Street.

If this occurs with enough companies, you have an out-of-control *Bull Market*, in contrast to a significant decline in the opposite direction, known as a *Bear Market*. The two creatures are constantly at odds with each other. Leading up to the collapse of the stock market, the bulls reigned. After that, the bears growled for almost a decade.

However, how do you buy and sell stocks? A person living in San Diego, California (a seller) cannot be in direct contact with someone in Pittsburgh, Pennsylvania (a buyer). Both need an intermediary known as a broker. He is in the business of buying and selling stocks on the stock market. All this occurs through a stock exchange, the most famous of which is the New York Stock Exchange (NYSE) located on Wall Street. Millions of transactions are conducted daily as buy and sell orders come in worldwide.

THE NEW YORK STOCK EXCHANGE

Sounds good. People invest their own money hoping for two things. The stock they own will appreciate; that is, go up in value as demand pushes the price upward. Moreover, of course, there are dividends paid quarterly or yearly. If you sell at a price greater than the purchase price, the difference is your profit after broker fees. This all sounds good unless…

What if people are not using their own money to buy stocks? How could that happen? Driven to get rich quickly, individuals borrowed money to buy stocks with money they did not have. How was that done? It was called buying on margin. If, by way of example, a guy named Joe wanted to buy 10 shares of a stock selling at $10.00 per share, he needed $100.00. However, he only had $10.00. Where will Joe get the additional $90.00? He will borrow, of course, from a bank, investment firm, or broker. Joe is now buying on *margin*. The shares he bought are his *collateral*. Eventually, Joe hopes to sell the stock at a profit, pay off his loan, and still be ahead of the game with a tidy profit. Now think of hundreds of thousands of people doing this with millions of shares, and the amount of indebtedness involved. The entire enterprise is based on a *bull market* that is ever-increasing in prices. Joe's small initial investment and borrowed funds have given him wealth, at least on paper. As long as the boom lasts, Joe is okay. Getting rich was never easier, right?

The frenzy of buying on margin was out of control by late 1929. Investors could borrow money (which they didn't have), as much as 75% of the purchase value of the stock. Stockbrokers and banks funded the reckless speculation, heedless of the warning signs. Tempted public members were often willing to pay 20% interest rates on their margin loans. As might be expected, they were "dead certain" that the risk would be worth the eventual reward. Lenders were equally sure that these transactions would pay off. Greed was driving the stock market despite concerns by many government officials.

Though it might seem improbable, the *Ladies Home Journal* bolsters the thirst for stocks and the right to get rich in an article entitled, "Everyone Ought to be Rich." The article was written by a wealthy financier, John J. Raskob. He advised every American to invest 15 dollars a month in the market. By his calculations, those monthly investments would be worth approximately $80,000 after twenty years. Many followed his advice. After all, the total value of the New York Stock Exchange was $27 billion in 1925. By September 1929, the Exchange was $87 billion. During that period, the average stockholder more than tripled the value of his stock portfolio. With gains like this, the fever to own stocks swept the nation. The Bulls, it was argued, were in control. Join the parade to prosperity.

The Secretary of the Treasury, Andrew Mellon, supported this view with a speech on December 31, 1929, even after the "Crash."

I see nothing in the present situation that is menacing or warrants pessimism... I have confidence that there will be a revival of activity in the spring and that during this coming year, the country will make steady progress. There is nothing to be worried about.

As of November 1929, brokers had lent small investors more than 2/3rds of the face value of the stock they bought. That amounted to $8,000,000,000. That is billions we are talking about. However, what would happen if the market turns bearish and Joe's stocks begin to lose value? If that happens, will his collateral start to disappear? Joe's broker can call and ask Joe to pay off the loan. Now Joe has a problem based on fear. Should he hold on to his shares and hope the hemorrhage on Wall Street will stop, or should he sell and cut his losses? Either way, his broker must be paid off. If Joe cannot did this, the broker loses money, but he is not alone. Where did the broker get the money to lend to Joe in the first place? Probably from investment banks that earned interest on the loans to the broker. If the broker can retrieve his loans, he cannot pay them down, and now the banks are in a fix. However, so are the bank's depositors if their money was used indirectly to help Joe buy his stock. What will happen to the millions of small savings accounts if the banks cannot get their money back? Will they go bust as the bank goes bankrupt?

Imagine this happening to thousands of brokers and hundreds of banks as millions of shares slid downward as measured by the Dow-Jones Index. Do what, you are asking? It measured many industrial stocks that generally indicated the market's direction, bear or bull. It originates from Charles Dow and Edward Jones, who devised the measurement before the turn of he century. The stocks used to calculate the index represented different sectors of the larger economy. If the index rose, the market appeared strong, and vice versa. Investors paid attention to it.

CHARLES DOW AND EDWARD JONES

The graph below explains statistically what happened. There was a big sell-off on *Black Thursday*, October 24, 1929. Some 12,894,650 shares were traded, and fear set in that the market would continue declining. On *Black Monday*, October 28, 1929, the sell-off was so significant that brokers made margin calls. The Dow-Jones Index lost 38.33 points that day, or 12.82%. The rout was on. On October 29, 1929, the market crash took hold. It is known as *Black Tuesday*. The selling was so great that the ticker tape could not keep up with the actual value of a stock. The tape fell behind the sales. Investors across the country did not have real-time information. In time and with some stocks, there were no buyers. You could not give away the paper. Billions of dollars in paper wealth disappeared. By the presidential election in 1932, the market had fallen from a high of 350 to 41 points. The total value of the New York Stock Exchange was $27 billion in 1925. By September 1929, that figure had skyrocketed to $87 billion. By 1932, the total value had plunged to $41 billion.

The joy ride was over. Sorry Joe. Your market prosperity was built on nothing more than a "house of cards."

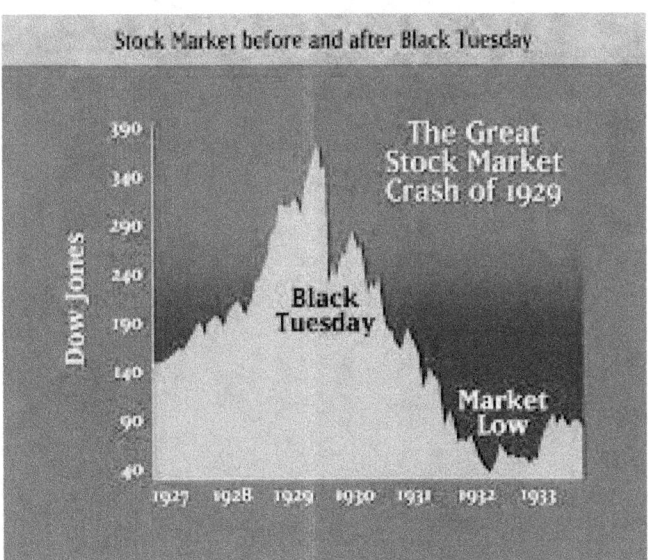

Few anticipated the magnitude of the stock market crash. One who did was Roger Babson, an economist, investor, and lecturer. In retrospect, he is now considered a "prophet of doom" whose warnings went unheeded. In September 1929, he stated his views before the National Business Conference in Massachusetts. He spoke directly and without equivocation:

Sooner or later, a crash is coming, which will take in the leading stocks and cause a decline from 60 to 80 points in the Dow Jones barometer. Someday, the time is coming when the market will begin to slide off, sellers will exceed buyers, and paper profits will begin to disappear. Then, there will immediately be a stampede to save what paper profits then exist.

That same day, the stock market declined by almost 3%. This moment in economic history is known as the "Babson Break." Regretfully, it was too late to prevent the Wall Street Crash of 1929.

THE PROPHET

Though not the sole cause of the Great Depression, Wall Street's collapse played a significant role. Demonstrating an "appreciable cause-and-effect linkage" between the Crash on Wall Street and the economic collapse is difficult. Many other factors were involved, and there is no question about that.

The spirit of the moment was captured by a few words in the *New York Times* on November 3, 1929:

As fall the leaves by
Autumn blown,
So fell those lovely

Shares I own.
Forlorn, disconsolate
I sing,O
Goodbye, goodbye to
Everything!

To car and plane and
Gleaming yacht
And rather ducal
Country cot
That all seemed surely
Mine by spring,
Goodbye, goodbye to
Everything.

The House of Cards had collapsed. In its wake were the troubling numbers. Over $7 billion in depositors' money was eliminated as banks went kaput. Over 150,000 homeowners lost their property in 1930, 200,000 in 1931, and 250,000 in 1932. The GNP fell by 50% between 1929 and 1933. Businesses only invested $3 billion in 1933 compared to $24 billion in 1929. Only 1/3rd as many automobiles rolled off the assembly line in 1933 compared to 1929. By 1932, iron and steel production had declined 60% from pre-crash levels. Also, 1932 residential and manufacturing construction plummeted to less than 1/5th of pre-crash levels. Finally, farm income fell from $6 billion in 1929 to $2 billion in 1932. The free fall was not encouraging and led to a significant decline in consumer confidence and spending. Invariably, this led to a decrease in sales and an increase in unemployment to over 12,800,000 by 1932. That amounted to 24% of the active labor force.

The onset of the Great Depression put millions out of work. However, who were these millions, at least statistically? A government study in 1933 indicated the following about our buddy, Joe.

- The typical unemployed city worker on relief:
- He was a white man.

- He was 38 years of age.
- He was the head of a household.
- He was either unskilled or semi-skilled.
- He had ten years of experience in his line of work.
- He had been out of work for one month or more for two years.
- He hadn't been working at his usual line of work for almost 2 ½ years.

As a group, the elderly were most affected by the loss of jobs. About them, the study said:

Through hardship, discouragement, and sickness as well as advancing years this group has gone into an occupational oblivion from which they will never be rescued by private industry.

The elderly were, the report concluded, now tied to permanent, structural unemployment that was related to technological changes, causing them to be removed from the job market as obsolescent workers. This raised difficult questions. What would happen to these people? What role, if any, should the government play in assisting them? Assuming assistance was provided, what would be the nature of that aid? What would be the cost of such government intervention? Where would the money come from? The Hoover Administration was not immune to the problems of the elderly. It simply did not have a satisfying answer.

Women, of course, were affected by the economic downturn, but not always in the same way as men. Before November 1929, very few women worked in the steel industry or the building trades. Nor were they driving rivets or swinging hammers in physically demanding occupations. Women were nurses and teachers, secretaries, and telephone switchboard operators. Their hours might be cut along with their pay, but they still had a check. These positions were less affected than other occupations. Still, women faced challenges due to the notion of the "breadwinner." At the onset of the Great Depression, many businesses and the federal government attempted to assist only "heads of households." Those meant men, for the most part. That meant firing any woman deemed a family's "secondary wage earner."

Black women and men were inordinately affected by the depression. The prevailing notions of race, class, and gender colored hiring practices. As an example... In Washington, D.C., one of the most coveted positions by Black women was that of a "charwoman." The federal government employed this worker to clean government offices instead of part-time domestic work. The position paid more than general domestic service and offered retirement benefits. With the onset of the Great Depression, white women competed with Blacks for these jobs that they once considered beneath them. As often happened, whites received preferential treatment.

From a sociological standpoint, there were also dramatic changes in the bedroom, so to speak. Marriages by young people were either postponed or canceled because of the uncertain economy. Make that their future. By 1932, marriage applications had declined by 22%. Those who are married have decided to put off having children. There was a 15% decrease in new birth rates. Kids are lovable. They are also expensive. Even the divorce rate fell by 25%. It is better to stay together in an unhappy relationship than to be single and unemployed.

As to the unemployed white male... The loss of a job by a former breadwinner struck at a man's sense of self-respect. As one man said:

When a father cannot support his family, supply them with clothing and good food, the children are bound to lose respect. When they see me hanging around the house all the time and know that I can't find work, it has its effect all right.

In the end, perhaps that is what the Great Depression was all about: self-respect. The collapse of the economy had humbled a great nation. What would be done to restore the American dream? Did the private sector have the answer? President Hoover thought so, stating:

While the crash only took place six months ago, I am convinced we have now passed through the worst — and with continued unity of effort we shall rapidly recover. There has been no significant bank or industrial failure. That danger, too, is safely behind us.

Sometime later, he said:

Economic depression cannot be cured by legislative action or executive pronouncement. Economic wounds must be healed by the action of the cells of the economic body, the producers and the consumers themselves.

THE CRISIS

By the 1932 presidential election, President Hoover's assumptions were called into question. The market crash and the human toll of the Great Depression had reached a crisis point. Something had to be done. The economic situation was aptly captured in photo and song.

SELLING AN APPLE FOR A NICKEL TO SURVIVE

Brother, Can You Spare a Dime?

They used to tell me I building a dream.
And so I followed the mob.
When there was earth to plow or guns to bear
I was always right on the job.

They used to tell me I was building a dream
With peace and glory ahead
Why should I be standing in line
Just waiting for bread?
Once I built a railroad, I made it run

Made I race against time
Once I built a railroad, now it's done
Brother, can you spare a dime?

CHAPTER 5 – DEARFIELD

It's a ghost town now. Traveling along State Highway 34 in Colorado, you'll come across a monument just south of Greeley. If you look closely at the commemorative stone out of curiosity, you'll notice it remembers and honors a lost experiment in Black self-sufficiency. The etchings in the stone shatter stereotypes and debunk biases about Blacks held by many Americans in 1929, and unfortunately, many of those in government. The legacy of one small town might have altered the implementation of New Deal policies, assuming that the Roosevelt Administration even knew about Dearfield.

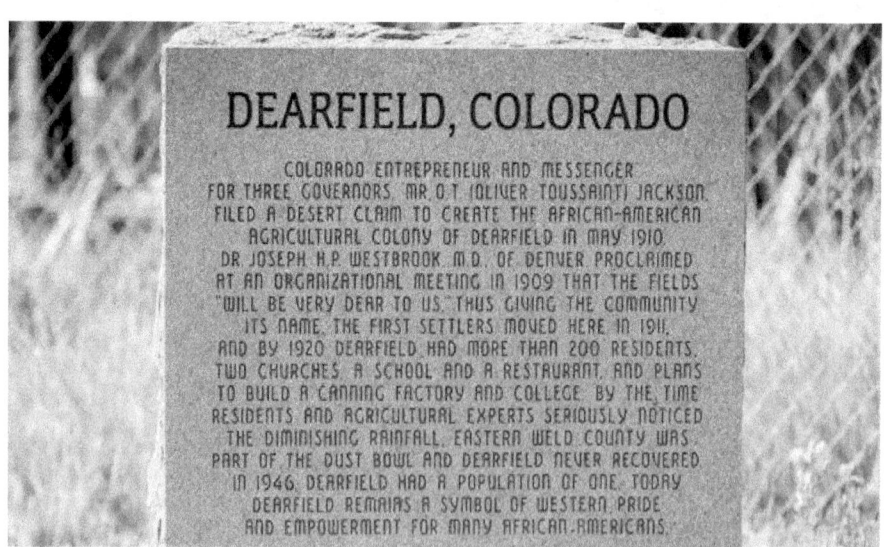

You'll notice a name: Mr. O.T. Jackson. He wanted to create a Black agricultural community. You'll notice another name, Dr. Joseph H.P.

Westbrook, M.D. of Denver. He proclaimed the agrarian fields would be *dear* to Blacks in that community. And that's how the place got its name --- Dearfield. The stone along the highway etched out the promise of the community and its ultimate demise, leaving the reader wanting to know more. Who was this fellow Jackson? What role did he have in establishing a self-sufficient Black community in Colorado in 1909 when Black communities across the country were besieged by the ugliness of the Jim Crow era and the rise of the Ku Klux Klan in Colorado and other states west of the Mississippi? How was it possible to build an oasis in the desert at a time when Blacks were marginalized and disenfranchised? When voter suppression was rampant, or if you voted, was your ballot counted? When were better white schools off limits to Blacks? When violence, whether riots in the cities or a lynching in rural areas, occurred, it all too often occurred. The answer lies with the vision of one enterprising man.

Oliver Toussaint Jackson was born on April 6, 1862, in Oxford, Ohio, a free slave state. His birth coincided with the first bitter years of the Civil War that eventually led to President Abraham Lincoln's Emancipation Proclamation. Jackson's parents were formerly enslaved people. He lived until 1948, the same year President Harry Truman ended segregation in the armed forces. In Cleveland, Ohio, he learned about the restaurant business. In 1887, he moved to Denver, Colorado, where, in time, he opened the Stillman Café that was described as one of the most select dining resorts in town." Business was good. At one time, he had seventy-five employees. In 1904, his first wife died, and a year later, he remarried Minerva J. Matlock, a schoolteacher. She would be critical in the development of the Dearfield community.

THE HUSBAND AND WIFE TEAM

Jackson was strongly influenced by Booker T. Washington's book *Up from Slavery*. Inspired by his reading, Jackson envisioned a community where Blacks farmed and owned their land. He wanted to move beyond sharecropping and tenant farming. After strenuous lobbying of Governor John Franklin Shafroth and taking advantage of the revised Homestead Act of 1909, Jackson purchased 320 acres of land in Weld County. A year later, that spot in the dry, arid land was named Dearfield.

The challenge was to find settlers. He attracted people from Denver and as far away as Minneapolis and Kansas through advertising. To encourage Blacks to move to Colorado, Jackson said:

We are building the Townland Settlement of Dearfield in Colorado, and we solicit your cooperation to establish a municipality owned and controlled by colored people to prove that we can control, govern, and administer a part of the state government the same as other people.

Continuing, he said:

We want 10,000 good farmers, truck gardeners, poultry, dairy, hog raisers, businessmen, and women to join in this race undertaking in Colorado… so that we can have a school of government to learn all the principles of government.

The Dearfield program is a home for every family and every man and woman working out of his or her own problems by creating a future for his or her old age and a job for their children.

We are soliciting all real honest-to-goodness race-loving and talking people to join in some way to build up the Dearfield community. There is plenty of work, talk, and occupation for everyone.

What could be more American? Self-help… Enterprise… Hard work… A pioneer spirit… A willingness to take a chance…

Those first Black settlers did not have it easy. They were forced to live in tents or caves in the nearby hillsides until wooden shacks could be built. There was always a shortage of fuel and water. Bitter winter conditions also took their toll. Somehow, the community took root. The settlers proved apt at dry farming and, spurred by high demand during World War I, the community prospered. There was a demand for corn, wheat, melons, squash, strawberries, sugar beets, oats, and beans. By 1921, there were over 700 residents.' The town included a blacksmith, a dance hall, a restaurant, a gas station, a cannery, and a soap factory. The property was valued at about $750.000. As to governance… While her husband continued to work in Denver, Minerva served as the unofficial mayor of Dearfield, where she ran the day-to-day operations.

The town also had another business besides agriculture to help pay the bills. It was known as "Beerfield" because bootlegging was a community industry during Prohibition. It was the best-kept secret in town that everyone knew about.

The old photographs that follow provide some insight into the town's life.

THE SETTLERS

WORKING THE LAND | GROWING WATERMELONS

PROSPEROUS TIMES

DRESSED UP | LOCAL CITIZENS

The photographs cast doubt about the many stereotypes held by whites, such as that Blacks had no work ethic, that they were lazy, uneducated, lacking in business skills, and certainly unable to govern a community. Implied was the perception that Blacks couldn't live in harmony with their white neighbors. That was patently not true of Dearfield and the local white community. In many cases, Black farmers were hired by white farmers because of their hard work and skills and paid fairly for their labor. One of the Dearfield farmers had a mechanical reaper that was shared with white farmers. By all accounts, informal interdependence evolved between the two groups, leading to a degree of integration. For example, both races attended the same dances, though couples adhered to prevailing social mores. Blacks danced with Blacks. Still, everyone was on the same dance floor.

Sadly, the good times didn't last. A series of disasters hit the town. Farm prices crashed. The Dust Bowl scattered the precious topsoil to the four winds. Natural rainfall dwindled. The seasonal creeks dried up, as did they well. People left. They sold their homes for lumber. By 1940, there were only twelve residents left. The last resident stayed until she died in 1973. Her name was Jenny Jackson.

The once thriving African-American community is no more. Only a lonely signpost reminds us of its past.

What's left of the community is painful to see, as it is with any ghost town.

LONG AGO DREAMS

As to the connection of Dearfield to the Hoover and Roosevelt administrations' efforts to deal with the Great Depression... Blacks, if given the opportunity and not limited by policies inherently biased or prejudiced, can be productive citizens." O.T. Jackson had proven that. Would the New Deal encourage Jackson's vision?

Presently, there is an effort by the National Park Service to restore and maintain a Dearfield Historic Site. According to the NPS:

Our national parks are sacred spaces that hold the power of interpreting, interrogating, and honoring our past and present. Preserving Dearfield for current and future generations is integral to a better understanding of the unique and relatively unknown African-American experience in Colorado's eastern plains and this work is also a bridge that can connect us toward a fuller, more representative story of our nation.

CHAPTER 6 – THE GOOD SAMARITAN

In the Gospel of Luke (10:29 – 32), there is a story of a man on a journey from Jerusalem to Jericho. Along the way, this Jewish man is attacked, beaten, and robbed. He is left on the road, stripped of his clothes and half dead. A Jewish priest comes by but fails to render aid. A Levite comes across the man but avoids stopping to help him. Later, a Samaritan comes upon the traveler. What will he do? Samaritans and Jews are not on friendly terms. Enmity exists between the two groups. The Samaritan, however, stops and helps the injured man. He renders aid despite the hostile relationship.

Jesus told this story in response to a provocative question: Who is my neighbor? The appealing answer is this: show mercy toward your fellow man. Moreover, as a corollary, we should overcome our anger and distrust of others, even showing a universal love for another. In doing so, we are in a relationship with God, transcending earthly discord. Of course, this is a challenging ethic in a world of cynicism and skepticism where greed and self-interest often motivate our moral compass. However, if there is a lesson here, it is the belief that there is a Good Samaritan in all of us. This view was at the ethical core of Herbert Hoover.

In the bruising world of partisan politics, it is often difficult to discern the better aspects of our nature. Though it might appear counterintuitive to ascribe a cloak of a Good Samaritan to President Herbert Hoover, given the harsh criticism he endured for his failure to deal better with the Great Depression, that would be a misleading characterization of the man.

That he was demonized by the Democrats and castigated by those in the breadlines, again, those characterizations fall short of the real person who had to deal with the aftermath of the Stock Market Crash. Indeed, when he was elected to the White House, the only time he ever ran for office, his reputation was already established as the "Great Humanitarian."

Born on August 10, 1874, in West Branch, Iowa, Herbert Clark Hoover was raised within a Quaker household emphasizing hard work, community involvement, spirituality, and nonviolence. Orphaned at ten by the death of his parents, he was sent to Oregon, where he lived with Henry Hinthorn, a physician and part-time real estate agent. He attended a relatively new university in Palo Alto, California, Stanford, after his high school graduation. There, he worked his way through school. He ran a laundry service, delivered newspapers, and worked for the U.S. Geological Service during the summers. He graduated in 1895 with a degree in geology. He met his future wife, Louise "Lou" Henry, at Stanford. She was also studying geology. Over the next two decades, he had jobs with mining companies worldwide, including Western Australia and China. By the time he was forty, he had his own company and was a millionaire. If ever the saying a self-made man" applied to anyone, it certainly did to Herbert Hoover.

His work as a geologist, engineer, and businessman influenced his philosophy of life and his behavior once in government. He applied the standards of engineering to the world in general. He sincerely believed that scientific expertise, if used "thoughtfully and properly," would lead to the betterment of society. Parallel to this, he had faith in the power of the individual to work to this end. Conscientious work by public officials and a reliance on private charity were at the forefront of his initial response to the economic crisis that besieged him only seven months after he won a landslide victory over Al Smith in 1928. In that presidential election, he stood tall and firm against the bigotry and scurrilous anti-Catholic rhetoric, anti-Irish charges thrown against the "Happy Warrior" from

New York State. He denounced those forces of bigotry, particularly in the South, where the ugliness was most entrenched. At that precise moment in November 1928, prosperity reigned, and the Roaring Twenties appeared headed for another decade. Enacted overwhelmingly, a Republican controlled Congress was prepared to go along for the ride.

ELECTION RETURNS – 1928

HOOVER		SMITH
21,391,993	POPULAR VOTE	15,016,169
441	ELECTORAL BALLOTS	87

1928 PRESIDENTIAL CANDIDATES

Though Hoover made few speeches during the presidential campaign, he did assert his views.

We in America are nearer to the final triumph over poverty than ever before in the history of any land… We have not yet reached the goal, but, given a chance to go forward with the policies of the last eight years, we shall, with the help of God, be in sight of the day when poverty will be banished from the nation.

In his inaugural address, Hoover proclaimed:

Ours is a land rich in resources, stimulating in its glorious beauty, filled with millions of happy homes, blessed with comfort and opportunity. In no nation are the institutions of progress more advanced. In no nation are the fruits of accomplishment more secure. In no nation is the government more worthy of respect. No country is more loved by its people. I have an abiding faith in their capacity, integrity, and high purpose. I have no fear for the future of our country. It is bright with hope.

The Great Humanitarian was in office, a reputation justifiably earned. For example… Europe went to war in August 1914. The slaughterhouse that would mark the European continent for four brutal years entrapped and stranded over 120,000 American citizens in Europe and Britain.

At the time, Hoover and his wife were living in London. They could not get out. German submarines in the watery depths and British ships on the high seas were strangling shipping in the North Atlantic. Those already in Britain could not get home. Panic set in. After hundreds of U.S. citizens demonstrated at the American Consulate, Hoover was asked by the U.S. Consul to organize the evacuation of all Americans. Using skills honed in the mining business, Hoover pooled over $1,000,000 of his money and funds from wealthy friends to provide housing in London, food for those stranded, financial assistance, and eventual transportation by ship to New York. This effort included working with the French and German authorities to permit the safe passage of Americans to London and later to America. All Americans were home within six months. Hoover's untiring and competent efforts made the front page. He was portrayed as a man with a big heart who could accomplish big things. As to the funds he provided… All was paid back. Those whom he had helped appreciated what he had done.

The war in Europe began with a large-scale German advance through the Low Countries in 1914. Caught in the middle was Belgium. With Berlin occupying the country, Belgium was cut off from the world. As a highly industrialized nation of 7 million people, it depended on imports for three-quarters of its food. Brussels was caught in a vice. On one side, Germany would not feed the nation or permit food to be imported.

On the other hand, the British navy blocked and turned away merchant ships bringing food to the beleaguered nation. As food supplies dwindled, an entire people faced starvation. Emissaries from non-belligerent countries pleaded with both countries to permit food to reach Belgium. After weeks of negotiations, an agreement was reached to resolve the humanitarian crisis.

Belgium would receive aid. However, how would this be done? Walter Hines Page was the American ambassador to Great Britain. Already impressed by how Hoover handled the stranded Americans' problem, he asked the geologist to engineer another, more important project. Hoover quickly founded a neutral organization "to procure and distribute food to the Belgian populace." It was called the Commission for Relief in Belgium (CRB). Ships would be permitted to go through the naval blockade unmolested. For its part, Germany would not get in the way of the shipments destined for the helpless noncombatants. The effort would go on for four years and need a billion dollars in funding.

BELGIUM RELIEF

The CRB had some of the characteristics of a government. It had its flag. It negotiated treaties with the countries at war. It dealt with cabinet ministers on almost equal terms. Hoover headed the whole business. Within a few months, Hoover had created what one British diplomat called "a practical state organized for benevolence." Hoover also requested and received informal diplomatic immunity. He could and did travel freely through enemy lines. He was the only American to do so during the war.

Hoover's stewardship of the CRB enhanced his reputation as a person who could resolve a complex problem. What did Hoover have to deal with? First, funds had to be raised worldwide through charitable appeals, primarily through subsidies from the Allied governments. With these funds, purchases of wheat and other foodstuffs from North America, South America, and Australia were made. Shipping had to be acquired to transport the grain to the Dutch port of Rotterdam. The ships, some twelve at a time, had to navigate carefully through dangerous minefields and blockades. Once the food was unloaded, it had to be transported to Belgium for distribution to mills, dairies, and bakeries to be prepared for human consumption. Distribution meant reaching over 2,500 villages, towns, and cities. The CRB had to verify that the food was sent to the people of Belgium and not to the German military. This required dealing with financial problems, competent bookkeeping, inspections, and endless checks to prevent corruption and abuse.

Remarking on the work of the CRB, Hoover later said:

The knowledge that we would have to go for four years, to find a billion dollars, to transport five million tons of concentrated food, to administer rationing, a novel relief organization, which went by the name of the Commission for Relief in Belgium (CRB), possessed some of the attributes of a government. It had its own flag, it negotiated "treaties" with the warring European powers, and its leaders parleyed regularly with diplomats and cabinet ministers in several countries.

Hoover had another responsibility during the war. In 1917, President Woodrow Wilson appointed Hoover to "immediately place in operation his plans for food control in the United States." An Executive Order did this on August 10, 1917. In this position, he served from 1917 to 1918 as the head of the U.S. Food Administration. The purpose of the new agency was to substantially reduce American consumption of food to feed our soldiers at the front and European civilians caught up in the ravages of war. The Allies (Britain, France, and Italy) needed food to keep them in the conflict. Unless Americans reduce their wheat consumption, food will not meet the demand. It was Hoover's job to make that happen. He had to convince Americans to participate.

In the Ranks.

(Copyright by Life Pub. Co.)
Courtesy of Life and Charles Dana Gibson.

Hoover enlisted the help of America's ladies and sent them into battle. Often referred to as "America's Food Czar," Hoover instituted a voluntary program of compliance rather than a heavy-handed, highly regulated government program. He wanted the business community involved rather than depending on bureaucrats to staff his agency. He called for patriotism and sacrifices. The effort was known as "Hooverizing." He declared, "Food will win the war." This is where the ladies came into the picture. He called for "Meatless Mondays" and "Wheatless Wednesdays." He asked the women of America to assist in reducing the consumption of key staples, saying, "Food is ammunition --- do not waste it." He added:

Be patriotic; sign your country's pledge to save food. Eat more corn, oats, and rye products. Eat more fish and poultry, fruits, vegetables, potatoes, baked, boiled, and broiled foods. Eat less wheat, sugar, and fats to save for the army and our allies.

In his memoirs, he wrote:

It was my job to ask people to go back to simple food, simple clothes, and simple pleasures. Play hard, work hard, and sleep hard. Do it courageously and cheerfully.

Though difficult, the country reduced food consumption by 15%. The women did their part in the kitchen, exceeding Hoover's expectations. Of course, there were problems, especially in the working class and immigrant neighborhoods where family budgets were already squeezed. Inflation had raised its ugly head. It was 40% in 1916-1917, a tremendous jump in food prices. This led to food riots in New York, Philadelphia, and Boston. As always, inflation fell hardest on those with the smallest wallets. Without question, Blacks fell into this group. There was little Hoover could do about this. As always, the immutable laws of supply and demand were at work. He could not overturn the stark reality of impoverishment in the cities.

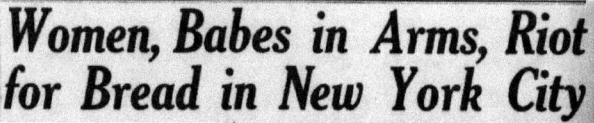

Women, Babes in Arms, Riot for Bread in New York City

"Sweet Marie," Leader, Arrested
After She Leads 300 Followers
to City Hall and Police Station

NEW YORK, Feb. 20.—Crying "We want bread, we want bread," more than 300 women, bareheaded, scantily clad—their warmest garment being a shawl thrown about their shoulders, stormed up the steps of the city hall today demanding relief from Mayor Mitchel from the high cost of food.

Some declared their families were starving.

Most of the women carried babies, their faces showing the pinch of hunger, in their arms.

For a time there was the greatest confusion about the building. The women demanded to see Mayor Mitchel. Police reserves were called, and arrangements were finally made for a committee to enter the hall.

THOUSANDS WATCH WOMEN

Within a few minutes after the hundreds appeared a crowd of thousands had gathered in City Hall park, watching the demonstration. Marie Ganz, known as "Sweet Marie," led the women.

On November 11, 1918, the guns fell silent on the Western Front. The slaughter of millions of young men ceased with the Armistice. Celebration and jubilation in London and Paris... The Great War was over. Soon, dignified men in diplomatic attire met at Versailles to formally conclude a treaty to end the conflict and usher in a new order among European nations. Triumphant soldiers marched in victory parades as bands played patriotic tunes and adoring crowds waved tiny flags. Peace at last...

Beyond this transient moment, the dark shadow of starvation hovered over Europe, particularly the new country of Poland and the revolutionary government of Soviet Russia. The Wilson Administration decided to provide relief. The Congress established and funded the American Relief Administration (ARA) on February 24. 1919. About 100 million dollars was appropriated. That amount was supplemented by an additional $100 million raised through voluntary efforts. Once more, President Wilson called upon Herbert Hoover to administer the program. Having run the Commission for Relief in Belgium, he was the most experienced person for the job. He had fed seven million Belgians and over two million French citizens during the war. No other person was more suited for the task. Under his leadership, over four million tons of relief supplies would eventually be provided to 23 war-torn European countries, including the Soviet Union. Though Hoover detested Bolshevism and Vladimir Lenin's takeover of Russia, he staunchly supported aid to the famine-stricken population. Indeed, this was a case of the Good Samaritan at work. The Congress appropriated $20,000,000 for relief funds under the Russian Famine Relief Act of late 1921. In time, 300 Americans and more than 120,000 Russians were employed by the ARA to feed 10.5 million people daily. The program continued until June 15, 1923, when Russia could feed its citizens.

THE GOOD SAMARITAN

Political cartoonists in America also noted the quiet man who made things happen under challenging circumstances.

THE CANNING SEASON

For millions of Americans, Hoover would make a great president, one you could count on in a crisis. However, the unfair fickleness of history anointed him with the stock market crash and the ensuing Great Depression. Of this, he said with regret:

Once upon a time, my opponents honored me as possessing the fabulous intellect and economic power by which I created a worldwide depression all by myself.

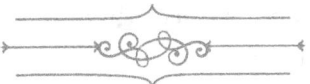

CHAPTER 7 – THE GREAT FLOOD

He had never held an elected office until he was pressured to run in 1928. He was not a career politician. While he raised millions for worthy causes, he never solicited funds for political campaigns. When nominated by Republicans to represent their standard, he never barnstormed across the political landscape seeking votes, promising a "goodie" to every voter he encountered. Though conservative to the bone, he was essentially nonpartisan in his politics. He believed in the smallest government possible, the strongest military necessary in an unsafe world, and maximum adherence to individual rights and liberties. All this worked for him as a capitalist, believing in the virtues of a free market and a private sector economy. In many ways, he was a progressive following in the footsteps of Theodore Roosevelt. He worked for President Woodrow Wilson and supported the president's efforts to join the League of Nations. He also endorsed Wilson's domestic efforts to iron out the sharp edges of unfettered capitalism. Though he later worked with President Warren G. Harding's people, Hoover was never tied to the scandals that beset that president."

Hoover's political philosophy can be summed up in his own words:

I do not believe that the power and duty of the general government ought to be extended to the relief of individual suffering.

As with any politician echoing strong positions, Hoover was faced with a singular question: What would he do with a crisis affecting many suffering citizens? One answer came with the Great Flood…

We must begin with a map depicting the length and breadth of the Mississippi, the "Mother River. "

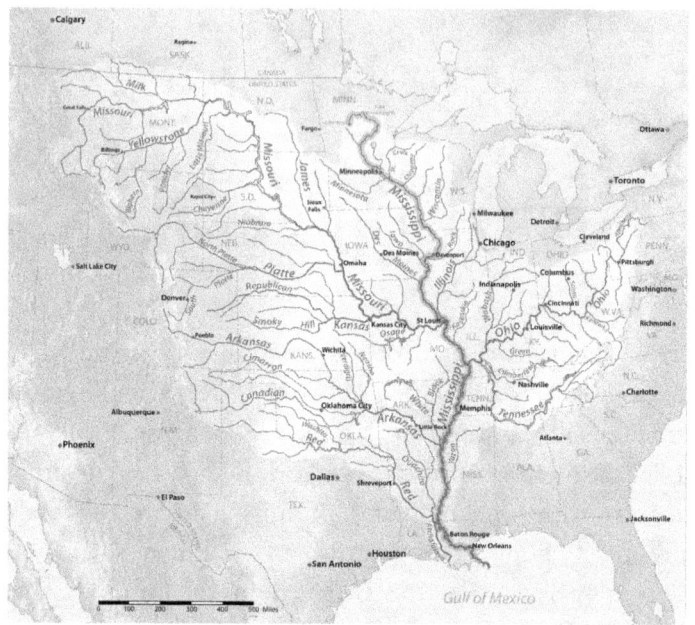

The great river begins in northern Minnesota, a few miles north of Minneapolis. From Lake Itasca, it flows south for 2,340 miles to the Mississippi Delta in the Gulf of Mexico. Given the many tributaries that flow into the river, the Mississippi watershed drains some 32 states. It is the thirteenth-largest river by discharge in the world. The river passes through Minnesota, Wisconsin, Iowa, Illinois, Missouri, Kentucky, Tennessee, Arkansas, Mississippi, and Louisiana. The river provides water to nourish the thirst of millions, and the soil tilled along its banks. It is the beating heart of agriculture, industry, and transportation in the middle of America.

In the summer of 1926, rainfall in the Midwest drenched the land. Tributaries, especially in Kansas and Iowa, were swollen to capacity. On Christmas Day, the Cumberland River at Nashville, Tennessee, exceeded 56 feet above flood stage. Flooding waters poured into the Mississippi. Levees broke along the river in 145 locations. Within a short period, over 27,000 square miles were flooded. The river averaged 35 feet above flood level. The rampaging waters directly affected over 650,000 people.

Some 94% of these people lived in Arkansas, Mississippi, and Louisiana. Approximately 200,000 Blacks were displaced from their homes along the Lower Mississippi River. As a group, they composed 75% of the Delta's population. About 94% lived in the three states already noted. They supplied 95% of the labor force in the vast area. In the relief camps later established, Blacks accounted for 69% of the 325,000 people receiving assistance.

FLOODED FARMS AND TOWNS

It was called the Great Mississippi Flood of 1927. It was the most destructive flood in our history. Over 500 people lost their lives, and over 700,000 people were homeless. In several states, over 27,000 square miles were inundated. The damage exceeded $1,000,000,000, or about 1/3 of the federal budget. Arkansas was the worst hit. Over 14% of the state was flooded. Below Memphis, the Mississippi reached a width of 80 miles. It wasn't until August that the floodwaters began to subside.

At the time, Herbert Hoover held a cabinet position in the Coolidge Administration. He was the Secretary of Commerce. President Calvin Coolidge quickly turned to Hoover, as Wilson had once done. Would he organize relief for the affected states and their citizens? Given his previous experiences during World War I, Hoover was the natural choice for the job.

Hoover immediately called upon the nation to assist in the vast relief project. He worked closely with the American Red Cross and sought public involvement on the radio.

HOOVER AROUSES THE NATION

Housing was the most immediate problem. The Commerce Department established tent cities in the devastated areas. This was needed for poor whites and the Black population. These impromptu enclaves required water, food, clothing, and bedding. Sanitation issues were always present. Hoover enlisted grassroots support to assist the government in dealing with these problems. That was most difficult in the rural areas, where political leadership and citizen involvement were most unprepared to manage the chaotic circumstances. Eventually, Hoover was forced to place the camps under federal supervision. In doing so, he aided vast numbers of poor whites and Blacks. Because of the circumstances, he engineered aid to individuals suffering from forces beyond their control. Clearly, Hoover understood the gravity of the situation, his personal views notwithstanding. The whole country followed his efforts.

A TENT CITY FOR BLACKS

MEDIA COVERAGE

Housing and feeding a displaced, flooded-out population were necessities. It was Belgium again; once more, Hoover was up to the task. People would be fed.

The refugee camps were not immune to extreme racial inequality. Local control in the southern states essentially meant white control of the relief programs. White citizens received immediate attention. Blacks received the leftovers. This was a heritage of Jim Crow policies and a history of racial discrimination. In far too many cases, Blacks did not receive supplies without providing the name of their white employer. Without that, they needed a voucher from a white person. As a group, they were not permitted to leave the camps. In addition, they were forced to work against their will --- and at gunpoint --- by assisting white landowners with their flood damage.

FORCED LABOR

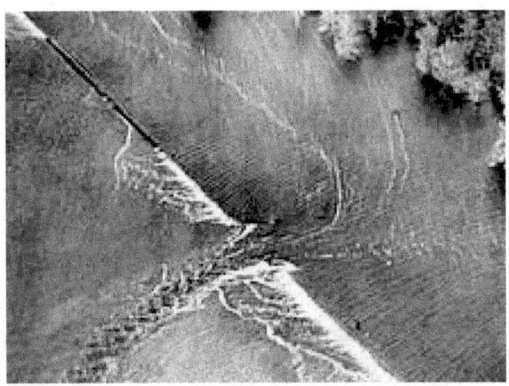

BROKEN LEVEES

In time, the poor treatment of Blacks reached Hoover. This was mainly the work of Robert Russa Moton, who headed the Colored Advisory Commission to Coolidge. Moton was born in 1867 in Amelia County, Virginia. He was the grandson of an African chieftain who had grown wealthy by engaging in the slave trade before he himself was sold into slavery. That's how the Moton family got to the Americas. Following the death of Booker T. Washington in 1915, Moton became the head of Tuskegee Institute, where he reformed the curriculum to emphasize a liberal arts program leading to a Bachelor of Science degree. Once America entered the war in Europe, he was sent to Europe by President Wilson to investigate the condition of Black soldiers. His report documented discriminatory practices within the military. Little was done to alleviate these conditions. In 1922, Moton was one of the keynote speakers at the dedication of the Lincoln Memorial. He closed his speech saying:

I believe that all of us, black and white, both North and South, are going to strive on to finish the work which Lincoln so nobly began to make America an example for the world of equal justice and equal opportunity for all who strive and are willing to serve under the flag that makes men free.

Moton gave his speech outdoors to a segregated crowd. He was not allowed to sit with the other speakers, who were white.

MAY 30, 1922 – LINCOLN MEMORIAL DEDICATED

On April 21, 1927, the floodwaters broke the levee at Mound Landing, Mississippi, near Greenville, Mississippi, a town of approximately 13,000. Moton was dispatched to cover the situation, particularly related to Blacks. One white resident told him:

We couldn't warn Negroes when we telephoned all subscribers yesterday. They had no telephones. Others thought the levee might hold. We don't know what happened to them. Negroes are coming out of the lowlands in boatloads.

The "lowlands" referred to areas of the Delta where Blacks lived in their segregated communities. These areas were directly in the path of the Mississippi River's regular flooding. Black residents were the first to be displaced by the torrent of eroding water. They were also the least able to respond to the crisis.

Moton also learned that the disaster was beyond the scope of local governments and relief agencies. Dennis Murphree, the Governor of Mississippi, summarized the situation in his urgent message to President Coolidge.

Unprecedented floods have created a national emergency. This territory will be water-covered one to twenty feet in twenty-four hours and contain a population of 150,000... beyond the capacity of local and state agencies in relief and control.

In response, Coolidge said:

The government is giving such aid as lies within its powers, but the burden of caring for the homeless rests upon the agency designated by government charter to provide relief in disaster: the American National Red Cross.

Coolidge appointed Hoover to oversee the Red Cross's efforts. He also chaired a quasi-governmental commission of five Cabinet members and the Red Ross vice-chairman, James Fieser. The group quickly developed a plan of action. The military would round up refugees and move them to local Red Cross camps. Each Red Cross chapter would be in charge of relief in a specific area, with power over all available local resources.

Moton's report focused on the levee at Greenville, Mississippi, that was held against the flooding waters. It was the only high, safe place for thousands of refugees, the majority of whom were Black. They were desperate for food, potable drinking water, and shelter. Given the situation, they should have been evacuated. They were not. They were virtually imprisoned on the levee. Again, at gunpoint, they were forced to maintain the levee. This camp was the worst of all the refugee sites. Where possible, white refugees were placed in indoor facilities. Blacks were detained in outdoor camps on the levee in tents. Ample evidence indicates they were systematically denied adequate food and shelter.

The abuses occurring at Greenville did not go unnoticed. Moton's report delineated them. Reporters for the *Chicago Defender,* a northern Negro newspaper, chronicled the situation and called into question the work of the Red Cross. Hoover was also criticized for his inability to stop the unequal treatment of refugees. The scandal threatened to tarnish Hoover's image and possibly his presidential ambitions. In time, Moton's findings were presented to Hoover. He advocated for immediate improvement to aid the flood's victims in most need. Moton's report was never made public. Hoover's supporters, already looking ahead to the 1928 Republican Party convention, wanted a tight lid on the investigation. They tried to maintain Hoover's image as a Great Humanitarian. In exchange for Moton's acquiescence, he was promised that Hoover, if he became president, would include Blacks in his administration on an unprecedented basis. There was even a suggestion that Hoover would divide the land of bankrupt planters into small, privately owned farms. Accepting Hoover's promises at face value, Moton's report never fully revealed the full extent of the abuses in the Delta? This essentially kept his worst findings out of the media. He went on to fully support Hoover's quest for the White House. Once elected, the Hoover Administration ignored the promises made to Moton. That is a matter of record. Four years later, Moton switched to the Democratic Party. By then, he was encouraging Blacks to leave the party of Lincoln and emancipation for the Democrats. He also strongly encouraged Blacks to move northward, especially to Chicago.

Of course, the question arises as to what Hoover could have done to resolve the unfair treatment of Blacks in the Delta? He did oversee a federal response in conjunction with the Red Cross. However, relief efforts were generally in the hands of local white politicians, relief workers, and military contingents embedded with racial attitudes. Hoover had little control over this. As to the promises made to Moton, that is a more difficult question to answer. There is little evidence supporting the view that Hoover was racist in outlook or the author of racist policies. On the other hand, the question remains: could he have done more to assist those trapped by the Great Mississippi Flood of 1927?

The tragedy of the Greenville levee was immortalized in a song entitled: *When* the *Levee Breaks.* It was a country music song written and first recorded by Memphis Minnie and Kansas Joe McCoy in 1929, a husband and wife country music couple. The lyrics reflected the experience of Blacks during the Great Flood. Minnie lived with her family near Walls, Mississippi, when the local levee broke. The lyrics in the song recounted the personal toll on a Black man who had lost his home and family.

WHEN THE LEVEE BREAKS

If it keeps on raining, levee's goin' break
If it keeps on rainin, levee's goin' break
When the levee breaks, I'll have no place to stay.

Mean old levee taught me to weep and moan, Lord
Mean old levee taught me to weep and moan
It's got what it takes to make a mountain man leave his home
Oh well, oh well, oh well.

Don't make you feel bad
When you're tryin' to find your way home
You don't know which way to go?
If you're going down south
They go to work to do
If you're going down to Chicago

Cryin' won't help you, prayer won't do you no good
No cryin' won't help ou, prayin' won't do you no good
When the levee breaks, mama, you got to move on.

All last night sat on the levee and moaned
All last night sat on the levee and moaned
Thinkin' 'b out my baby and my happy home

I'm goin' to Chicago
Goin' to Chicago
Sorry, but I can't take you, ahhh

Goin' down, goin' down now.

THE LEVEE

Should Hoover have done more for Blacks? The fundamental truth is that, as with any crisis, more could be done. But Hoover wasn't the president. He held a cabinet position. His authority was limited. He had to work with the military, the Red Cross, government bureaucrats, and local people. It would have been challenging to circumvent them, especially in the racially charged Delta. Keeping Moton's report out of the public eye raises questions, including a most difficult one. Would it have made any difference? Except in the Black community, who would have cared what was happening to impoverished people living in the lowlands? In an imperfect world, Hoover did what was possible as he encountered the social and racial forces beyond his control. The Great Mississippi Flood of 1927 was a crisis that challenged Hoover's views on assisting those in distress. In the capriciousness of history, one question did, however, remain. How would Hoover respond to an unprecedented economic disaster if elected to the presidency?

ALWAYS THE RACE ISSUE

CHAPTER 8 – THE SOLID SOUTH

In the 1930s, the novelist, satirist, and columnist H.L. Mencken described what was called the Solid South and the oppression of Blacks living under Jim Crow law.

To a large number of American citizens life in certain parts of the country becomes intolerably hazardous. They may be seized on any pretext, however flimsy, and put to death with horrible tortures. No government pretending to be civilized can go on condoning such atrocities. Either it must make every possible effort to put them down or it must suffer the scorn and contempt of Christendom.

Historians have generally alluded to sectional, one-party rule in the South as the mainstay of Southern political power.

In the United States, the continued influence of the old elite meant that southern politics fell under the domination of the Democratic Party that glorified the Confederacy, the Lost Cause, the Ku Klux Klan, and resistance to Reconstruction. White supremacy was made into the fundamental cause of the South, and racism became the tool to enforce white unity behind the Democratic Party. Conformity to white supremacy, segregation, and Democratic Party rule was a social imperative for generations of southerners who were indoctrinated in the belief that they had suffered a grave injustice with the defeat of their glorious Lost Cause.

Many had tried to circumvent the political power of the Solid South. All have failed. Whether it was Teddy Roosevelt, Warren Harding, Calvin Coolidge, Herbert Hoover, or Franklin D. Roosevelt, these presidents couldn't pass, by way of an example, a federal anti-lynching law. While all were asked to throw their political weight behind such a law all either quietly refused or demurred to one overwhelming political reality. A block of southern states (see map below) with control of key congressional committees in Congress could and did stymie efforts to enact anti-lynching legislation, or any legislation that altered race relations in the South.

As a group, they represented what was called the Solid South. With a representation of nearly 40% in the Senate, they stalled or voted down potential legislation in committees or ignored efforts in that direction. Elected again to office, they were armed with seniority, giving them the chairmanship of major committees. Again, these southern Democrats functioned in a one-party system and had a veto on any legislation that disrupted social and racial conditions in the South. They sought to maintain the status quo, relegating Blacks to second-class citizenship characterized by segregation and discrimination in Jim Crow country.

Southern representatives were opposed to any law-making lynching a federal crime punishable by a jail sentence and/or a fine. They argued such laws would infringe on states' rights since murder was a state offence. They claimed this was federal overreach and amounted to the political targeting of southern states that once composed the Confederacy.

The presidents noted that they knew what was taking place in the South. All too often, there was no attempt to hide or mask a lynching. Ads were placed in newspapers explaining where an extralegal execution was going to take place. Flyers were distributed to the local white population announcing an impending lynching. Mailers were sent through the USPO. Special trains and buses brought law-abiding citizens to the appropriate site. Southern sheriffs, majors, and state officials openly aided and abetted the lynch mobs. Most people understood that lynching wasn't a legal hanging. No jury had found the victim guilty of a crime punishable by death. Vigilantes executed people without legal authority. They did so regardless of whether that person had committed a crime. Between 1882 and 1951, some 4,730 people were lynched in the United States. Of that number, 3,437 were Black men.

LYNCHING

Why were there so many lynchings of Blacks? The basic reason was to keep an easily identifiable minority in a subordinate position through a systematic system of legal oppression supported by violence to intimidate an entire group. In particular, this meant keeping Blacks from voting. The South, by force of arms, was forced to accept emancipation and the end of slavery. However, it fiercely opposed suffrage and the notion of equality of races, whether in social interactions or on constitutional rights. Following the withdrawal of federal troops from the South in 1876, sixteen former slave states began a violent process to disenfranchise the freemen regardless of the Fifteenth Amendment. This effort was backed up by fraternal organizations such as the KKK, the Redeemers, the White League, and the Red Shirts. Lynchings became their hallmark in an effort to maintain white supremacy. In actions today noted as systemic racism, they excluded Blacks from voting by way of poll taxes, literacy tests, residency requirements, and grandfather clauses that still permitted poor, illiterate whites to vote. Where such efforts failed, violence always hovered in the shadows.

Over the years, the Republican Party had pledged itself to enact an anti-lynching law to "exterminate the hideous crime." President Hoover was quoted as saying, "Every decent citizen must condemn lynching as an evil undermining of the very essence of both justice and democracy (September 23, 1930)." Even though Hoover was generally sympathetic to the needs of the Black community, his administration was unwilling to expend political capital on civil rights. What could he have done to dislodge the southern grip on Congress if he had been more forceful? As with other presidents, he accepted what amounted to American apartheid in the former Confederacy. His successor in the White House was also unable to support an anti-lynching law publicly. Without the blessings of the Solid South, Roosevelt's New Deal programs would have been jeopardized. To get along, as Hoover had to, he had to go along.

The Solid South was a political force to be reckoned with. However, defiance occasionally occurred, though muted and often from unexpected sources.

An unusual incident occurred on June 12, 1929. First Lady Lou Henry Hoover hosted the traditional tea party at the White House. Members of Congress were invited along with their wives. One who showed up with his spouse was Oscar DePriest, the elected Congressman from Illinois's 1st Congressional District. His presence shocked many people, particularly those invitees from the South. Why was that? DePriest was the first elected Black person in Congress outside the southern states. He was also the first and only Black member of the House of Representatives in the 20th Century. During his three terms in Congress, he was the only Black member. Another point must be added. White members of Congress would not dine with him in the cafeteria run by the government. At the time, he could invite Blacks to join him for a meal, but he could not invite Blacks and whites to do so simultaneously. Diversity was out. Pseudo segregation was in. In any event, Mrs. Hoover received sharp criticism in southern newspapers.

TEA AND POLITICS

Whatever his true feelings were about Blacks' civil rights, Hoover found himself in a political storm in 1930. On March 8th of that year, Edward T. Sanford visited his dentist to remove a tooth. After the extraction, he rose from the dentist's chair and collapsed. He died that day. He was 64 years old. He wasn't just another government worker.

He was an Associate Justice on the U.S. Supreme Court. The southerner from Tennessee needed to be replaced. To do so, President Hoover chose a politician from North Carolina, John J. Parker. He was a Republican who had run for governor and other offices and always lost in this Solid South state. He was always accused of courting Black voters. That was a fatal charge in North Carolina.

JOHN J. PARKER

Almost immediately and unexpectedly, Hoover's nominee came under incessant attack from two powerful groups: The NAACP and the AFL. The NAACP was founded in 1909. It was incorporated on February 12, 1909. This was, of course, Abraham Lincoln's birthday. Its charter proclaimed:

To promote equality of rights and to eradicate caste or race prejudice among citizens of the United States...

The organization opposed Parker based on his statements in earlier political campaigns to garner white votes.

Experience has demonstrated that the participation of the Negro in the political life in the South is harmful to him and is a fruitful source of racial prejudice, which works to his injury. As a class, he has learned this lesson. He no longer desires to participate in the state's politics.

He also added:

> *The participation of the Negro in politics is a source of evil and danger to both races and is not desired by the wise men in either race or by the Republican Party of North Carolina.*

Parker had also antagonized the American Federation of Labor (AFL). He had delivered anti-union opinions as a judge at the state level. Parker supported "yellow dog" contracts that forbade worker participation in unions. These contracts were an agreement between an employee and an employer. Signing one was a precondition if you wanted to be hired. An employee agreed not to become a labor union member or act in collaboration with other employees. In many cases, unemployed workers had no choice but to sign. A paycheck meant food on the table for the family.

On April 28, 1930, an acrimonious debate began in the Senate. Everyone knew it was going to be a close vote. How close? The Vice-President of the United States was Charles Curtis. He was also the President of the Senate and entitled to vote in case of a tie. The debate closed on May 7, 1930. Hoover's nominee was defeated 41-39. Curtis's vote was not needed. The first high court nomination was lost on a Senate roll call since 1894. From the perspective of the NAACP, a racist had been kept off the high court. The AFT was pleased that another anti-labor judge was not on the court. Following the defeat, Hoover nominated Owen Roberts. He was easily confirmed. It should also be noted that "yellow dog' contracts were eliminated by the Norris-LaGuardia Act (1932) as part of the New Deal. By that time, public opinion shifted in favor of labor. Political sentiment was now against employers who sought to prevent workers from joining a union. It was also against judges who used their power to limit union activities. It was the first national pro-labor law and the precursor to the Wagner Act of 1935 that recognized the right of workers to unionize and negotiate collectively for higher wages and safer working conditions.

On the issue of civil rights, it is challenging to evaluate Hoover. He saw little need for significant civil rights legislation during his presidency. Believing in individualism, he thought that Blacks would benefit more from education and assimilation than from any federal program. In a perfect world, that was an appealing case. Educational opportunities would have enhanced not only the underclass but also those still tied to the legacy of slavery. Here, Hoover failed to fully see that in the absence of federal legislation, segregated schools would prevail, especially in the South. Equality in educational opportunities was simply not present. Assimilation was indeed a legitimate goal that required two for this societal dance. Too much of the country held assimilation at arm's length. The presence of ghettos and barrios attests to this due to inequalities in housing patterns and income. With respect to a federal anti-lynching law, Hoover was absent from the fray. Given the inordinate influence of the Solid South in Congress, this would always be a losing proposition for the president. Ultimately, he was unwilling to ensure equal opportunities through federal legislation. It would be up to future presidents to take on the task.

It is important to note that Hoover gave special attention to improving the lives of Native Americans. Based on the Indian Citizenship Act of 1924, he supported the concepts of self-sufficiency and full assimilation. He also selected Charles Curtis as his running mate in 1928. Curtis was a member of the Kaw Tribe and the first Native American to hold that elected office.

THE REPUBLICAN CANDIDATES

As noted earlier, before entering the White House, Hoover was the Secretary of Commerce under President Coolidge. At that time, the government policy prohibited segregation in the federal workforce. There was however an "unwritten rule" to avoid any integration of the white and Black employees to the extent possible. This was especially true in southern cities, including Washington, D.C. In March 1928, Hoover received a contingent of Blacks from the NAACP. Neval Thomas was the leader of the organization. He presented Hoover with several recommendations that would assist the Black community. Central to the recommendations was the Census Bureau, which was a division of the Commerce Department. Thomas claimed the Bureau was segregated. Hoover requested a full report on the matter. The report indicated that the Bureau had two segregated offices with 23 employees. Hoover ordered the two offices to be broken up. Employees would work in the same room.

Hoover's action was seen as a significant departure from the status quo. Following the decision, Thomas wrote Hoover:

The colored people of the country are deeply sensible of the high-minded statesmanship you showed in your abolition of the humiliation they suffered in the Census Bureau.

The *Washington Eagle*, a Black newspaper, editorialized:

Mr. Hoover did not vehemently deny the existence of segregation. He promised to investigate, which he did with the result that he quickly abolished the segregated area and the clerks who were Jim-Crowed were assimilated in the bureau among the other clerks. What Mr. Hoover has done in his department all of the other Cabinet officers could do was they so minded. The only difference between the others and Mr. Hoover is that he has the necessary backbone to do the right thing.

Hoover described his action as simply a matter of fairness. He pointed out that he had received no protest in the matter from either white or Black employees. Senator H.D. Stephens of Mississippi replied, representing the Solid South's determination to preserve the prevailing social order.

You may have received "no complaint" but your knowledge of human nature and your sense of decency and propriety must cause you to know that the breasts of many of the employees in the bureau are seething with unuttered protests against the condition that you have brought about. This criticism is not a political one. It is made in the interest of decency and of the welfare of the Government. History cannot be trifled with. Whenever there has been a step toward social equality between the races, dire results have followed, and both have suffered.

Hoover's action did not end segregation in most government offices. It was merely a first step in what would be a long and difficult road. So where does that leave us? Hoover was a product of his time. He was elected during prosperous times. The public wanted the Harding-Coolidge policies of normalcy to continue. They wanted a president to limit government interference and to allow the capitalist system to function unhampered. Given that Hoover was the perfect man for the White House as long as good times lasted. Along with others, he never foresaw the clouds of a looming Great Depression. By the time his administration understood the depths of the depression, Hoover had only attempted some timid moves to involve the federal government. He stopped short, however, of directly relieving millions of people without work. That, of course, did not benefit the very poor and certainly Blacks. Unfairly or not, Hoover would be blamed for starting the depression (which he did not) or for failing to respond to the needs of the unemployed (for which a case can be made). Nevertheless, Hoover would reap, unjustly or not, the blame for the Great Depression.

A contemporary humorist and actor, Will Rogers, stated the feelings of many. He said:

If Americans were lucky enough to find an apple to eat in the Depression and bit into it only to find a worm, they would blame Hoover for it.

HARSH POLITICAL CARTOONS

For Hoover and Roosevelt, the political strength of the Solid South was always a factor to be weighed in dealing with any legislation that would alter race relations. The Solid South was always resistant to change and the constitutional amendments that were forced upon them: the Thirteenth Amendment (abolition of slavery), the Fourteenth Amendment (defining citizenship), and the Fifteenth Amendment (granting the right to vote). That was the reality both Hoover and, later, Roosevelt faced.

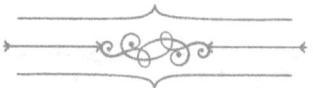

CHAPTER 9 – HOOVERVILLES

Donald Francis Roy was at the University of Washington in 1934. He was working on his M.A. in Sociology. He did ethnographic fieldwork in a "shantytown" adjacent to Terminal 4, Elliott Bay in Seattle. He paid $15 to buy a beat-up wooden shack. That was quite a lot in 1934. He could have paid the monthly rent for a house for the same money. Roy, however, wasn't interested in living in Seattle proper with more affluent folks. He wanted to live in a community of unemployed men and women in what were disparagingly called "Hoovervilles." Charles Michelson first coined the term in 1930 to describe gatherings of "down and out" folks bewildered and damaged by the Great Depression. At the time, Michelson was a newspaper reporter and the PR director of the Democratic National Committee.

What did Francis Roy get for his purchase? He was now the owner of a homemade stove, a 5-gallon kerosene can that leaked smoke. He also got a bunk padded with burlap that wasn't much better than sleeping on concrete. For his cash, he now owned a few plates and utensils that had seen better days. But all of that was okay with Roy. He was right where he wanted to be. He was now the resident of one of the largest encampments for those down on their luck. It was where he needed to be. He wanted to study the attitudes and behaviors of people who had lost everything but were still trying to keep their self-respect. He could do so without appearing to conduct an academic study. His work produced the best-known view of homelessness and shanty towns in the 1930s.

Of course, homelessness existed before the Great Depression. Where it existed, local governments built municipal lodgings to aid people. Unemployment during the depression outstripped the available housing. Shantytowns dotted the landscape without public assistance, from about 500 in 1929 to over 6,000 by 1932.

SEATTLE SHANTYTOWN

Almost all the shanty homes were constructed from old wood crates, cardboard, and other materials. At best, they had a small stove, bedding, and simple cooking implements. Satirists of the day coined other demeaning terms for the Hoovervilles. What was a Hoover blanket? Answer: an old newspaper. What was a Hoover flag? Answer: an empty pocket turned inside out. What was Hoover leather? It was old cardboard used to line worn-out shoes. What was a Hoover wagon? Horses pulled an automobile because the engine had been removed.

SHANTY TOWNS

Hooverville became a common term for shack towns and homeless encampments. The term emphasized that President Hoover and the Republican Party were responsible for the nation's economic crisis.

As Roy discovered, the shanty communities initially had no formal government. Over time, an informal system allowed diverse groups, including migrants and immigrants, to live in close quarters. All nationalities, ethnic groups, and races functioned in reasonable harmony. Unlike in general society, integration existed in the camps. Blacks and whites got along. Being down on the ground, down by the depression, was what they all had in common.

Roy's research chronicled the history of Seattle's shantytowns, which began in 1931 and would exist for almost a decade. In 1931, an unemployed lumberjack and twenty other men started building shacks on vacant land owned by the Port of Seattle and adjacent to Pioneer Square. Within a few days, they constructed 50 shanties. Very quickly, squatters arrived. Informally, they accepted Jesse Jackson, the unemployed lumberjack, as their mayor.

There was pushback from the City of Seattle. The Health Department posted notices on every shack. The residents were told to vacate in one week. A week later, the Seattle Police arrived. They poured kerosene and burned down all the shacks. The squatters immediately rebuilt their shanty homes. Once again, the city burned them down. The squatters now tried a different tactic. They burrowed into the ground and built roofs made of tin or steel. This time, the city relented. The squatters were allowed to stay if they adhered to safety and sanitary rules.

Jackson later wrote about his tenure as the mayor, saying:

I was just a simple person, living among simple people, whose status in life is the same as theirs, trying to do the best I know how to administer in my poor way to their wants. The men often seek my advice and bring their troubles to me. I advise them the best I can on many occasions. I am often able to prevent many little rows that might develop into big ones.

The city of Oakland, California, has the most unusual shantytown. The out-of-work men lived in huge concrete sewer pipes that were stored above ground. The American Concrete Pipe Company owned the pipes. The company agreed to let the squatters use the surplus pipes, which they did between September 1932 and April 1933. The pipes were six feet long. Each section became a "homeless shelter." Nearly 200 squatters lived in the community that was called Pipe City. The ends of the pipe were covered with burlap or cardboard. The residents survived on mulligan stew made from discarded vegetables from nearby grocery wholesalers.

PIPE CITY, PORTLAND, OAKLAND

The *Oakland Post-Inquirer* published an article about Pipe City on December 3, 1932, shortly before the Christmas holidays. What was written applied to all the shantytowns across the country.

To qualify for citizenship in Pipe City you must be jobless, homeless, hungry, and preferably shoeless, coatless, and hatless. If one also is discouraged, lonely, filled with a terrible feeling of hopelessness and helplessness, one's qualifications are much stronger. One belongs. Not all of Pipe City's inhabitants are that way. Some of them have learned that a philosophical attitude helps. One may tinge his philosophy with drop of iron, even bitterness, and the concrete may seem less hard and the blankets less thin and the mulligan less watery. Bit it takes a lot of philosophy, you bet, to make concrete either soft or warm.

In 1938, William Lee Con Conley wrote and sang a song called *Unemployment Stomp*. It provided a realistic picture of being unemployed and what it could mean for family life.

I'm a law abiding citizen, and my debts I sure will pay,
I'm a law-abiding citizen, and my debts I sure will pay.
I hope war don't start and Uncle Sam have to send me away.

I haven't never been in jail, and I haven't never paid no fine, baby,
I haven't never been in jail, and I haven't never paid no fine, baby.
I want a job to make my livin', cause stealin' ain't my line.

I've known a time when I have raised my own meat and meal,
I've known a time when I have raised my own meat and meal,
My meat was in my smokehouse and my meal was in my field.

When Mr. Roosevelt sent out those unemployment cards,
When Mr. Roosevelt sent out those unemployment cards,
I just kowned sure that work was goin' to start.

Broke up my home 'cause I didn't have no work to do,
Broke up my home 'cause I didn't have no work to do,
My wife had to leave me' cause she was starvin' too.

It had all started out so well for President Hoover, prosperous times and a landslide victory. A well-earned reputation for humanitarian work is appropriate for a decent man who found his way to the White House, lauded by most of his fellow citizens and deeply caring about them. And then the Wall Street crash and all that followed, desperation on Main Street, despair in the countryside, and bitterness in the squalor of Hoovevilles. Things had all gone so quickly, and they were about to worsen for the embattled Quaker from Iowa.

HISTORY CAN BE CRUEL

What Ray witnessed and what one song suggested was a country in need. America was crying out for leadership. Most people wanted temporary assistance, not charity. If the private sector could do so, that would be okay. But what if such aid were insufficient? What would happen next?

PRIDE ON THE LINE

CHAPTER 10– THE
BONUS MARCHERS

In 1924 the Congress overwhelmingly passed the World War Adjusted Compensation Act. It promised to pay each veteran $1.25 for each day served in Europe, or $1.00 if their service was restricted to the United States. Those owed $50 or less would be paid immediately. The maximum payment would be $625. The payments, described as a bonus, would be in the form of a certificate. The total number of certificates issued was 3,662,374. The face value of the certificates was $3.64 billion. To provide for this huge amount, Congress set up a trust fund. Each year, tax revenues would be added to the fund. The enabling legislation permitted a veteran to borrow up to 22.5% of the certificate's face value. The key component of the law was this. The certificates would not be redeemable until 1945.

Out in Oregon in 1932 was an out-of-work, 34-year-old veteran down to his last dime. His name was Walter W. Waters. Since the November Armistice, he had found work as a mechanic, car salesman, baker, and in a cannery. Over a period, he spoke to other men, all of whom had served in the American Expeditionary Force (AEF) and were now unemployed. As a group, they agreed the promised bonus should be paid now rather than in 1945. Waters emerged as a leader of what would later be described as the Bonus Marchers. He organized over 200 men to travel to Washington to pressure the White House to begin the redemption process. Travelling from Oregon to the nation's capital was not easy. Many of the men rode on boxcars or hiked along dusty roads, hoping to hitch a ride. Over 20,000 veterans eventually reached Washington. Many Americans embraced the veterans as they trekked across the country. In preparation for an encampment near the Capitol, Waters insisted on order. He demanded discipline from the men. There would be no panhandling, no liquor and no radical talk. As he told reporters, "I love this country. I'm emphatically not advocating revolution."

WATERS AND THE BONUS MARCHERS REACH WASHINTON

Waters kept a diary of what he called the Bonus Expeditionary Force (BEF). One of his entries stated his case straightforwardly.

It mattered not that the Bonus was not due, legally, until 1945. What man, having a promise to (be paid) at a later date would not ask his debtor for it in advance if he believed that the debtor could afford the money and if his own need was not only great but critical? These men felt that the Government had the money. Newspapers, which can always be picked out of trashcans in the parks and public polices, published stories of extensions of credit to foreign nations. Headlines told of loans to railroads and to large corporations.

Concerning Black soldiers… Over 380,000 had served during WWI. Over 200,000 had been sent to France. As a group, they represented slightly more than 13% of all inductees, though they were only 10% of the general population. The eventual encampment was racially integrated. Blacks and whites lived side by side at a time when this was verboten in much of the country. The Great Depression was the common thread that brought the veterans together, as well as the misery of the unemployment line.

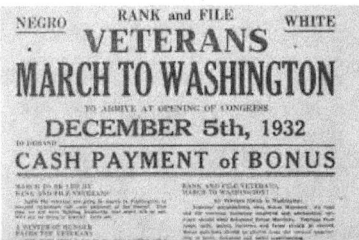

MARCHING TO WASHINGTON

IN FRONT OF THE WASHINGTON MONUMENT

Once the veterans reached Washington, they formed Hooverville on the Anacostia Flats located in a historically Black area of the city. The area was muddy and swampy. Strictly speaking, the encampment was illegal. It was against Federal law to do so. However, the Director of Public Buildings and Public Parks made no objection. His name was Ulysses S. Grant III. Representative James Hamilton Lewis of Illinois requested that the War Department set up billets to assist the veterans. The request was denied. As had been done elsewhere, the veterans had to use materials from a local junk yard where they found old lumber, packing boxes, scrap tin and thatched straw to be used for roofs. The encampment was named Camp Marks after the friendly police captain, S. J. Marks. Food, of course, was a challenge. Pelham D. Glassford was the Superintendent of the Washington, D.C. police force. He worked with the camp leaders to supply Camp Marks with food, water, and other supplies.

VIEWS OF CAMP MARKS

The veterans tightly controlled Camp Marks. Streets were laid out in an orderly fashion. Sanitation facilities were constructed. An internal police force was created. Every morning started with reveille and a flag-raising ceremony. The Salvation Army provided a lending library, as well as a place to write letters home. A makeshift post office was created. To be in Camp Marks, you had to register. Veterans needed to show and prove they had been honorably discharged, or provide a bonus certificate. Once accepted, veterans received a membership card. The media of the day covered the B.E.F. in detail.

What would happen next? The veterans were encamped. Their pleas for the immediate redemption of the certificates had been made. The public was generally sympathetic toward the doughboys of the Great War. Now it was up to the White House and the Congress. The first act took place in the House of Representatives. Wright Patman of Texas, himself a veteran, introduced a bill to provide $2.4 billion to fund the certificates. The bill was passed on June 15, 1933, by a margin of 211-176. Including interest that amounted to about $1,000 per veteran. In support of the bill, Representative Edward Eslick of Tennessee delivered an impassioned speech. As he was ending his speech, he suffered a heart attack and died on the House floor. The veterans, of course, were jubilant that the bill had passed. They fully expected the Senate to do so. Many gathered at the Capitol. Others milled around in the makeshift town.

On June 17, 1933, the Senate rejected the Wright Patman Bonus Bill by a 61-18 margin. In the camps, jubilation quickly turned to despair and anger.

The Senate, taking a cue from President Hoover's speech almost a year earlier, resisted all overtures of the veterans:

March 19, 1932

Informal polls of the House of Representatives have created apprehension in the country that a further bonus bill of $2 billion or thereabouts for World War veterans will be passed. I wish to state again that I am absolutely opposed to any such legislation. I made this position clear at the meeting of the American Legion in Detroit last September 21 and the Legion has consistently supported that position. I do not believe any such legislation can become law. Such action would undo every effort that is being made to reduce Government expenditure and balance the budget. The first duty of every citizen of the United States is to build up and sustain the credit of the United States Government.

Following the rejection of the Bonus Act, President Hoover ordered the D.C. Police Commissioner to clear all veterans from government buildings rather than just letting them disperse on their own. In response to the heavy-handed police action the veterans rioted. Two veterans were killed, William Hushka and Eric Carlson. They were eventually buried in Arlington National Cemetery.

The situation was quickly getting out of control. The D.C. Police Commissioner asked for Federal troops. Hoover passed on the request to Patrick J. Hurley, the Secretary of War. He, in turn, ordered General Douglas MacArthur to disperse the protesters. On July 28, 1933, MacArthur ordered General Perry Miles to assemble troops on the Ellipse just south of the White House. It was 1:40 p.m. Also involved were then Major George S. Patton and a youthful Dwight D. Eisenhower. They crossed the Memorial Bridge with a sizable contingent of soldiers. As this was happening, the 13th Infantry arrived by steamer. By 4 p.m., the troops were fully assembled. Supported by light tanks and machine guns, the troops assembled on Pennsylvania Avenue, even as thousands of civil servants craned their necks to view the spectacle. Initially, the Bonus Marchers thought the army was parading to honor them. Patton then ordered his troops to advance, bayonets drawn and with tear gas canisters. As they did, many watching yelled, "Shame, shame!" The veterans were forced back across the Anacostia River to Camp Marks.

THE US MILITARY ATTACKS WAR VETERANS

At that point, things were out of control. Hoover ordered the assault ended. The veterans had been driven out of the capital. MacArthur chose to ignore the order and proceeded with plans to attack Camp Marks. He later said he hadn't received any orders. He also said the veterans wanted to overthrow the government and that Communists had infiltrated the Bonus Marchers. Once again, Hoover ordered MacArthur not to cross the Anacostia Bridge. Once again, he was ignored. In truth, the general was insubordinate. General Miles was ordered to attack. In the end, 55 veterans were injured and 135 were arrested. Camp Marks was destroyed, and the veterans were forced to return to their homes.

THE VETERANS ROUTED

On July 29, 1932 President Hoover gave a news conference in which he said the following:

After months of patient indulgence, the Government met overt lawlessness as it always must be met if the cherished processes of self-government are to be preserved. We cannot tolerate the abuse of constitutional rights by those who would destroy all government, no matter who they may be. Government cannot be coerced by mob rule.

The Department of Justice is pressing its investigation into the violence, which forced the call for Army detachments, and it is my sincere hope that those agitators who inspired yesterday's attack upon the Federal authority may be brought speedily to trial in the civil courts. There can be no safe harbor in the United States of America for violence.

On another occasion, during his efforts to be reelected, he said:

Thank God there is a government in Washington that knows how to deal with a mob.

Walter W. Waters, the unemployed lumberjack and leader of the Bonus Marchers, took a different tack, saying later:

The methods of eviction on that day revealed a stupidity and cupidity among Washington politicians, which was almost unbelievable.

Historians generally believe that Hoover should have dealt differently with the veterans. As one stated the case:

The spectacle of the United States Army routing unarmed citizens with tanks and firebrands outrage many Americans. The Bonus Army episode came to symbolize Hoover's supposed insensitivity to the plight of the unemployed.

A cruel joke at the time symbolized all that had gone wrong for President Hoover. The president asked for a nickel to make a telephone call to a friend. An aide flipped him a dime and said, "Here, call them both."

Many Americans were disheartened by Hoover's policies. How could the government treat veterans of the Great War with such violent disrespect? The president's words rang hollow for most citizens. He believed "political agitators, anarchists, and communists dominated the mob." Those claims were contradicted by the facts. The vast majority of the men were simply vets trying to survive, the boys you knew in the neighborhood now grown older by war and the depression. Nine out of ten Bonus Marchers were vets. Twenty percent of them were disabled. Hoover clearly "overestimated the threat posed to national security." As the 1932 presidential campaign progressed, an already unhappy public turned against the president. The sight of regular Army troops firing on their fellow Americans saw to that. There is no doubt that Hoover's harsh response to the Bonus Marchers played a pivotal role in the November presidential election, leading to a political upheaval with the landslide victory of the Democrats and Franklin D. Roosevelt.

Though the new president was opposed to redeeming the certificates, he dealt differently with the veterans. He explained he didn't want to assist one group and not others. Once elected, he welcomed a second "bonus march." A special camp was set up at Fort Hunt, Virginia, for the veterans. It had 40 field kitchens and served three meals per day. Bus transportation was provided so that the veterans could travel to the capital. A military band was also at Fort Hunt for the veterans' entertainment.

The new president sent an emissary to meet with the veterans. It was his wife, Eleanor. The date was May 16, 1933. Unaccompanied by the usual mix of politicians and bureaucrats, she visited Fort Hunt alone. Had they known, the Secret Service would have objected strenuously. There she had lunch with the veterans, and very importantly, she listened to their grievances. Though unable to make any promises, she said the president would do what he could. One veteran captured the moment, saying, "Mr. Hoover sent troops. Roosevelt sent his wife." As Mrs. Roosevelt recalled her visit:

I walked right into the camp and headed for a line of men waiting for food. They looked at me curiously, and one of them asked my name and what

I wanted. When I said I just wanted to see how they were going on. They asked me to join them. Pretty soon they were reminiscing about the war, and I joined them in singing old Army songs, such as "There's a Long, Long Trail a-Winding" and "Pack UP Your Troubles in Your Old Kit Bag."

The First Lady apologized for not being able to tell the men anything about the bonus they desired. She did explain that she understood their frustration. She then spent an impromptu tour of the veterans' camp. She waded through ankle-deep mud to visit their living quarters and the camp hospital. Before she left the camp, she said:

I would like to see fair compensation for everyone, and I shall always be grateful to those who served their country. I hope we will never have to ask such service again.

However, the president was still opposed, as was Hoover, to the early redemption of the bonus certificates. On May 11, 1933, an executive order was issued that permitted 25,000 veterans to be enrolled in the Civilian Conservation Corps (CCC), a federal relief program later known as the "tree army." The veterans were exempted from the regular requirements. They could be older than 25, and they could be married. Thousands of vets joined up. They received $1.00 per day. Married men received $35 per month, of which $30 was sent to their families. It was the beginning of a number of New Deal relief programs that put men back to work, many of whom were veterans.

In 1936, Congress overrode Roosevelt's veto of the Adjusted Compensation Act. It authorized the immediate payment of $2 billion to qualified veterans. The override vote was 324-61 in the House and 76-19 in the Senate.

The long wait and difficult battle were over for the boys who were once sent to the killing fields of France, whether Black or white.

SOLIDERS IN 1917 - BONUS MARCHERS IN 1932

ENTERING WASHINGTON

CHAPTER 11 – KEYNES

Most politicians running for an elected position are loath to admit they lack expertise in all the issues facing the public. They have abundant generalizations and "red meat" solutions that they feel will appeal to the voters. They are always long on possibilities and short on details. Politicians are practitioners of nuancing when asked hard and very direct questions, suggesting they have all the answers without disclosing much. They are also practiced chameleons, appearing to tell different groups exactly what they want to hear. This, of course, is a necessary part of getting elected. Both Presidents Hoover and Roosevelt fell prey to this political need. However, once in office, each would discover he needed expertise from others. This was especially true when FDR entered the White House. In the presidential campaign of 1932, he had claimed he would tackle the Great Depression and that it was time for new ideas to deal with the economic calamity. Certainly, there was an abundance of challenges facing Hoover's successor.

But what new ideas? As often happens in history, the unpredictable became a possibility when a staid, bookish economist in London linked intellectual arms with president-elect Roosevelt in embracing the notion of "countercyclical" fiscal policies, which would have momentous implications for the New Deal.

In 1938, John Maynard Keynes published his seminal study of economics. It was entitled *The General Theory of Employment, Interest, and Money.* This British economist presented a number of economic concepts that had percolated to the surface even before the Wall Street crash. Those ideas would play a pivotal role in shaping Roosevelt's New Deal. Concerning the Great Depression, Keynes believed traditional economic theory could not explain the causes of the economic collapse, nor did it have a response to the massive unemployment that descended on industrial countries. In addition, as he pointed out, conventional policymakers had no adequate strategy to jumpstart the economy. He held in disregard the conventional view that the Business Cycle would automatically provide full employment through an inherent self-correcting mechanism. He concluded that a new approach was needed to the unprecedented economic situation.

What would be called the Keynesian view was that aggregate demand was the most important driving force influencing the economy. This was a measurement of the sum of all spending by households, businesses, and government. Keynes believed that the government could influence aggregate demand through its economic policies. That meant government policy could influence the Business Cycle, and that the economy was not held hostage waiting for the self-correcting forces to take place over the long run. It meant that government policies could and should make up the difference between real GNP and the potential GNP by moving the economy out of a recessionary gap and lagging aggregate demand through increased federal expenditures.

The chart below illustrates this point. Simply put, when the real GNP falls below the potential output, the government can attempt to make up the difference through fiscal policies. In 1929, the economy was in balance (see chart below). Prosperity reigned, and there was no recessionary gap. By

1939, the gap remained, though it had been reduced. Beginning in 1940, it was all but eliminated. In 1941, the potential output exceeded all previous measurements. The years between 1929 and 1939 saw improvements in the economy, but not yet at the end of the depression. So, of course, what happened in 1941 that put every man, woman, and teenager to work? There was only one answer. The country had gone to war against the Axis Powers, and Keynesian concepts were functioning on steroids.

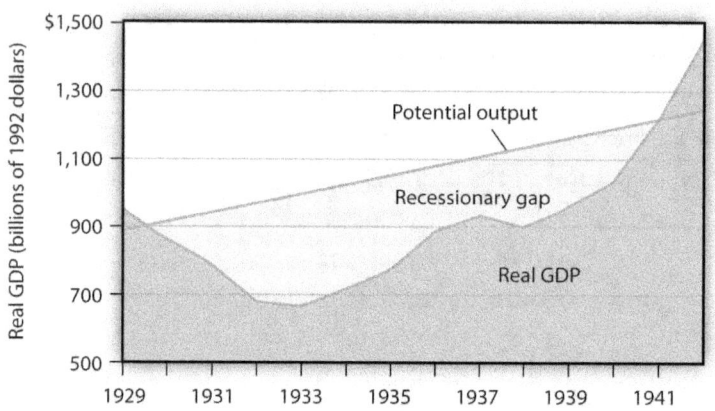

Keynes proposed "countercyclical fiscal policies. This meant that the government would push against the direction of the Business Cycle. During a recession or depression, when demand was dampened, the government, through deficit spending, would mitigate the gap between real GNP and potential GNP (total output). This would require an unbalanced federal budget and additions to the national debt. In theory, expanded government expenditures would make up for declining private sector consumption. During prosperous times, a reversal in policy was necessary to cool economic expansion and to control inflation. This would be done by raising taxes or through monetary policy to raise interest rates. In short, the federal government could spur consumption (demand) or reduce it as it followed "countercyclical" fiscal policies.

What was Keynes trying to accomplish? First, the goal would be to take the country out of a recession or depression (that is, a lack of consumption). Second, to do this, decreased taxes and increased government expenditures would be necessary to increase consumption.

Third, where necessary, increased government consumption would prod greater production, both industrial and agricultural, while at the same time decreasing unemployment. Fourth, increased employment should lead to increased purchasing power, which should lead to an increase in consumer confidence. People would spend their cash, which in theory would put even more people to work. By buying a new pair of shoes, another salesperson might be needed, including more shoe factory workers. Multiplied by many thousands of newly purchased shoes, the economy would expand, and the bad times would relinquish their hold on the economy. Fifth, the economy should experience an increase in total spending (the GNP) as consumer confidence increases and investors return to the market. Sixth, the increases in demand should bring the actual and potential GNP into balance.

Essentially, the federal government would have to spend money it didn't have to create a healthy economy where employment was maximized and inflation was minimized, always a difficult hat trick to pull off. If adopted by the New Deal policymakers, the government would be going against traditional economic orthodoxy, a balanced fiscal budget and limited government involvement in dealing with a recession, let alone a depression. In the end, the New Dealers sided with Keynes. They needed to end bank failures, business bankruptcies, a lack of investment, and a dearth of corporate profits. They needed the economy to improve and for consumer confidence to return. Indebtedness, they understood, would not come without costs. Borrowed money was a future obligation that had to be met with interest payments. That was the nature of the fiscal beast Keynes postulated. If the economy improved and social distress was reduced, that was worth the tradeoff, the followers of Keynes argued.

Critics, of course, pointed out the obvious. Government policies, once in place, are difficult to rescind, especially when individuals and groups are loath to lose some form of public assistance. That was another trade-off. The chart below shows the tenacity of deficits even in prosperous times. No politician wants to raise taxes and/or cut expenditures to reduce deficits, Keynesian "countercyclical" fiscal policies notwithstanding. Continued deficit spending and an increased national debt are almost always seen as more appealing, even when the country was not at war, as in 1917-1918 and 1941-1945.

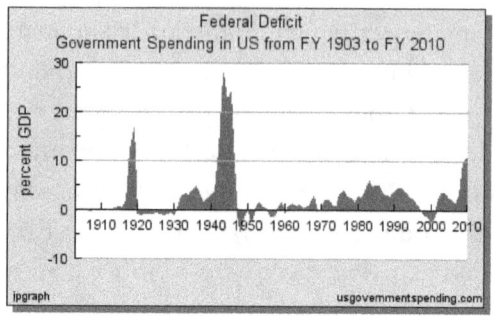

The New Deal policymakers adopted the Keynesian view to meet the immediate emergency of the Great Depression. The tradeoffs were acceptable. A society beset with massive unemployment was a fire that needed quenching. The federal government would spend what was needed to overcome the Great Depression. The chart below indicates the massive expenditures undertaken and the indebtedness incurred.

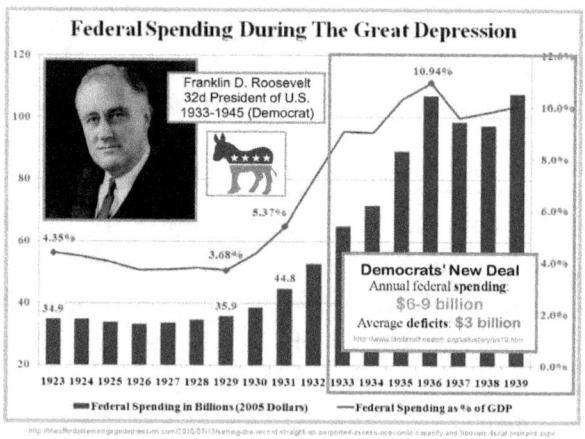

Ironically, in the last days of the Hoover Administration, there was a timid move toward a Keynesian response to the depression. In 1932, the president signed legislation to create the Reconstruction Finance Corporation. Half a billion dollars was allocated for banks, corporations, and state governments for public works projects, two of which were the Golden Gate Bridge and the Los Angeles Aqueduct. From the standpoint of the Keynesians, Hoover's new approach was necessary, but it was too little and too late. Also, it stopped short of providing federal aid to individuals who were out of work. Hoover sincerely believed that government aid would "stifle initiative and create dependency where individual effort was needed." It had worked for him. Why couldn't it work for others? Way, indeed?

The country demanded action as the 1932 presidential election loomed. Candidate Roosevelt was determined to provide the action required if elected. Armed with a Keynesian approach to the Great Depression, he was ready to battle. In a poetic sense, it was full steam ahead.

ON THE RIGHT TRACK

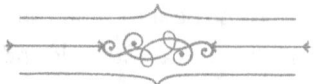

CHAPTER 12 – AFFLICTION

Empathy is the ability to emotionally understand what others feel. It is the ability to see things from another person's point of view, and perhaps even to imagine being in his place. In the end, it is the ability to feel what another person is feeling. It is not necessarily a universal response to the feelings of others. We're not born with it. It comes about as we experience life. And so it was, many would contend, in the case of Franklin D. Roosevelt.

First, an aside…

Many argued that the Great Depression created a "culture of despair." The social landscape provided numerous examples. There was a dramatic rise in crime as many jobless men resorted to petty theft to put food on the table. The suicide rate increased for those so depressed that no other alternative seemed possible. Alcoholism increased as some sought to find solace in a bottle. Cases of malnutrition rose, as did other health issues. Seeing a doctor costs money. Medical needs were put off. Visits to the dentist were avoided. Prostitution increased as desperate women looked for ways to feed their families. On the lighter side, those who smoked expensive cigars made the switch to cheaper cigarettes. *Lucky Strike* prospered, though not the economy. Higher education, already out of the reach of most Americans, saw a considerable drop in attendance. Paradoxically, high school attendance remained relatively stable. Why drop out of school if there were no jobs? Marriages were delayed even as the divorce rate dwindled. Why get married if you didn't have a job? Why leave an unhappy relationship? Better to stay together until better times. As might be expected, the birth rate declined. Children were wonderful but expensive. Moreover, there was a massive migration as thousands took the open road seeking work in some promised land. There must be work in California, isn't that so? A bare statistic indicated that over 600,000 people were caught hitching rides on trains during the Great Depression. How many more were never caught?

Now, as to FDR and the notion of empathy…

The whole business began in the summer home of the Roosevelt family. It was located on the Canadian island of Campobello just off the coast of Maine. The year was 1921, and Roosevelt was 39 years old, a successful practicing attorney, and a young man with aspiring political interests. Roosevelt was on the island with his wife and young family, plus his trusted political advisor, Louis Howe. Some would say he was handsome, charming, and perpetually optimistic. Perhaps that occurs when you're born into a wealthy family, sent to the most exclusive private schools, and have access to the "good life" in the tradition of America's aristocracy. All that changed on August 10th. After a full day of strenuous activity, Roosevelt came down with an illness characterized by fevers, numbness, and hypersensitivity of the skin. He was close to death, caused by poliomyelitis or polio for short. Though he survived the illness, it left him paralyzed from the waist down. From that moment on, he was shackled to a wheelchair or steel braces to enable him to stand upright. For the next seven years, the future president of the United States struggled to rehabilitate his body and political career, and, it is fair to say, to give meaning to his life. On October 3, 1924, he visited a small town in Georgia known for its healing waters and hydrotherapy. There in Warm Springs, Roosevelt met other polio victims, many of whom were children. That experience tapped into Roosevelt's innate sense of empathy.

WITH THE CHILDREN AT WARM SPRINGS

While wearing iron braces on his hips and legs at Warm Springs, he laboriously taught himself to walk short distances by swiveling his torso. This "two-point walk" permitted him to walk by gripping the arm of a strong person with his left hand and bracing himself with a cane in his right. The waters, it seemed, helped.

A CHANGED MAN

As Roosevelt reentered the political world, he did so as a physically disabled person. He was always aware of this and concerned about the public's perception. He took great pains to convince his closest friends and political cronies that he could again campaign for elected office. His public appearances were carefully choreographed. Photographs of him were generally taken at a distance and, if possible, only at certain angles. In private, he used a wheelchair. He was careful not to use it in public. This was a strategy to minimize the extent of his handicap. In public, he used his crutches. When he needed to stand up, he was always assisted by an aide, sometimes even by his sons. Often, he had to make a major campaign speech. On those occasions, an especially solid lectern was placed on the stage. This permitted Roosevelt to support himself. To emphasize a point, he gestured with his head, not his hands, which were gripping the lectern.

Roosevelt's disability was no secret. The public was aware of his situation, and he used that fact to his advantage. As one historian wrote:

But he could show himself to be a fighter and better yet, an underdog. Not a man to pity; not a man to envy, but a man to cheer.

Another observer noted:

With steel and fire, he forced his arms to take him across the room, across the lawn, and down the steps. He knew he would never be walking at the head of the Labor Day Parade, but he kept on pouring his will into what was left of his muscles, trying to walk that walk again.

By 1928, Roosevelt felt strong enough to reenter politics. Now it would be up to the voters to decide his fate. In 1920, he had last run as the vice-presidential nominee of the Democratic Party. At the time, he could walk down a grand avenue, a glorious picture of health, robust and charming as he waved to the crowd.

CAMPIGNING IN 1920

The team of James Cox (for president) and Roosevelt was badly beaten by Warren G. Harding. The Republicans would hold the White House through Harding, Calvin Coolidge, and Herbert Hoover, the period through which Roosevelt endured his affliction. The political events of 1928 would, however, extricate him from his self-imposed wilderness. In that year, Alfred E. Smith, the governor of New York State, decided to challenge history and tradition and become the first Catholic to seek the White House. That decision opened the door for Roosevelt. He would, if the voters agreed, replace Smith's position as governor of the Empire State.

ROOSESVELT AND AL SMITH (RIGHT)

Roosevelt's devastating illness, many came to believe, might serve as a metaphor for the pain so many were going through during the Great Depression. What would be called the New Deal was a political, economic response to a country in distress. Similarly, it might be understood as an emphatic response to the ills of the 1930s. In the mix of politics, social unrest, and a public plea for action, the New Deal would be many things, including one overriding point. The power of the Federal Government, Roosevelt believed, could be used for the betterment of the public where all other efforts had failed. But first, he had to show the American people he could govern with energy and appropriate policies. If elected to Albany, he would be tested as Governor of New York State. In doing so, he would be reminded of a quote from *Twelfth Night* (Act II, scene 5) where Shakespeare wrote:

Be not afraid
of greatness.
Some are
born great,
some achieve
greatness,
and others
have greatness
thrust upon
them.

Of course, perhaps the future president had already been tested.

FDR AND FRIEND AT WARM SPRINGS

CHAPTER 13 – ELECTIONS

In 1928, Alfred E. Smith ran against Herbert Hoover. It wasn't even close. The final results were:

Hoover (R) 21,281,993

Smith (D)   15,961,161

Hoover ended with 444 electoral votes and entered the White House. Smith got 87 electoral votes and went into retirement.

In the other election… No one knew what to expect of Roosevelt. If elected, what kind of governor would he be of New York State? Good times reigned, and the Empire State was prospering. How bad could Roosevelt be? Would his health hold up? What did he want to accomplish? One columnist noted in the *New York Post* soon after Roosevelt entered the gubernatorial race:

There's something both pathetic and pitiless in the drafting of Franklin D. Roosevelt. Even his own friends, out of love for him, will hesitate to vote for him.

Roosevelt had to prove himself on the campaign trail. He did. He barnstormed the state, traveling 1300 miles by car and making as many as 14 speeches each day. He displayed physical energy and political charisma as he turned the campaign into a battle of ideas: progressivism versus the status quo and reactionary policies. In time his views settled on these issues: (1) he championed hydroelectric power under public control, not private utilities; (2) he supported a minimum wage for all workers; (3) he believed in the right of labor to organize and for unions to engaged in collective bargaining; (4) he threw his political weight behind a plan to give he elderly the right to an old-age pension; and (5) he promoted the need to aid farmers in the state. In a very tight election, he won the race by the narrowest margins, some 25,608 votes out of more than 4,000,000 cast by New Yorkers.

Roosevelt (D)	2,130,193	48.6% of the Popular Vote
Ottinger (R)	2,104,129	48.3% of the Popular Vote

During his first two-year stint as governor (1928-1930), he met severe opposition from the Republican-controlled legislature. Sixteen of his major proposals were rejected. His conservative opponents were adamantly opposed to his progressive platform. Roosevelt decided to take his issues to the public. Again, he barnstormed across the state by car, barge, and boat to meet farmers, small business owners and local political leaders. He also took to the radio and spoke directly to New Yorkers. This was a precursor to what he did during his later "fireside chats" as president.

In 1930, Roosevelt won a second term. This time it was not close:

Roosevelt (D)	1,770,342	56.5% of the Popular Vote
Tuttle (R)	1,045,341	37.6% of the Popular Vote

With his overwhelming victory, Roosevelt was now able to achieve his goals. He immediately pushed through a bill to establish an old-age insurance program for New Yorkers over 70 years of age. He signed the Water Authority Act authorizing the construction of a hydroelectric dam on the St. Lawrence River controlled by the people of New York. Because of the swelling unemployment in New York, he created the Temporary Relief Administration to provide relief to those out of work. New York became the first state to have its own emergency relief program. It assisted 1 out of 10 New Yorkers through direct payments or with infrastructure jobs at prevailing wages. In the 1930 Governor's Conference, he pushed for an unemployment insurance program on a national scale. He stated:

This form of insurance should not, of course, take the shape of a dole in any respect. Our American aged do not want charity, but rather old-age comforts, to which they are rightfully entitled by their own thrift and foresight in the form of insurance.

He also proposed regulating banks to protect deposits by separating commercial deposits from personal savings, and requiring banks disclose the true value of securities they sell. This proposal, along with the programs also reviewed suggested where a Roosevelt Administration might take the country. They certainly reflected his philosophy of government.

More and more those who are the victims of dislocation and defects of our social and economic life are beginning to ask respectfully but insistently of us who are in positions of public responsibility, why government can not and should not act to protect its citizens from disaster? I believe that the question demands an answer.

As Roosevelt delved into the challenges of implementing his ideas, he recognized that he needed outside expert assistance. One of his supporters also recognized this.

He was a man who you could talk to you. He had sense enough to talk to a man who didn't have any education, and he had enough sense to talk to the best-educated man in the world, and he was easy to talk to. He could talk about anything.

In time, Roosevelt began meeting with bright academics from New York colleges and universities. Over Sunday dinner, they discussed issues pressing on the Governor. As one said:

Roosevelt was at once a student, a cross-examiner, and a judge. He would listen with rapt attention for a few minutes and then break in with a question whose sharpness was characteristically blurred with an anecdotal introduction or an air of sympathetic agreement with the speaker.

What came out of these meetings was a rich diversity of ideas and a host of options in dealing with perplexing social problems, leading Roosevelt to one inevitable conclusion, which he articulated on August 28, 1931:

When widespread economic conditions render large numbers of men and women incapable of supporting either themselves or their families… aid must be extended by Government, no as a matter of charity, but as a matter of social duty.

By 1932, Roosevelt had a strong record in New York. He had dispelled questions about his health. Still, questions remained. Would the party bosses nominate him as the party's standard-bearer? Would the voters cast aside the Republicans after three consecutive victories? And, if elected, would a Roosevelt Administration be up to the daunting task of dealing with the Great Depression?

Roosevelt got the nomination and immediately broke tradition. He flew to Chicago to accept the nomination in person. This had never been done before. It was a strategic move. He demonstrated that he was physically fit for the impending campaign despite still stricken with polio.

He also wanted to show that he was the candidate of change, a candidate who was willing to break precedents. Before the convention, he struck a responsive chord in those present:

The country needs and unless I mistaken its temper, the country demands bold, persistent experimentation. It is common sense to take a method and try it; if it fails, admit it frankly and try another. But above all, try something.

By implication, Roosevelt's presidency would take the lead in dealing with the Great Depression. Congress, though a constitutional partner, would relinquish a degree of authority to the White House. From the perspective of Roosevelt, that was as necessary as in war. Another cartoonist illustrated the situation.

Once he was nominated, the party bosses advised Roosevelt to run a front porch campaign. That is, stay at home. Let others hit the campaign trail in your stead. Roosevelt rejected those admonitions. Disregarding their advice, he made 27 major speeches around the country, always proclaiming "ours must be the party of liberal thought, of planned action, of the enlightened international outlook, and of the greatest good to the greatest number of our citizens." He also became the first presidential candidate to recognize the power of the radio. Over 18% of his campaign funds went into political radio blurbs. That amounted to $343,415 or about $7.5 million in today's dollars. He was a natural on the radio, a communication platform beyond the ink press, and the short movie newsreels. The radio brought him into every home with the device.

Election Results Table

Candidate	Total Votes	Popular Vote (%)	Electoral Votes
Roosevelt	32,821,277	57.4%	472
Hoover	15,761,254	39.6%	59

In addition, the Democrats gained 110 seats in the House of Representatives and 12 seats in the Senate. Roosevelt became the first Democrat in 80 years to simultaneously win the popular vote and the electoral vote. Franklin Pierce had last done it in 1852. The instruments of power were now in the hands of the Democrats.

THE END AND THE BEGINNING: HOOVER AND
ROOSEVELT ON INAUGURATION DAY

In his acceptance speech before the Democratic Convention, Roosevelt suggested what he would do if elected:

I pledge to you, I pledge to myself, to new deal for the American people.

The words caught on, as did the lyrics to the Democratic Party's official anthem, "Happy Days Are Here Again."

CHANGE IN THE AIR

Happy Days Are Here Again

So long sad times
So long bad times
We are rid of you at last
Howdy gay times
Cloudy gray times
You are now a thing of the past.

Happy days are here again
The skies above are clear again
So let's sing a song of cheer again
Happy days are here again.

Happy days are here again
Your cares and troubles are gone
There'll be no more from now on
From now on.

Roosevelt ascended to power, but what would it mean for Smith? Hoover had assumed the continued loyalty of the Black vote. After all, the Republicans were the party of Lincoln, emancipation, and the Civil War amendments: the 13th – abolishing slavery; the 14th – granting citizenship to the former slave; and the 15th- granting the vote to former slaves. In contrast, the Democratic Party was split on issues of race. The Southern wing favored maintaining Jim Crowism at any cost, while the Northern wing was more progressive, seeking, if it could, the end of segregation and discrimination. In 1928, Al Smith had made a determined effort to encroach on the Black vote. He had worked with James Weldon Johnson, the president of the NAACP. Johnson didn't want the Black vote taken for granted by either party and made that known to Blacks. In the end, Hoover garnered a majority of the Black vote, but Smith had made inroads. In 1932, despite the Great Depression, a majority of Blacks still voted for the Republicans, though the numbers were decreasing. The problem was that Roosevelt had no civil rights record as New York's governor. He had also chosen John Nance Garner to be his running mate. Garner was from Texas, a Jim Crow state that had systematicaly denied suffrage to its Black citizens.

Most Blacks lived in the South, an area of the country that seemed perpetually impoverished. In 1929, at the height of good times, the average per capita income in the South was $365. The section had the least educated population and the least skilled. Southern lacks and poor white farmers were trapped growing corn and cotton, two crops that depleted the soil. In the extractive industries of coal, oil, and iron ore, wages were the lowest in the country, in contrast to the same work in the North. As one wit said, southerners were "underpaid, underfed, and undereducated." He might have added that poor whites were still doing better than poor Blacks.

Paradoxically, the depression wasn't something new for Blacks. It didn't mean much to them. The Great Depression only became official when it hit the white community. Blacks already earned the least, had the worst jobs, and lived in the least hospitable areas. They already faced poll taxes and lynching violence, and the principle of "separate but equal" facilities. Some 77% of Blacks worked the land, mainly as sharecroppers, providing them with little more than subsistence living. That said, what would a New Deal mean for agriculture and them? Would the agricultural South support changes that uplifted all citizens and potentially altered the embedded caste system? These questions awaited the Roosevelt Administration.

FDR had promised relief. Those in need, whether in the city or in rural America, awaited a new White House fulfilling that promise. When he spoke of a New Deal, what exactly was he implying? Reshuffling the cards meant what?

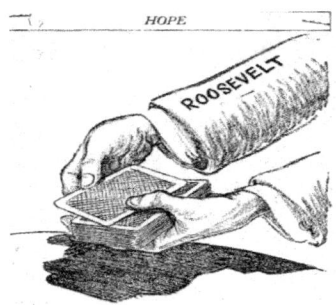

Contrary to public understanding the new president had "no grand strategy" to end the Depression. The political skills and policies he had displayed in New York as governor, he would bring to Washington. What were the skills? He was a bold experimenter. Try this, try that ... Find out what works. He was willing to listen to a diversity of views, evaluating them on their merits, not his presupposed assumptions. Think big and work out the details later. Once convinced of a policy, he delegated responsibility and authority to competent officials. He did so with steady confidence. Though he used the radio while in New York, he had connected with the voters. He did so with confidence that proved contagious. Broadcasting skills homed in Albany would be harnessed during his later Fireside Chats with the American public. Out of all this emerged the New Deal and a degree of government empathy perhaps last shared by Abraham Lincoln.

On November 19, 1863, President Lincoln delivered his Gettysburg Address several months after the Union Army defeated the Confederate forces commanded by Robert E. Lee. What Lincoln said that day defined the issue of the Civil War; the conflict was a struggle for "a new birth of freedom" for a nation that ensured equality for all its citizens. Certainly, that was true of President Roosevelt seeking "a new birth of economic freedom" for all Americans. In this, both presidents connected with the suffering and pain they experienced, slavery in an earlier century, and unprecedented unemployment in the 1930s. In this, they were fellow travelers, each seeking to continue the American experiment.

... that this nation, under God, shall have a new birth of freedom --- and that the government of the people, by the people, for the people, shall not perish from the earth.

CHAPTER 14 – HISTORY INTERVENES

All of us know what happened on April 14, 1865, at Ford's Theater in Washington, DC. John Wilkes Booth assassinated the 16th president of the United States. One shot from the famous actor and history was altered. President Abraham Lincoln was dead. However, most people don't know what happened on July 2, 1881. On that terrible day, James A. Garfield was killed by Charles J. Guiteau, an attorney. And what about September 6, 1901, when Leon Czolgosz fired an anarchist bullet into William McKinley, our 25th president? On November 22, 1963, Lee Harvey Oswald killed the nation's young president, John Fitzgerald Kennedy.

In every case, the assassin, whether provoked by a personal grievance or some political motive, sought to alter history. That's why the Zangara's name is of interest. On February 15, 1933, only seventeen days before the president-elect would take office, a shot fired by Zangara came close to killing Franklin D. Roosevelt. Had he been successful, history would indeed have been dramatically altered. Would there still have been a New Deal? Would John Vance Garner, the vice-president elect, have been able to pursue Roosevelt's policies? Would Congress have sought a preeminent role in crafting a response to the Great Depression? Would the headlines on February 16, 1933 been different? Questions and speculation…

What happened on that fateful day? Roosevelt was riding in the back of an open car in Bayfront Park near Miami, Florida. He was going to give an impromptu speech that night. A crowd estimated at nearly 10,000 had come to cheer on Roosevelt, all but one. Standing on the running board of the vehicle was the mayor of Chicago, Anton Cermak. In addition to him, there were the usual Secret Service agents who protect our presidents.

THE PRESIDENT-ELECT AND THE KILLER

Standing in the crowd was Zangara. The day before, he had bought a .32-caliber revolver for $8 at a local pawnshop. He mixed in with the crowd. Because he only stood five feet in height, he had to stand on a wobbling metal folding chair to see the motorcade. He was about 25 feet away as Roosevelt's car approached. In front of Zangara was a woman with a large hat that obscured his vision. Her name was Lillian Cross. Zangara placed his gun on her right shoulder and then fired his first shot. She and others tried to grab the gun. He was able to fire five more wild shots before being subdued. Five people were hit, including Mayor Cermak. Critically wounded with his head resting in Roosevelt's arms, the stricken mayor was rushed to the nearest hospital. Cermak died 19 days later and two days before Roosevelt's inauguration. His last known words to Roosevelt were, "I'm glad it was me, not you."

Who was Zangara, and what was his motive in the attempted assassination? He was an Italian immigrant and nationalized citizen living in Patterson, New Jersey. He was poorly educated and worked as a bricklayer. During World War I, he served in the Italian Royal Army. During his trial, he told the judge, "I have the gun in my hand. I kill kings and presidents first and next all capitalists." He pleaded guilty to four counts of attempted murder and was sentenced to 80 years in prison. In response to that, he told the judge, "Four times 20 is 80. Oh, judge, don't be stingy. Give me a hundred years."

In a later hearing, it was determined that he would be executed. To that, he responded, "You give me the electric chair. I'm not afraid of that chair! You're one of the capitalists... You are crooked, man, too. Put me in the electric chair. I don't care." He was sent to the Florida State Prison in Raiford. Because there was another man scheduled to be the executive, he had to wait. That led to a term we are all aware of --- Death Row.

On March 20, 1933, "Old Sparky" ended his life. Zangara was electrocuted. No news cameras were permitted. This enraged the doomed man. His last words were, "Viva I'talia! Goodbye to all poor people everywhere! Push the button! Go ahead, push the button."

It was just a moment in history, as it had been with other presidents. As always, the "ifs" of history challenge us. Had stricken presidents lived, how would history have changed?

LINCOLN AND GARFIELD (TOP)
MCKINLEY AND KENNEDY (BELOW)

CHAPTER 15 – THE FIRST 100 DAYS

"The number one hundred is forever tied to the first three months of FDR's administration and his aggressive efforts to deal with the Great Depression. That number was symbolic of the policies quickly implemented and would be the gauge by which future presidents, unfairly, would be judged. The number came to mean different things to different people. For the supporters of Roosevelt, the public had thrown the dice in the November elections. They came up seven, and hopefully, they were a good omen. The government would finally wage war on depression by using its immense fiscal power to alter the business cycle. For the critics of FDR, the same period represented a constitutional overreach by Washington and was unfortunate for conservative economic philosophy. What is often forgotten, however, is the frightful numbers weighing on the new president as he took office. Over 25% of the workforce was unemployed with continuing bleak prospects. Over 250,000 families had defaulted on their mortgages, and the numbers were climbing daily. More than 1.2 million Americans were homeless, and that figure was increasing daily. Well over 9,000 banks had failed, and the hemorrhage showed no evidence of stopping. Over 27,000,000 families had lost their savings. In many cases, their life savings… On top of this, farm foreclosures were averaging 20,000 per week."

What are elections, if not a gamble? Do we really know what a new president will do? Once elected, a new president has a four-year ride, does he not? But what will he accomplish? Beyond the campaign rhetoric and partisan accusations back and forth, where does he really stand on the issues? Presidential elections provide a ballot box victory, but not necessarily a clear picture of the future. You vote and hope for the best. Some vote for the candidate who will help them the most. Others vote for the candidate who will harm them the least. That is not a cynical view. It is a harsh reality.

Roosevelt had been eloquent in his inaugural speech, pointing out that:

All we must fear is fear itself, nameless, unreasoning, unjustified terror which paralyzes needed efforts to convert retreat into advance." But what does that really mean to hungry families and destitute millions?

And:

I am prepared under my constitutional duty to recommend the measures that a stricken nation among a stricken world may require.

I need broad executive power to wage a war against the emergency, as great as the power that would be given me if we were, in fact, invaded by a foreign foe.

The eloquent words would lead to the passage of seventy-seven new laws during the first one hundred days of the Roosevelt Administration. With strong Democrat majorities in Congress much would be accomplished during a unique period of strong bipartisan support." Over time, these first legislative accomplishments would form a pattern that gave structure and purpose to the New Deal under three headings: relief, recovery, and reform. Relief referred to putting people back to work as quickly as possible and doing subsidized government work. Recovery meant rebuilding a prosperous economy sustained by private sector consumption. Reform would be an effort to cleanse the system of those ills that led to the Great Depression. Separate but overlapping legislation would fall under the "3 R's rubric." The key components of the legislative agenda are shown below.

Relief	Recovery	Reform
Emergency Banking Act, 1933	National Recovery Act, 1933	Glass-Steagall Banking Act, 1933
Federal Emergency Relief Act, 1933	Home Owners Loan Corp, 1933	Securities Exchange Act, 1934
Public Works Administration, 1933	Federal Housing Administration, 1934	Social Security Act, 1935
Works Progress Administration, 1935		National Labor Relations Act, 1935
Civilian Conservation Corps, 1933	Agricultural Adjustment Act, 1933 and 1937	Fair Labor Standards Act, 1938
Tennessee Valley Authority, 1933		

It is important to keep in mind the spectre that loomed over the incoming president, and Congress called into the emergency session. facing the government. There couldn't be a repeat of the Wall Street crash and all that followed, especially Hoovervilles and encampments of Bonus Marchers. At stake was the ability of a democratic form of government to meet an unprecedented emergency. The new president had promised relief. Beyond the rhetoric, would there be action?

During the emergency session of Congress and later, the new Administration faced many challenges. Those challenges were ultimately reflected in the programs implemented as the Roosevelt Administration reshuffled the economic cards.

The Solid South

The first and most serious challenge Roosevelt faced was geographical and political. The Solid South was essentially a one-party section of the country. Only

Democrats could win state and local elections. In presidential elections, an electoral voting bloc existed. Southerners would cast their votes only for candidates that would not disrupt the social-economic-racial policies prevailing in the region. What did that mean? White supremacy would exist as Blacks and poor whites were systematically disenfranchised. The less educated, least organized, and most impoverished were excluded from voting by restrictive voting registration in the form of poll taxes, residency requirements, and literacy tests. For Blacks in particular, this meant segregation and discrimination in every aspect of Southern life. After 1890, the Plessey v. Ferguson codified such practices and the notion of "separate but equal." The racist policies catered to the preservation of white political and economic control by building on a legacy dating back to the Civil War that emphasized "Yankee Invaders," and the noble service of Southerners who fought valiantly in the glorious "Lost Cause." The policies also reacted against the Civil War amendments enacted during the Reconstruction Period. The southern states were forced to accept abolition and citizenship, but resisted suffrage and the integration of public facilities, especially in public schools and housing. By every means possible, both legally and through violence, the Black vote was all but eliminated in the South.

What did this mean for Roosevelt? Since southern politicians, as noted earlier,

They were elected and reelected to Congress, and they gained seniority and chairmanships based on tenure. This, in turn, permitted them to gain control over powerful committees in Congress, where they could stymie any civil rights proposals. Any effort to alter the socioeconomic patterns in the South would be challenged. Any effort to substantially improve the lot of southern Blacks would be resisted. Voting as a block, Southerners could and did block such legislation. They could also block other legislation, including Roosevelt's New Deal bills and later his efforts to rearm the country, unless they accepted these realities.

A leading representative of the Solid South and a staunch opponent of civil rights legislation was Senator James Strom Thurmond, Sr. of South Carolina, who served in the Senate for 48 years. He consistently voted to maintain the racial status quo in the South as demanded by his white constituents. His views were representative of those who came before him in the 1930s. His adherence to the Southern political landscape reached into the 1960s. Though he denied he was a racist, he voted against the Civil Rights Act in 1964 and the Voting Rights Act the next year. He justified his support for racial segregation based on states' rights, and as a fearless opponent of the expansion of federal authority into areas properly within the purview of the states.

As to whether Thurmond was a racist, that was always a question that cannot be fully answered; there was no ambiguity as to whether he was opposed to the integration of the races on that score. His own words substantiated his position.

Segregation is not discrimination. It is separation. We must keep the bloodlines pure to maintain our racial purity. States' rights are not only justifiable, but necessary. There are not enough troops in the army to force Southerners to break down segregation and admit the Nigra race into our theaters, into our swimming pools, and into our homes. We don't advocate violence, but we do say sometimes violence is justifiable, and that in the highest traditions of our ancestors, violence is sometimes necessary. I don't think that a society that exists in America today ought to try to integrate the races. There will always be racial discord as long as we have people of different races.

Roosevelt had to contend with the Thurmonds and others in Congress. It wasn't that every Southerner felt this way. Nevertheless, a majority wanted to maintain the status quo when it came to racial issues. That was the reality Roosevelt faced. His eventual strategy was to take a middle ground on civil rights issues. He wasn't overtly for integration or blatantly for maintaining the status quo. Was he wishy-washy? Yes, one could argue. He deplored lynchings and the poll taxes, but pragmatically resisted taking on the Southerners in Congress. To have done so would have put his New Deal policies in jeopardy. He needed southern votes. As the governor of New York State, he had taken this modest approach. As president, he hoped his policies would assist Blacks at the margins; that is, indirectly. Programs such as the Civil Conservation Corps would hire hundreds of thousands of young men, hopefully providing jobs for all. The "kicker" was, of course, that all such programs, though federally funded, were implemented at the local level, and racial prejudice and bigotry could limit the access of Blacks to assistance. The White House had almost no control over this. That again was the political reality with which the New Dealers had to contend. It was almost as if the president were presiding over two countries.

CHAPTER 16 – THREE CHALLENGERS

Huey Long

He was nicknamed the "Kingfish." Many called him a demagogue. He was flamboyant. He thrust himself into the political world with the enthusiasm of a carnival pitchman. He showered Louisiana and Washington, D.C., with defiant arrogance, even some said as a vengeful zealot, as he fought for the rural poor in the cities. Huey Long was all this and certainly a thorn in Roosevelt's efforts to deal with the Great Depression. By 1935, he seriously considered running as a third-party candidate 1936 if the New Dealers didn't move more to the left, especially regarding the redistribution of wealth in America. A secret poll by the Democrats indicated he would get from 3 to 4 million votes, enough to call Roosevelt's reelection into question. Jim Farley, a close adviser of Roosevelt, said:

It was conceivable that his third-party movement might constitute a balance of power in the 1936 election. What he might have done in 1940 is difficult to conjecture. He was high in our political thoughts.

Huey Pierce Long was the 40th governor of Louisiana. He was also elected to the United States Senate. As a populist and champion of people experiencing poverty, he consistently favored left-wing policies within the Democratic Party. He denounced wealth inequality in the country and criticized both Republicans and Democrats for maintaining an inequitable economic system. Initially, he supported Roosevelt. He traveled through the South to help FDR get the nomination and electoral votes below the

Mason-Dixon line. He gave 39 speeches and traveled over 2100 miles as he spoke to more than 200,000 people. His campaigning was essential to Roosevelt's victory in 1932. In that year, he also garnered votes for Hatti Caroway of Arkansas. She became the first woman elected to a full term in the Senate.

THE POPULIST

His support of the president dwindled as the New Deal took shape. For Long, it wasn't radical enough. As he said:

Whenever the administration has shifted to the left, I have voted with it, and whenever it has shifted to the right, I have voted against it.

In a 1934 radio address, he spelled out his views in what would be known as the "Long Plan." Essentially, he wanted to liquidate large personal fortunes. He tried to make "every man a king." He wanted every family to have a house, a car, and a radio. How would he accomplish this? He would redistribute wealth in the country. He would cap fortunes at $100,000,000. He wanted to limit annual income to $1,000,000. He proposed capping inheritance at $5,000,000. With the funds realized through these "caps", he would guarantee every family a basic household grant of $5,000. College education and vocational school would be free. He wanted to emphasize aid to farmers and veterans. He supported major public work projects, such as $10,000,000,000 to reclaim the land lost to the Dust Bowl. Increasing federal regulation of the economy was also a high priority for him. All that was in addition to assisting older people with a $30 monthly pension. He also favored free medical services.

Of course, there were challenges to his program. The Senate balked. The House was more amenable. The White House was prepared to implement some of its programs short of income redistribution. Long had touched a nerve. He could not be ignored. By way of example, legislation providing for Social Security was undoubtedly a response to his populist leanings. Not to be outdone by his critics, Long formed the *Share Our Wealth Society* in 1934. It was a national network of local clubs to oppose Roosevelt's modest programs. By 1935, there were 7.5 million members and over 27,000 clubs nationwide. Each day, Long received 60,000 letters addressed to his Senate office. In short, as James Farley had said, Huey Long had to be taken seriously, as shown in the cartoon below.

THE PIED PIPER IS WILLING TO PASS OVER HIS PIPES

Huey Long never ran against Roosevelt on a third-party ticket in 1936. Fate intervened. On September 8, 1935, Long traveled to the Louisiana state capitol to support a bill to gerrymander the district of an opponent, Judge Benjamin Pavy. Pavy had been in office for 28 years. At 9:20 p.m., the bill was passed to remove the judge. This angered Dr. Carl Weiss, a supporter of Pavy. Weiss approached Long and fired one shot at him. Long was hit in the torso. His bodyguards, sometimes known as "skullcrushers," then killed Weiss, pumping at least 60 rounds into him. Still able to walk,

Long left the Capitol, hailed a car, and was immediately taken to Our Lady of Lourdes Hospital. Though the surgeons tried, they could not stop the internal bleeding. Huey Long died at 4:10 a.m. on September 10, 1935

Upon hearing of Long's death, the president said, "He regarded the assassination as a providential occurrence." Though Long was gone, his influence on the Roosevelt Administration was substantial. Millions supported Long and wanted the president to move sharply to the left. FDR's challenge was to do so without alienating powerful business interests and the generally conservative attitude of most Americans, or at least those working. The eventual plan for Social Security would be a compromise between what Long desired and what was politically possible.

Father Coughlin

He hardly looked like a demagogue who used the radio to incite millions of disgruntled Americans to action. He was a quiet Catholic priest from an impoverished parish in a Detroit suburb. He spoke with a passionate voice and a tinge of Irish burr. But once before a radio, his impassioned voice marked him as an effective spellbinder second only to Huey Long. Father Charles E. Coughlin was known as Detroit's "Radio Priest," who spoke out against the economic sins of his day with zealous conviction. He preached a religious-economic doctrine that promised earthly salvation and a heavenly future. He combined Catholic humanism with Marxist socialism to mobilize those most harmed by the Great Depression. With fervent belief, he claimed capitalist greed had brought the country to its knees. That greed, he believed, stood in the way of a better secular world and the fulfillment of Christ's promise of a just world.

Essentially, he wanted a fairer materialistic world while maintaining a spiritual life.

THE RADIO PRIEST

What did Father Coughlin want to achieve in the political world? He believed strongly in a centralized banking system under government control, not just a highly regulated system. This was a direct challenge to the New Dealers. He wanted Congress to pass legislation guaranteeing an annual wage. He wanted the cost of living to be stabilized to end the threat of inflation. He felt the tax burden should shift dramatically from the middle class to wealthy individuals and prosperous corporations. He also wanted the government to nationalize the major industries, including banks and the railroads.

In time, his small radio audience increased until millions listened to him on Sunday. That audience was estimated to be from 20 to 30 million listeners who tuned in to his show, The *Shrine of the Little Flower.* His ratings were better than most radio entertainers of his day. He received over 30,000 letters each week. Radio success encouraged him to create The National Union of Social Justice, where he combined theology and politics. Initially, he had supported Roosevelt and the New Deal, calling it "Christ's Deal." However, his support for Roosevelt dwindled when he realized the president would prop up the existing capitalistic system. He was going to maintain the economic status quo with some minor changes. Uncharacteristically, his agitation with Roosevelt led to harsh attacks. With vehemence, he called the president a "liar" and the "great betrayor." Unlike Huey Long, Coughlin had no ambitions to start a third party. He wanted his organization to remain what he called a "people's lobby." At the heart of his anger was disdain for free-market capitalism. Of that he said:

We maintain the principle that there can be no lasting prosperity if free competition exists in industry. Therefore, it is the business of the government not only to legislate for a minimum annual wage and maximum working schedule to be observed by the sector, but also to curtail individualism, so that, if necessary, factories shall be licensed and their output shall be limited.

Of course, all this was too much for the New Dealers. Given a choice between regulating business and banking or nationalizing these entities, they choose regulation with various degrees of severity. Roosevelt's policies were tied to reform rather than revolution. He wasn't out to end capitalism. He attempted to save the system by curing the ills that led to the Great Depression. Still, he was cognizant of Coughlin's influence and that of Huey Long. In a tight election, he needed the votes of their followers. He was not immune to their potential political clout. Roosevelt, as always, was pragmatic. He would move cautiously to the left, especially regarding a pension for the country's elderly citizens. Long and Coughlin pushed him even as another challenger arose in the West.

Francis Townsend

Dr. Francis Townsend lived in Long Beach, California. As a senior, he was influenced by the "old folks lobby" spurred by Huey Long's and Father Coughlin's proposals. In his memoirs, Townsend recounted a story that provoked a latent anger to do something about the abject poverty of older people. As the story goes… He looked out of his window and saw two older women. They were dressed in what were once very nice dresses. Now their clothes were tattered. The women were picking through his garbage cans looking for food. That image stuck with him. It also motivated him to do something.

A critical mass had emerged throughout the country. There was an urgent need for a system of old-age pensions and unemployment insurance. Dr. Townsend proposed a plan that was simplicity itself. With the zeal of an evangelical preacher, he wanted every senior 60 or older to receive $200 each month. The money would come with one major stipulation. It had to be spent within a month. The money couldn't be hoarded. The plan would be financed with a general sales tax of 2%. Townsend defended his plan by stating the obvious: seniors (1) needed the assistance; (2) they would spend the money and in the process stimulate the economy; (3) they would leave the workplace, thereby providing jobs for younger workers; and (4) the problem of old-age dependency would be resolved.

Older people were a sizable group, accounting for 6.6 million citizens or 5.4% of the country's population. Townsend's plan spread like wildfire throughout the country. Townsend Clubs sprang up everywhere, with meetings held in private homes, church basements, and school auditoriums. Millions of letters flooded the daily newspapers. Local politicians everywhere took notice. In the 1934 congressional elections, 12 seats were won by supporters of Townsend's ideas.

DR. TOWNSEND

Roosevelt and his New Deal planners took notice. A stark choice confronted the president. He could seize the moment and gain the initiative, or a plan for unemployment and old-age insurance would emerge from the Congress, possibly one he wouldn't like. Pressured by Long, Coughlin, and Townsend, Roosevelt publicly stated in late 1934 his commitment to such legislation in the coming year. To that end, he formed a committee within his Cabinet to study the problem and make recommendations. The committee was chaired by the Secretary of Labor, Francis Perkins, the first and only woman in the Cabinet. He confided in her:

We have to have it (Social Security). Congress can't withstand the pressure of the Townsend Plan without a real old-age insurance system.

In discussing the difficulties of creating such a program, Roosevelt told her:

You want to make it so simple that everyone will understand it. The system ought to be operated through the post offices—just simple and natural... The rural free delivery carrier ought to bring papers to the door and pick them up as they are filled out.

Continuing, he said:

There is no reason why everybody in the United States should not be covered. Not just industrial workers.... Everybody ought to be in on it, the farmer and his wife and family. I see no reason why every child from the day he is born shouldn't be a member of the social security system.

In his State of the Union message in 1935, Roosevelt took a historic leap toward what would be called the "welfare state." He requested that Congress pass legislation to create an unemployment insurance system under the joint control of the federal government and the states. In addition, he asked for a system of old-age annuities to be exclusively under federal control. Lastly, asked Congress for a permanent program of federal grants to the states for aid to dependent children and blind people. In defending his proposals, he said:

We pay now for the dreadful consequences of economic insecurity---and dearly. This plan presents a more equitable and infinitely less expensive means of meeting those costs. We cannot afford to neglect the plain duty before us.

It was now up to the Congress to act. Roosevelt's plan was presented for a vote. Long's influence was in the air. The Townsend Plan evoked support.

CHOICES: TOWNSEND AND LONG

Roosevelt seemed to have a knack for gauging public sentiment, never getting too far ahead of it, nor too far behind. In the case of unemployment insurance and aid to the elderly, it was just a matter of figuring out how to implement such programs." The time for a decision could not be put off.

Though challenged by vested interests and political foes, Roosevelt would accomplish much during his first Hundred Days. As one historian stated:

He pushed 15 major bills through Congress. The bills would reshape every aspect of the economy, from banking and industry to agriculture and social welfare.

Roosevelt appealed directly to the American people during this time of dramatic change. On March 12, 1933, he held his first of many radio "fireside chats." He explained his actions in plain, simple terms and told the public to have "confidence and courage." His calming voice endeared him to millions. It also brought a malestrom of protest from his political foes.

The political cartoonists of the day generally supported Roosevelt, at least those in the Democratic Party's progressive ranks.

PHIA RECORD, FRIDAY, MARCH 3, 1933

CHANGE – OUT WITH THE OLD, IN WITH THE NEW

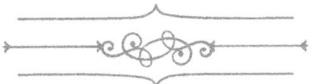

CHAPTER 17 – SOCIAL SECURITY

The headlines spread the word. A new president was in town. He had promised a New Deal. Would he keep his word? Political action and economic change were coming for many, who meant some form of social security program. It would take three years before the Social Security Act was proposed and passed by the United States Congress. How did people survive before this legislation and the involvement of the federal government?

Individuals were expected to care for themselves. What did that mean? They were expected to put aside a little money from each paycheck to help them in retirement. Of course, that depended on two things. First, you had a job. Second, after paying the bills, you had something to save. Since most Americans were living paycheck to paycheck, that was an almost impossible task; those few with a pension program through their employer were most fortunate. Essentially, you worked until you were infirm. Assistance came through family and friends. Unfairly or not, you became a "drag" or others. Under these circumstances, as a destitute, one might lose what little he had of this self-respect. Growing older deserved a better outcome. Britain and Germany were already experimenting with old-age pension plans. Would America also do so?

The New Dealers were up to the task. They envisioned it as a "contract between generations." Simply put, the current generation of workers would pay into a fund. The retirees would receive a monthly stipend. At age 65, individuals would begin receiving payment based on the amount they contributed to the fund over the years. Both employees and employers would contribute to the system, 1% at first and later 3%. The system would be a mandatory.

The Social Security Act was approved by Congress on August 14, 1935, and signed soon afterwards by President Roosevelt. The legislation was revolutionary. It was designed to mitigate the worst effects of the Great Depression by providing income to unemployed workers and assisting older people to prevent numbing impoverishment in their "golden years." The legislation was an omnibus bill containing 11 titles (or parts) that authorized seven distinct programs. Every aspect of the bill resulted from heated debate, intense lobbying, and a series of compromises sufficient to guarantee its passage.

At the time, the president said:

Long before the economic blight of the depression descended on the Nation, millions of our people were living in wastelands of want and fear. Men and women too old and infirm to work either depended on those who had but little to share, or spent their remaining years within the walls of a poorhouse. The Social Security Act offers to all our citizens a workable and working method of meeting urgent present needs and of forestalling future needs. And what's more, there is no reason why everybody in the United States should not be covered, not just industrial workers. Everybody ought to be in on it, the farmer and his wife. And family. I see no reason why every child, from the day he is born, shouldn't be a member of the social security system.

FDR SIGNS THE LEGISLATION

Title I provided federal grants to the states to assist elderly citizens. It was, therefore, a state-based welfare program. Initially, the New Dealers wanted this to be a federally run program. That proved too difficult a legislative rock to lift. Southern Senators feared the measure "might serve as an entering wedge for federal interference with the handling of the Negro question in the South." In addition, they didn't want Washington to be able to curtail the funds because a state might discriminate in administering the grants. States also shared these concerns in the North and West.

Concerning Title I, the president said:

It is impossible under any social insurance system to provide ideal security for every individual. The practical objective is to pay benefits that provide a minimum degree of social security---as a basis upon which the worker, through his own efforts, will have a better chance to provide adequately for his individual security.

Title II provided for old-age benefits. A system was created in which both the employer and the employee contributed to an insurance fund that would pay the worker benefits in the future once he reached 65 years of age. Here, the New Dealers won a major victory. The federal government would have exclusive control over the program. It would be difficult for the states to discriminate in how the funds were used. In theory, the poor house would become a thing of the past.

Title III provided grants to states for unemployment compensation. The program would be administered by the states. Given the different cost-of-living numbers and widely different wage scales across the nation, state control made sense. Washington would provide funding and standards, but the states would implement the program.

Southern employers voiced concerns that federal benefits (of all types) would "discourage Black workers from taking low-paying jobs in the fields, factories, and kitchens in the South." From their perspective, they had a strong economic argument. Over 60% of Blacks in the country (and mainly in the South) worked in the agricultural or domestic service sectors. Tied to this was a strong desire to avoid upsetting the prevailing racial socioeconomic system in the region. Again, this view was shared perhaps less overtly in other areas of the country. Ultimately, the final Social Security Act excluded domestic workers, sharecroppers, and tenant farmers. This meant that 65% of the Black workforce was excluded from the initial program. It also excluded 27% of white workers. The exclusion of workers without coverage looked like this in 1935.

Occupation	White	Negro	Other	Total
Agriculture	8,192,181	1,987,839	291,978	10,471,998
Domestic Service	3,268,725	1,576,205	197,521	5,042,451
Total Workers	11,460,906	3,564,044	489,499	15,514,449

Statistically, the Black population was inordinately excluded from coverage. Here, questions arise. Did the South want to exclude Blacks based on race or economic status, or was it a combination of factors? Was this about race or the type of jobs available to Blacks? Was it even possible to administer a tax program given the diversity of domestic service? Was the implementation of Social Security too complex for agricultural pursuits based on sharecropping and tenant farming? However, one thing was clear. Blacks in poorly paying domestic services, as well as those who tilled the land, were initially left out of the Social Security System. Their lives were still insecure for these people, and what the president said after signing the legislation was only half-true in their case.

President Roosevelt understood the drawbacks of the initial Social Security Act, which transcended Blacks and poor whites.

We can never insure one hundred percent of the population against one hundred percent of the hazards of life, but we have tried to frame a law, which will give some measure of protection to the average citizen and to his family against the loss of a job and against poverty-ridden age.

Here, a troubling question arises. Concerning the Social Security Act, was the domestic worker, sharecropper, and tenant farmer an "average citizen," particularly those living in the Jim Crow South, where segregation and discrimination reigned?

Once the Social Security Act was law, a monumental task faced the government. How would employers and employees be registered by January 1, 1937, when workers would begin acquiring credits toward old-age insurance benefits? Millions of businesses and millions of workers would be involved. To reach as many people as possible, the United States Post Office was contracted to distribute the necessary applications beginning in November 1936. The Post Office collected completed forms and turned them into local or regional Social Security offices. The forms were then forwarded to Baltimore, Maryland, where all Social Security Numbers (SSN) were registered. As a matter of record, the lowest SSN was assigned to Grace Dorothy Owen --- 001-01-0001. Thanks to the postal service, over 30,000,000 people were registered. It would have been difficult, but not impossible, to register domestic workers. That was also true of sharecroppers and tenant farmers, representing a unique segment of the nation's workforce.

GRACE DOROTHY OWEN (RT)

A bit of history… Years earlier, an attempt had been made to assist Blacks with a quasi-Social Security program. In the last days of the Civil War, General William T. Sherman hatched a plan in Georgia to aid the formerly enslaved people. He granted 40 acres to each freed family in the state's coastal areas and on adjacent islands. The Union Army donated mules that were no longer needed for military purposes. This was Sherman's "40 acres and a mule" plan. Had the program been continued, it would have enabled the emancipated Blacks to have land ownership and a degree of economic independence. Following Lincoln's assassination, however, President Andrew Johnson ended the program. He ordered that all land under federal control be returned to the previous owner in the summer of 1865. Potential Black ownership ended.

SHERMAN'S 40 ACRES AND A MULE

What social assistance might replace Sherman's efforts? Indeed, the Freedman's Bureau during Reconstruction provided basic aid during its relatively short existence. Something more was needed and came about because of the unique situation in the South following Appomattox Courthouse.

The devastated South faced many problems. For the former white landowner, where would he get workers? For the formerly enslaved person, where would he find work? Without capital and little if any education, he couldn't purchase land. He would need to work for someone who did.

The former enslaver, almost bankrupt, couldn't afford to hire workers. He was stripped of cash. He needed workers who wouldn't be paid until the crop came in. Out of mutual need, a system of sharecropping evolved. Labor contracts were drawn up to formalize a new relationship. Typically, a landowner divided his land into smaller plots of approximately 10 acres. He provided tools, a mule or other draft animal, clothing, food, housing, seeds, and fertilizer in exchange for labor. The "cropper" was allowed to keep 1/3rd of the harvested crop for use of the land. However, another third of the crop was deducted for tools, housing, and seeds. In the end, the formerly enslaved person was left with very little. He often ended the year in debt, especially if the weather was harsh to the two main crops, cotton and tobacco. The crop was sold and applied toward settling the sharecropper's account, which the landowner kept. The quasi-social security system wasn't ideal, but it provided stability in a world turned upside down.

SHARECROPPERS, BLACKS, AND POOR WHITES

The tenant farm system was different. The farmer owned the land he worked on or paid rent for. He made his own decisions as to what he would plant. He owned his crops outright. He paid the rent following the harvest. He had a degree of independence. However, he was generally in debt at the end of the year. That was because of the crop lien. Without cash and few banks willing to provide loans, the tenant farmer depended on local merchants' credit. All of the things noted earlier were bought on credit. A lien was placed on the property to protect the merchant. The eventual crop was used as security or collateral. Usually, the farmer pledged his unplanted crop at the county store each spring. The merchants charged a hefty 37% interest or more for their risk. At the end of the year, accounts were settled. If the crop did not cover the lien, the farmer had failed to "pay out." His debt was carried over until the next planting season.

Many merchants were unscrupulous, as were the landlords. They kept the records, and a few tenant farmers could read. Even if they could, they couldn't challenge the white merchant or landowner. That was not tolerated in the South. In some cases, local laws made it even illegal to sell crops to others besides the landowner whose land you worked. If you were in debt, many local ordinances prohibited you from moving until the debt was paid. Again, though not ideal, this third quasi-social security system did provide poor whites and Blacks a degree of certainty in their lives.

In 1935, there was a New Deal program to interview formerly enslaved people and their descendants who were sharecroppers. What follows explains the difficult circumstances faced by those who tilled the land for others.

After freedom, we worked on shares for a while. Then we rented. When we worked on shares, we couldn't make anything, just overalls and something to eat. Half went to the other man... A man who didn't know how to count would always lose. He might lose anyhow. They didn't give an itemized statement. No, you just had to take their word. They never gave you no details. They just said you owe so much. No matter how good account you kept, you had to go by their account. They kept you in debt. But you better not leave him, you better not try to leave and get caught.

As to whether the Social Security Act was intentionally racist? Did the New Dealers purposely build institutional racism into the legislation? There is scant evidence to suggest this. The final law was, however, a series of compromises that were necessary to pass the legislation. Title I funds for old age assistance provided some security to Blacks, where the states treated all groups equitably. Was this always true in the South, where the program was under local control? Not always. Title II, as a federal program, was available to all citizens. Since the Postal Service was used to distribute the registration forms and a degree of literacy was needed to fill them out, there was a challenge for many Blacks, and room for local authorities to hamper the process. Title III grants to the states again open the door to unfair local control of the funds. All of this is acknowledged. In sum, the White House policymakers always had to play with the cards dealt them. That was the political reality in 1935.

Two other Titles to Social Security assisted Blacks and others in time. Title IV provided grants to states for aid to dependent children, while Title V gave the states funds for maternal and child welfare. These programs have become increasingly important over the years."

In evaluating the Social Security program, where does that leave us?" As is often said, democracy is messy, and compromise is necessary to achieve anything. You don't always get all that you want. Conservatives railed against the legislation, claiming it was socialist, that it created too significant a role of government in the lives of people, and that it would create a sense of entitlement. Progressives were disappointed that the program was so limited. There was no 'cradle to grave' security as a birthright of all citizens. They were disappointed that many groups, such as migrant workers, civil servants, day laborers, and merchant seamen, were left hanging in the wind. The tax scheme was seen as regressive, hitting too significant a tax burden on people experiencing poverty. What we must remember is that this was day one of school. The program had the potential to grow and evolve, as it has. In many ways, it was aspirational. However, political cartoonists of the day nailed the contentious arguments, pro and con.

WEIGHING THE ARGUMENTS

Concerning deficits and the need to support Social Security, Roosevelt said of his political foes with a glint in his eyes:

We have heard much about a balanced budget, and it is interesting to note that many of those who have pleaded for a balanced budget as the sole need now come to me to plead for additional government expenditures at the expense of unbalancing the budget.

No government program is free. Indeed, that was the case of Social Security. In 1937, a payroll tax was dedicated to Social Security on the first $3,000 of earnings (that would be about $65,462 in today's dollars). Both the employees and the employer paid an equal amount into the program. The tax was referred to as a "payroll tax." Currently, 7.65% is deducted on the first $168,600. Medicare gets 1.45% of that amount, while Social Security receives 6,2% of the working population, earning more than the taxable maximum. The two taxes are a contribution under the Federal Insurance Corporation Act (FICA).

The New Dealers knew the Social Security System was not perfect—that was always obvious. The pensions that retirees received were modest, to say the least. In many cases, they were below the poverty level standards of different states. On the other hand, the program was "revolutionary." The federal government now accepts responsibility for assisting people in need. The relationship between the federal government and the American people was redefined.

In time, the Social Security System has embedded itself in our economic system, and the naysayers, though critical of its tax and solvency, came to understand how important it was to most Americans. Even the Republicans came around to this view:

> *Should any political party attempt to abolish social security, unemployment insurance, and eliminate labor laws and farm programs, you would not hear from the party again in our political history.*

Dwight D. Eisenhower

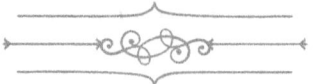

CHAPTER 18 – THE BANK HOLIDAY

In his inaugural address on March 4, 1933, President Roosevelt noted the two most important issues that needed immediate attention. The first was to put people back to work. The second was to reassure the public that the floundering banking system was safe for their deposits. Employing those out of work would take time. Securing the nation's banking system could not wait. On March 6, 1933, he issued Proclamation 2039 at 1:00 a.m. All banks in the country would be shut down to determine their solvency. On March 9, 1932, Congress passed the Emergency Banking Act. At 10 that Sunday evening, the president spoke to the nation by radio. It was the first of his many "fireside chats." Speaking as if he were sitting in your living room in a comfortable cushioned chair, he announced to a waiting nation that he was declaring a "bank holiday." In doing so, he set in motion an effort to stop "runs" on the banks and the further collapse of the banking system. At that moment, he had been in office less than 40 hours.

The president understood the skeptical public needed to understand what a "bank holiday" meant. People needed to be assured that their deposits would be safe and that the torrent of bank failures would end. But how did that work? Roosevelt's answer was to speak directly and candidly to the American people. The magic of radio transmissions would be the instrument of his upstate, New York aristocratic voice. In his first broadcast, he said:

I want to talk for a few minutes with the people of the United States about banking --- with the comparatively few who understand the mechanics

*of banking, but more particularly with the overwhelming majority who use
banks for the making of deposits and the drawing of checks. I want to tell you
what has been done, and what the next steps are going to be.*

And so he did…

A bank holiday… What was that all about? First, it is necessary to
understand how a bank functions to answer this question. The word
bank comes from the Italian word "banco." This word refers to a bench.
Italian merchants gathered by a bench to do business and to conclude a
deal, which generally meant borrowing or lending money. The transaction
was complete when the money was placed on the bench. Today, banks are
typically privately owned institutions that accept deposits and make loans.
Deposits refer to funds people put in the bank with an understanding
that they can get the funds back at any time or at an agreed-upon future
date. Money deposited in a bank does not remain locked up in the bank's
vault. The funds are put to use. Loans are made so people can purchase
a car, operate a business, or fund a home mortgage. In that sense, banks
are intermediaries between depositors (who deposit funds) and borrowers
(to whom the bank loans funds). Interest is what banks pay those who
deposit funds, or the interest they get on loans made. The "spread" is the
way banks make a profit. Depositors receive 3% on their funds, and the
bank charges borrowers 7%. The "spread" or profit before fees and taxes
is the difference. Banks offer various other services, including checking
accounts and mortgage services. Traditionally, money earned in interest
accounts for up to 65% of a bank's revenue.

What was a run on the bank? As banks failed during the Great Depression, depositors hurried to withdraw their money. If the banks had insufficient funds, they could only pay depositors a portion of their funds. For example, if you had $1,000 in Queen's Bank of Saratoga, New York, and the bank was only providing 10% of your funds, you got $100. The other $900 was lost. People scrambled to the bank to retrieve their funds before this happened, or worse, before the bank went under and no funds were available. The "runs" created a panic that only fueled more panic. Please make no mistakes about it. Depositors had seen over 659 banks fail in 1929, and by 1932, some 5102 banks were out of business. The savings of millions were lost. Still, solvent banks had little to loan and less to invest in profitable ventures. All of this dampened the economy and contributed to worsening the depression. Something had to be done to rescue the depositors. Something had to be done to prop up the banking system. Something had to be done to encourage the flow of capital into the economy. Something had to be done to resurrect confidence in the banking system. A sense of urgency pervaded the country and the New Dealers.

PANIC IN THE STREETS

Proclamation 2039 essentially shut down the nation's banking system. All banking transactions would be halted for four days. When reopened, the president promised the banks would be secure. The declaration was made. Could it now be fulfilled? The president called Congress into an emergency session. Almost immediately, the Emergency Banking Act was passed. Only one copy of the hurried legislation was available in the House of Representatives. It was read aloud in the House before it passed. A few hours later, copies were available in the Senate, and again the legislation passed.

Roosevelt's radio broadcast calmed the country. The radio audience included more than 60 million people. In concise and clear language, the president explained "what had been done in the last few days, why it was done, and what the next steps would be." Though seated in the White House, the president came across as if he were in your living room, chatting and explaining the day's news. Using the radio, the president had a powerful instrument to bypass the print press, where conservative ownership and editorials challenged the president. Roosevelt was determined to speak personally and directly to the American public. This first Fireside Chat accomplished that goal. According to most economic historians:

The public's confidence remarkably turned around. The contemporary press confirmed that the public recognized the implicit guarantee and, as a result, believed that the reopened banks would be safe.

For four days, the banks were on a "holiday." No one could access funds. No deposits were possible. Money couldn't be transferred in any form. Workers couldn't cash their paychecks. Somehow, people survived. In some cases, stores extended credit so people could buy the necessities. Railroads provided emergency credit to passengers who wouldn't be stranded. Public service workers were paid with vouchers, a sort of IOU. Ministers agreed not to pass the collection plates at church. Those with cash were in a better position to weather the situation. Surprisingly, the public went along with closures, having been told the banks would be safe when reopened. The tension of not knowing what would happen next dissipated. As one journalist for the *Boston Post* wrote:

Everybody seemed to take the bank closing with good nature. Police officers on duty at the banks with instructions to inform any prospective depositors just way they could not leave their money reported that there was little or no excitement because the doors of the bank were not open.

President Roosevelt had reached out to the American people. He explained the basics of banking and what was being done to safeguard deposits. He had said:

First of all, let me state the simple fact that when you deposit money in a bank, the bank does not put the money into a safe. It invests your money in many different forms of credit --- bonds, commercial paper, mortgages, and many other forms of loans. Your bank puts the money to work to keep the wheels of industry and agriculture turning. A comparatively small part of the money you put into the bank is kept in currency --- an amount, which in regular times is wholly sufficient to cover the cash needs of the average citizen... In other words, the total amount of all the currency in the country is only a small fraction of the total deposits in all of the banks.

What has happened during the last few days of February and the first few days of March? Because of undermined confidence on the part of the public, there was a general rush by a large portion of our population to turn bank deposits into currency or gold --- a rush so great that the soundest banks could not get enough currency to meet the demand.

The president then explained that Congress would develop a " rehabilitation program of our banking facilities." The Emergency Banking Act, passed by Congress, permitted the president to reopen solvent banks. Determination would be in the hands of the Treasury Department. Banks were divided into three groups. Class A banks referred to half of the nation's banks. They were classified as solvent and would be reopened. Class B banks would be reopened with federal assistance and reorganization. Class C banks were insolvent. They were unfit to reopen. Given this reassurance, the public's confidence was restored. The bank deposits would be safe. People now gathered at their banks to deposit funds. The banking panic was arrested but not forgotten.

The banks were back in business. Still, something more was needed. Banks had gotten into trouble with bad investments, questionable loans, and a combination of poor management and, in some cases, corrupt practices. Those possibilities still existed. Excessive greed, instead of reasonable profits, was always a cloud hanging over the banking industry. How could the depositors be safeguarded against another collapse of the banking system? The answer was four letters --- FDIC, standing for Federal Deposit Insurance Corporation. Created by the Banking Act 1933, the system worked as follows: A - The FDIC assesses premiums on member banks. B – assessments accumulated in a Deposit Insurance Fund (DIF). C – Funds from the DIF are used to pay depositors of failed banks. D – banks were required to fund the DIF to at least 2.35% of all insured deposits. E – The DIF invests its funds in guaranteed Treasury securities that earn interest. In short, the member banks pay insurance dues. If the FDIC did not have sufficient funds in the worst of all possible situations, it could and would borrow funds from the federal government. In addition to the insurance program, the FDIC examines and supervises financial institutions for safety and soundness. It also manages the receivership of failed banks. Banks needed cash to do business. FDIC encouraged that.

What does the FDIC cover? Initially, the insurance was $2,500 per account. It covered checking accounts, savings accounts, certificate of deposit accounts (CDs), cashier checks, and accounts denominated in foreign currencies. What wasn't covered? Stocks and bonds, money funds, and mutual funds were on their own. Since its inception, no one has lost any money in accounts insured by the FDIC. Today, accounts are insured to $250,000 in over 5200 institutions. In sum, the system worked. The banking emergency was resolved. The New Dealers had dealt successfully with one aspect of the Great Depression. What did this mean for Blacks? The FDIC did not discriminate on any basis. All accounts under its jurisdiction were protected. Whether Blacks could get a line of credit was another question not answered by the FDIC. Whether local banks would treat all customers equally was still to be resolved.

The president summed up his feelings about the Bank Holiday, stating:

It needs no prophet to tell you that when people find that they can get their money—that they can get it when they want it for all legitimate purposes— the phantom of fear will soon be laid. People will again be glad to have their money safely taken care of, and where they can use it conveniently at any time. I can assure you that keeping money in a reopened bank is safer than under the mattress.

The president offered a confession and a hope. He pointed out that:

We had a bad banking situation. Some of our bankers had shown themselves incompetent or dishonest in handling people's funds. They had used the money entrusted to them in speculations and unwise loans. Of course, this was not true in most of our banks. Still, it was true enough to shock people for a time into a sense of insecurity and to put them into a frame of mind where they did not differentiate but seemed to assume that the acts of a comparative few had tainted them all. The government's job was to straighten out this situation and resolve it as quickly as possible. And the job is being performed.

Confidence and courage are the essentials of success in carrying out our plan. You people must have faith; rumors or guesses must not stampede you. Let us unite in banishing fear. We have provided the machinery to restore our financial system; it is up to you to support and make it work. It is your problem no less than it is mine. Together we cannot fail.

Protecting depositors was accomplished through the bank holiday and implementing the FDIC. Tied to this effort was what to do about Wall Street and stock market manipulation that defrauded investors as hyper-speculation gripped the stock market. Though investing in stocks and bonds always carried a degree of risk, what the ancients had called "caveat emptor," or "Let the seller also beware." Investors needed protection against unscrupulous brokers and bankers. Recall that FDIC does not cover such investments; Wall Street has no guarantees. The question was how to do this? How do you maintain a fair, orderly, and efficient market? How do you limit "inside trading?" How do you increase public scrutiny? The answer to these questions was found in the Securities Act of 1933 and the Securities Exchange Act of 1934. By law, companies would have to publish quarterly and annual reports that included complete financial statements. The sellers of securities were required to disclose all pertinent information about them. The sale of misrepresented securities could be blocked. In addition, stiff penalties could be imposed on violators. All this, it was thought, would assist investors in making sound choices. The Securities and Exchange Commission (SEC) would enforce all this by requiring that all securities be registered with this government agency.

Initially, the question arose as to who would lead the SEC? It had to be someone who understood the investment world and the antics of shady players seeking a questionable, if not dishonest, return in the stock and bond markets. It needed someone who understood how insider trading and market manipulation occurred. In the end, Roosevelt picked a self-made Irish financier and multimillionaire. His name was Joseph P. Kennedy. His job was to restore investor confidence by restoring integrity to the securities market. This would be done by prosecuting and eliminating fraudulent and unsound practices targeting investors. Kennedy seemed like the perfect person for the job and the father of a future president, John F. Kennedy.

JOSEPH P. KENNEDY AND THE SEC

During the first 100 Days, the Roosevelt New Dealers accomplished their first task. The banking system was revived and reformed. Wall Street was now regulated. Because of the FDIC and the SEC, depositors and investors felt more confident about the placement of their capital. One important lesson had been learned. Wall Street and the banks could not reform themselves, nor could they be trusted to fully regulate their industries in an orderly manner to protect their clients. Only the government could do this by control and appropriate regulations. Even then, the patient might resist the needed medication. Those of a conservative bent were not altogether happy with Roosevelt's policies. The government was intruding on their domain. Constitutional questions were raised. In the end, however, the Congress and the president prevailed. Banks would be highly regulated.

William Woodin was the Secretary of the Treasury at the time. He put the importance of the Bank Holiday into perspective.

The emergency banking legislation passed by Congress today is the most constructive step toward the solution of the financial and banking difficulties that have confronted the country. The extraordinary rapidity with which this legislation was enacted by the Congress heartens and encourages the country.

The banking system was saved, as the chart below indicates.

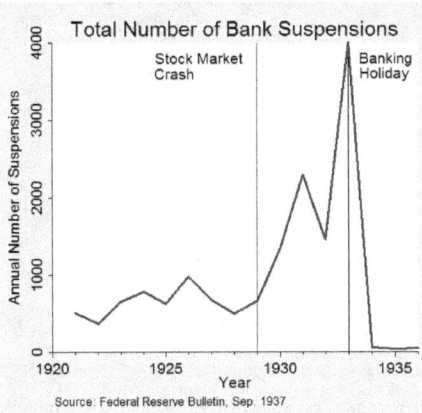

In response to these actions, letters flooded the White House from grateful Americans. Industrial workers and farmers alike were satisfied that their savings were protected. Bankers were relieved, too. The government would not nationalize the banking system as some had advocated. The banking system would be highly regulated to reduce risk. As one New Dealer said, "Capitalism was saved in eight days. Not bad considering that God took seven days for his creation."

CHAPTER 19 – THE TAXING PROBLEM

Once the banking crisis was resolved, another economic problem challenged the Roosevelt Administration, one that most Americans had scant knowledge about or felt they were little influenced by. Of course, there were a few who knew what was going on.

This is the way some remember the story. It was a lazy day in June 1931 in San Jose, California. No one seems to remember the exact day. Two men were having breakfast at Mike's Diner in what passed for downtown. Both men were conservative in their politics and Republicans with their votes. Three years earlier, they had campaigned for Herbert Hoover. They would not vote for Al Smith, the Catholic from New York State. One was a most prudent local banker in whom depositors had absolute faith since insolvency had not occurred. His name was Harold J. Stevens. His breakfast companion was Henry Taylor, the proprietor of a lumberyard still surviving the construction crunch wrought by the Great Depression. As always, they were talking politics as they ate their usual: pancakes, scrambled eggs, and a slice of ham. Perhaps grousing would better describe their conversation that morning. From all accounts, this is what appears to have transpired.

Stevens: "Those damn fools!"

Taylor: "They were warned about what would happen."

Stevens: "They wouldn't listen to Hoover. He told them to back off, but they wouldn't listen."

Taylor: "Even when those thousand economists objected strenuously. But they knew better, Smoot and Hawley."

Stevens: "Damn protectionists."

Taylor: "Didn't crusty old Henry Ford go to the White House?"

Stevens: "He pleaded with the president."

Taylor: "Hoover listened quietly and…"

Stevens: "… then signed the darn bill when it landed on his desk."

The two men paused to eat and drink coffee, always as black as the night and sometimes their thoughts. The threads of their conversation were not new. According to their friends, business associates, and wives, they had been at this for the past five months. What began as reasoned differences of opinion in Washington had turned into a smoldering anger that the Congress had been so shortsighted and the White House so bullheaded.

Stevens: "The legislation really affected your business, Henry?"

Taylor: "Christ, the price of Canadian lumber has tripled."

Stevens: "And construction costs?"

Taylor: "Sky high."

Stevens: "I see the results at the bank. Fewer applications for a loan… Fewer projects to invest the depositor's funds… Difficult time…"

Taylor: "I just don't know what they were thinking."

Stevens: "At first, it seemed so plausible. I must admit I fell for it, at least at the beginning. What about you?"

Taylor: "With the market down and all the unemployment, I was tempted to support the legislation. It took time for me to realize the implications."

Stevens: "Just like much of the country, I guess."

Sevens: "Damn, how could our Republican Party go for it? Aren't we the party of business, commerce, and banking? Aren't we the party of free trade? Isn't that what we tell the voters?"

Taylor: "That's what won elections, in 1920, 1924, and 1928. Right?"

Stevens: "But with this tariff hanging around our necks, I'm unsure about '32."

Taylor: "Well, maybe Congress will repeal the darn things before then."

Stevens: "You think so?"

Taylor: "No, but that Roosevelt guy in Albany will if he gets the nod from his party and the voters agree. He's already all but said he'd end Prohibition, or why not this 'tariff of abomination?"

Stevens: "Beer for votes?"

Taylor: "A lot of people would drink to that."

People overhearing that conversation might have asked, "What are those two old guys talking about?" What indeed.

————————

On June 17, 1930, President Herbert Hoover signed a bill to implement protectionist trade policies. Senator Reed Smoot, a Republican from

Utah, and Representative Willis C. Hawley of Oregon co-authored the legislation. The primary purpose of the Smoot-Hawley Tariff Act was to protect existing industrial and agricultural jobs in the United States. By raising US tariffs on over 20,000 imported items, the idea was to limit goods from other countries while exporting American products. In theory, American jobs would be saved from foreign competition, and overproduction for the domestic market would be siphoned to the world. The tariff was the second-highest in American history, exceeded only by the Tariff of 1828. The mechanism for achieving these goals was the tariff.

SMOTT AND HAWLEY

A tariff is a tax imposed by the government on imported goods. It works this way. If a Speedy Bike Company imports a bicycle from China at $50 per bike, a 10% tariff would raise the bike cost by $5. The company now pays $55 for the bike. In turn, it will pass along some, if not all, of that increase to the consumer. In reality, it is a hidden tax, regressive in nature, on the consumer. In protecting domestic bike manufacturing jobs from cheaper foreign competition, the consumer pays more and keeps domestic workers employed. The tariff or tax is not directly imposed on a foreign country. The company importing the bike pays the fare.

Some issues were raised during the debate over the passage of the Smoot-Hawley Tariff. Though not a member of the League of Nations, the United States had favored a declaration proposed by the World Economic Conference in 1927, held in Geneva. That declaration stated, "The time had come to end tariffs and move in the opposite direction." If nations abide by international trade, it would increase, thus benefiting all trading partners. Unfortunately, electricity, of all things, disrupted this vision. The advent of electrical power became a crucial factor in the mass production process and in assembly-line manufacturing. Exceptional gains in productivity occurred, leading to overproduction. Simply put, manufacturing exceeded the capacity of the domestic market to consume all that was produced. Excessive production needs to be exported while imports of similar products are limited. At the same time, the use of gasoline-powered trucks and tractors replaced mules and horses on farms. Greater agricultural production was possible thanks to the machines produced by the John Deere and Caterpillar companies. Land once used to feed animals was now freed up for greater food production, leading to overproduction in time. Again, the excess production needed to be exported while protecting the home market. Of course, prices would eventually go up, as stated by most economists at the time. In the end, consumers would pay the bill.

THE HIDDEN TAX

One thousand twenty-eight economists pointed out the flaws in the Smoot-Hawley Tariff and argued against it. The message to Congress went unheeded. As the story goes, Henry Ford went to see President Hoover and pleaded with him to veto the tariff. He called it "economic stupidity." Thomas W. Lamont, the Chief Executive Officer of J.P. Morgan, begged Hoover to use his veto power.

Though the president referred to the tariff as "vicious, extortionate, and obnoxious," he remained adamant about a veto. Even before Congress voted, 23 of America's most valued trading partners warned that retaliation would follow. Mexico, Canada, Britain, and others would also raise tariffs to protect their economies. They cautioned that the Smoot-Hawley Tariff would undermine America's commitment to international economic cooperation. Congress did not heed the warning. The bill passed the Senate 44 to 42. The House of Representatives voted 222 to 153. Caught in the middle was Herbert Hoover. In his presidential campaign, he had promised farmers he would do something to help them. He felt he couldn't break his promise. He had made promises similar to those of other industries. As he said:

The principle of a protective tariff for the benefit of labor, industry, and the farmer is established in the bill by the requirement that the Commission shall adjust the rates to cover the differences in cost of production at home and abroad, and it is authorized to increase or decrease the duties by 50% to effect this end.

Hoover, unable to extricate himself from the industries desiring a higher tariff and because of his election promises to protect American jobs, signed the tariff bill on June 17, 1930.

Retaliation followed. Canada immediately imposed a high tariff on 16 imported products, accounting for 30% of US exports to our neighbor. Britain and other members of the Commonwealth followed suit. Countries were engaged in protecting their own economies at the expense of others. US imports decreased 66% from $4.4 billion in 1929 to $1.5 billion in 1933. Exports decreased 61% from $5.4 billion to $2.1 billion in the same period. International trade influenced the decline in the nation's GNP from $103.1 billion in 1929 to $75 billion in 1932. That said, the Smoot-Hawley Tariff did not cause the "Stock Market Crash," nor did it cause the Great Depression. However, restoring a stronger economy and improving international trade made it more challenging. A political cartoon of the day captured the situation.

THE GAP IN THE BRIDGE.

In the 1932 presidential election, Hoover stood by his policies, while the Democratic Party promised lower tariffs. Roosevelt adopted this plank and campaigned on its behalf. Roosevelt was elected, and the Democrats were given overwhelming control of Congress. The Smoot-Hawley Tariff was thrown out. The Reciprocal Trade Agreement Act of 1934 replaced it. It permitted the president to negotiate tariff reductions on a bilateral basis. Such agreements were treated as regular legislation and only required a majority vote of approval by Congress. Before this, tariff agreements were defined as a treaty and needed a 2/3rds vote of the Senate. The president could now deal with individual countries with reasonable assurance of passage by Congress.

———————————

Back at Mike's Diner…

Stevens: "So?"

Taylor: "I'm undecided."

Stevens: "Hoover will get the nomination again."

Taylor: "Your vote again?"

Stevens: "The banking system is a mess."

Taylor: "Construction is down. I had to lay off three more guys yesterday."

Stevens: "So?"

History can't record how Stevens and Taylor voted. However, it can be stated that Roosevelt won a decisive victory and Smoot and Hawley lost their jobs in Congress. With the banking system secure and the Smoot-Hawley Tariff yesterday's painful memory, it was time for the New Dealers to move on.

CHAPTER 20 – THE MISGUIDED EXPERIMENT

It was 1932, and Franklin D. Roosevelt was hustling for votes in St. Louis, Missouri. With a glowing, optimistic face, he was touting what he would do if elected to the White House. Putting people back to work was his number one priority. That action was met with robust applause. Supporting the banking system and the deposits of millions was ever foremost on his mind. This he conveyed to those assembled. Heartfelt cheers greeted Roosevelt. Building a strong, enduring economy was also on his agenda. He spoke to this. Again, the crowd responded to FDR, applauding these obviously necessary actions. Pushing close to the Democratic Party's nominee for the presidency, an enthusiastic supporter bellowed, "Will you bring back beer?" With only the slightest hint of a smile, Roosevelt answered coyly.

I propose increasing federal revenues by several hundred million dollars a year by taxing beer.

The crowd read between the lines and exploded with gleeful smiles, sharp slaps on the back, and cries of delight. If elected, Roosevelt intended to end Prohibition. The country would go from "Dry" to "Wet." The curse of Carrie Nation and Andrew Volstead would finally be kicked into the wastebasket of history. No longer would the lexicon of Prohibition be necessary: speakeasies, bootleggers, and moonshiners. No longer would it be required for one to say quietly, "Joe sent me," the words needed to enter an illegal establishment selling prohibited alcohol. The despised Eighteenth Amendment would be extinguished once and for all. The proposed Twenty-First Amendment would end a misguided experiment in mandated social morality. As opposed to President Hoover's continued support for Prohibition, "happy days" would be here again if Roosevelt were elected. After a decade of temperance, most of America was ready to tip its glasses and drink to its demise.

What had America gotten into? Or, best said, what was the country trying to get out of? Many would say it began with Caroline Amelia Nation, known as Carrie Nation. She was also called the "Hatchet Granny." Born in 1846 in Kansas, she was the implacable foe of beer, wine, and liquor consumption. She was undoubtedly the most famous and radical member of the temperance movement. She hated what "booze" had done to families. She contended that hardworking husbands, the breadwinners of a family, wasted their modest income on "drink." Little was left for food and rent. Alcohol use led to domestic violence against women and children at a time when few legal protections existed for either. Excessive drinking led to job-related accidents and deaths. For many, it was noted that alcohol resulted in immoral sexual behavior.

What provoked Carrie Nation was a US Supreme Court decision that "favored the importation and sale of liquor in original packages from other states." From her divinely inspired view, this weakened the prohibition laws of Kansas. In her mind, the saloons were illegal; therefore, she could crusade against them. She would enter a saloon with her supporters, dressed in stark black and white clothing. First, she would besiege the saloonkeeper with sharp criticism. Then she sang, prayed, and hurled biblical-sounding utterances at those with bent elbows. If that didn't work, she took more radical steps. With a hatchet, she broke saloon fixtures and stock, yelling as she did so, "I'm here to save men from the drunken state." She began in Kiowa, Kansas, with a "mission from God." Later, she would move on to Topeka, Kansas. Saloonkeepers, their customers, and local officials did not take kindly to her antics. She was jailed thirty-two times and fined hundreds of dollars, but that did not stop her. As reported by the print press of her day, she slowly gained celebrity status. She hit the lecture circuit, protesting against tobacco use, foreign foods, corsets, and skirts of improper length. She vigorously supported suffrage and the rights of women. There was no doubt about it. Carrie Nation gave heart and soul to the early temperance movement and the creation of the Christian Temperance Union.

THE CRUSADER

Of course, the saloonkeepers objected to her actions. Livelihoods were at stake. In one somewhat humorous encounter with the upset wife of a saloonkeeper, Carrie Nation found herself attacked with a broom. She had bent over to see her bonnet when the proprietor's wife grabbed a broom and whacked the zealot on that portion of the anatomy "which chanced to be uppermost."

Led by the Anti-Saloon League and supporters of the lady from Kansas, the demand for a national prohibition law increased. The federal government passed the War Time Prohibition Act with America's entry into World War I in 1917. This temporary measure was enacted in November 1918. It barred the manufacture of beer and wine in the United States after May 1919. It prohibited the sale of beverages containing more than 2.75% alcohol by volume anywhere in the country after July 1, 1919. Dry Zones were established around military bases and camps. The Selective Service Act forbade the sale of liquor to men in uniform. Questionable justifications were given for the law. There was suspicion of foreigners, especially Germans, who owned many major brewers. It was claimed that beer drinking made you pro-German in the war against the Hun. It was stated that most saloons were owned by foreigners, most by Germans. Grain, it was said, was needed for food, not the manufacture of beer. A last argument was that the liquor industry had too much influence, most prominently on local politicians. Whatever his doubts about the law, President Woodrow Wilson signed the legislation.

The end of the war did not end the crusade for a national law against "evil alcohol." Even as President Wilson struggled to create a safer world through the Treaty of Versailles, other events overtook his administration. H.R. 6810 was passed by Congress and sent to the president's desk. The full name of the legislation was the National Prohibition Act. Stated succinctly, an act is proposed to:

Prohibit intoxicating beverages, and to regulate the manufacture, production, and sale of high-proof spirits for other than beverage purposes, and to ensure an ample supply of alcohol and promote its use in scientific research and in the development of fuel, dye, and other lawful industries.

The legislation, if signed by President Wilson, would require an amendment to the Constitution ratified by the states. The president vetoed the bill. Congress then overrode his veto, and the act became law on October 28, 1919. Now it was up to the states. Mississippi was the first state to ratify, and Utah was the last. That was January 16, 1919.

Only two states, Connecticut and Rhode Island, refused ratification. Much later, the Twenty-First Amendment repealed Prohibition, thereby making the Eighteenth Amendment the only amendment to have that inglorious honor. Prohibition began on January 17, 1920. Congress then passed the Volstead Act to implement the Twenty-First Amendment. Carrie Nation's hopes had come to pass. The forces of righteousness had won.

The Volstead Act was in three sections. Section I continued the War Prohibition Act. Section II declared the production, transportation, and sale of intoxicating liquors illegal. It did not, however, make the actual consumption of alcohol illegal. Section III indicated how alcohol could be used for industrial purposes.

The authorship of the act was attributed to Andrew Volstead, the Chairman of the House Judiciary Committee, 1919-1923. Though he was a "temperance evangelist," he had never taken a "dry pledge" demanded by the Anti-Saloon League. That said, he sponsored the bill and campaigned for it. There is no question that he helped facilitate its passage. He said:

I have no sympathy for the kind of liberty (the Wets) want, liberty to restore the saloon and nurse the brothel. Liberty to profit on suffering and insanity, liberty to gratify their alcoholic drink habit at the expense of ruined homes and wasted lives --- none of these are inalienable rights.

VOLSTEAD

In his official role, he felt it was his duty to write the act to implement the law. In doing so, he received hate mail and threats of a physical attack. One unhappy "Wet" wrote: "You will go to hell soon, you damned loafer." Another writer said: "Who, in God's name, would waste a good bullet, a knife thrust, or even a cup of hemlock on such an infinitely despicable specimen of the genius vermin of Andrew J. Volstead?" Some accused him of being in cahoots with the youthful Coca-Cola Company. Others said he drank when no one was looking. Photographs of him were sent showing a noose around his neck. From coast to coast, he was cursed for taking away their right to drink.

AN AMERICAN TRAGEDY

In a later interview with the New York Times after Prohibition ended, he defended himself. He said:

If I were to say that prohibition had been a mistake, there would be an awful uproar. And if I defended prohibition, the other side would be after me.

Implementation of the Volstead Act proved difficult to enforce. It was legal to own and use liquor obtained before Prohibition. It was legal to serve alcohol to friends in your own home if you had proof of purchase. Wealthier individuals stocked up. Physicians were restricted to one pint of spirits every ten days in treating their patients. Pastors, rabbis, ministers, and priests could use alcohol in religious practices with a permit. All that was in addition to the legal use for industrial purposes. Soon, of course, a black market was in full sway, as booze was imported from Mexico and Canada and wherever else it was legal. Tourism to Mexico's border towns flourished, as did a short hop to a Canadian province for some. Leave the country and have a drink. Stay at home and find a bootlegger selling legitimate liquor or a moonshiner making his own questionable brew. For a more formal environment, find a speakeasy through a friend where a password permitted entry and drinks were served. Initially, consumption of alcohol declined, and then the criminal world got involved, and gangs developed to supply whisky, wine, and beer to those with a thirst. Soon, the gangs were in a war with the Feds and themselves, and a guy named Elliot Ness would make the headlines along with his boss, J. Edgar Hoover.

There were other consequences, some ugly and unintended. Unemployment, at least in the restaurant and saloon business, increased. The proposition was simple: no liquor for sale, resulting in many concerns going out of business. An effort to promote social morality led to people consciously breaking the law as they rebelled against Prohibition. Crime increased as the Al Capone-type gangsters evaded the law and battled each other. Organized crime, as it was called, evolved to slacken the thirst or to help many drown the woes of the Great Depression. Police were bribed, politicians were paid off, and many were threatened to "just look the other way." And, of course, thousands of people died from drinking adulterated and poorly made "moonshine." From a fiscal standpoint, the federal government took a hit. Without the legal sale of liquor, there was no tax on liquor and nothing for the federal coffers. Prohibition was failing in its vision of a more virtuous society in many respects. The so-called "Roaring Twenties" resisted enforced morality and the criminalization of cold one on a hot day. By 1932, most of the voters and members of Congress were opposed to Prohibition. A momentous change was in the air.

ELLIOT NESS – THE LAW | AL CAPONE – THE GANGSTER

Change began with the Cullen-Harrison Act, which Congress enacted on March 21, 1933. Senator Pat Harrison and Representative Thomas H. Cullen sponsored the legislation. President Roosevelt, newly elected, signed the bill the next day. This act legalized the sale of beer in the United States, which has an alcohol content of 3.2% by weight. Wine of a similar low alcohol content was also legalized for sale, effective April 7, 1933. In signing off on the new law, the president said, according to some, "I think this would be a good time for a beer." Even most Republicans agreed. The new law left it up to individual states to pass similar legislation. This they quickly did. Newspaper reports of the day reported, "throngs gathered outside breweries and taverns to celebrate the return of beer." As a footnote… The return of legalized beer sales was celebrated on April 7th every year as National Beer Day.

By 1931, more than a dozen bills were introduced in the new Congress to amend or repeal the Volstead Act. For the next few months, there was a pitched struggle between those who still supported the Volstead Act and others who wanted it repealed. On December 6, 1931, Representative John J. Blaine of Wisconsin introduced a bill to end Prohibition. The formal title was Joint Resolution Proposing the Twenty-First Amendment to the United States Constitution. Congress adopted the Blaine Act on February 20, 1033. This initiated the political process of repealing the Eighteenth Amendment, including the Volstead Act. In the Senate, the vote was 69 to 25. In the House, it was 294 to 126.

The Blaine Act permitted the states to hold conventions to ratify the proposed repeal of Prohibition by passing the Twenty-First Amendment. Ratification required a two-thirds approval by the then 48 states. By December 5, 1933, this was done. Utah was the 36th and last state to ratify the amendment.

Years earlier, Senator Morris Sheppard had made a bold assertion about the lasting power of the Eighteenth Amendment. He had said:

There is as much chance of repealing the Eighteenth Amendment as for a hummingbird to fly to Mars with the Washington Monument tied to its tail.

Apparently, John J. Blaine was the hummingbird. What President Hoover had called a "noble experiment" was over.

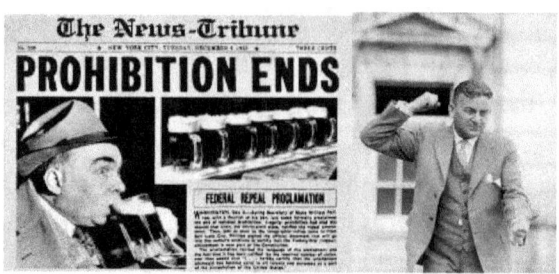

TWENTY-FIRST AMENDMENT | JOHN J. BLAINE

President Roosevelt celebrated "repeal" with his favorite drink, "a dirty martini." Around the country, others joined in. Even Uncle Sam was delighted with the thought of increased revenues.

A bit of necessary neglected history… The early foes of liquor who fought the saloonkeepers through the temperance movement included abolitionists, pro-suffrage, civil rights activists, ministers, teachers, and people of faith. They linked alcohol to immorality, criminality, and unpatriotic citizenship to the "drink." For them, addicting people to make a profit was a sin. Freed Blacks and later emancipated slaves found a degree of kinship with the anti-saloon movement. One Black man had something to say on ending the scourge of liquor. In his 1845 memoir published as *The Narrative of the Life of Frederick Douglass*, an *enslaved American*, he made his views clear. "Liquor," he said, "was the most effective means in the hands of slaveholders in keeping down the spirit of insurrection." Elaborating on this, before temperance groups in Scotland and England, he said:

In the Southern States, masters induce their slaves to drink whisky to keep them from devising ways and means by which to obtain their freedom. To make a man an enslaved person, it is necessary to silence or drown his mind. It is not the flesh that objects to being bound—it is the spirit. It is not the mere animal part- the immortal mind distinguishes man from the brute creation. To blind his affections, it is necessary to bedim his understanding. In no other way can this be so well accomplished as by using ardent spirits! On Saturday evening, it is the custom of the slaveholder to give his slaves a drink, and why? If they had time to think, it would leave them to reflect on the Sabbath day, and they might devise ways to obtain their liberty.

Following the passage of the Thirteenth Amendment, he wrote: "Black men should not take their emancipation and newfound freedom straight to the bar." He admonished the formerly enslaved person to avoid "passing the chains of Black bondage from the white master to the white saloonkeeper." Continuing, he said, "an unregulated saloon business ensured white dominance in keeping Blacks down." Douglas also pointed out the paradox afflicting Blacks. Freed Blacks in the North were often denied equal membership in white-majority organizations like the Sons of Temperance and the Washington Temperance Society. On the other hand, he noted, when traveling and lecturing in England, "he was welcomed to the temperance platform, side by side with white speakers, and received kindly and warmly as though my skin were white."

Douglas' message was straightforward. "People of color must be temperance people, otherwise they may expect to remain in degradation."

FREDERICK DOUGLAS

Prohibition was a grand vision and ultimately a failed effort to impose morality on American citizens. To a degree that had been anticipated in the 1840s when Abraham Lincoln spoke out against Illinois' statewide liquor prohibition. The future president said:

Prohibition goes beyond the bounds of reason in that it attempts to control a man's appetite by legislation and makes a crime out of things that are not a crime.

A few years later, the humorist and writer, Mark Twain, had this to say:

Prohibition only drives drunkenness behind doors and into dark places, and does not cure it, or even diminish it.

Somewhere in the pages of history, Carrie Nation's hopes and dreams burned brightly for a brief decade and then diminished. History can be brutal.

CHAPTER 21 – INITIALS

Once the banks and Wall Street had been stabilized, the next order of business for the New Dealers was to address acute unemployment. The graph below indicates the challenge before President Roosevelt. The choices before the White House narrowed to three. First, do nothing and wait for the business cycle to sort things out over time. That was unacceptable to the Administration. Second, it provides relief to avoid hunger and strife with private charities. Unacceptable. Joblessness was beyond the scope of private charities and limited public assistance. Third, in addition to providing immediate emergency assistance, provide massive funding for public projects that are clearly crucial to the country. Again, with 25% of the workforce idle, the first option was a nonstarter. Time was of the essence to avoid desperate men taking to the streets or clamoring for Huey Long or possibly a socialist candidate. Charities, regardless of their good intent, lacked the resources to deal with the massive homelessness and millions of hungry citizens. Immediate relief was necessary before an anticipated bitter winter arrived. The third option was essential and clearly a Keynesian effort to push against the business cycle with increased government expenditures, even if that meant running fiscal deficits and a flood of "red ink." Under these circumstances, the government would be the employer of last resort until the economy improved. This was the road the New Dealers took. There was no other choice as they saw it.

YEAR	POPULATION	WORKERS	JOBLESS	%
1929	88,010,000	49,440,000	1,550,000	3.14

| 1932 | 91,810,000 | 51,250,000 | 8.020,000 | 25.30 |
| 1935 | 95,460,000 | 53,740,000 | 9,030,000 | 16.80 |

UNHAPPY NUMBERS

One has to be careful with numbers. Suppose one person is out of work; that's personal. We can relate to that person. No paycheck. No food on the table. No place to live in time. No future for the children. We can empathize with that person. When 20,000,000 are jobless and millions more only partially working, that's a numbing statistic almost beyond our comprehension. We know that behind each number was a person caught up in a drama over which he had little control. All he was left with were questions. How can I be without work in the most prosperous country in the world? How can my family be one step ahead of homelessness and a bitter winter on the streets in such a wealthy nation? What has happened to all my dreams and hopes for my children? What is to become of us?

Writing about those without a job, one historian stated:

The jobless were the most conspicuous feature of that dismal social landscape, particularly in the cities. They clustered about pool rooms and taverns, sat in the park when the weather was fair, stood in empty doorways to get out of the wind, panhandled for nickels and dimes on the streets, haunted their union halls or the clubrooms of the Moose and the Elks, sat for hours over a nickel cup of coffee in dingy restaurants, staring out the window. You learned how to make a passable cup of tomato soup. You ordered an extra cup of hot water for your coffee and doused it with ketchup from the bottle on the table. If there was a complimentary tray of crackers on the counter, you had a meal that would do you for a day.

Though emergency relief was necessary in the short run, more was needed in the long run to maintain a healthy economy. Again, drawing on a Keynesian concept, the New Dealers promoted the "pump priming" theory instead of "trickle down" economics. What was the difference? The chart below will help.

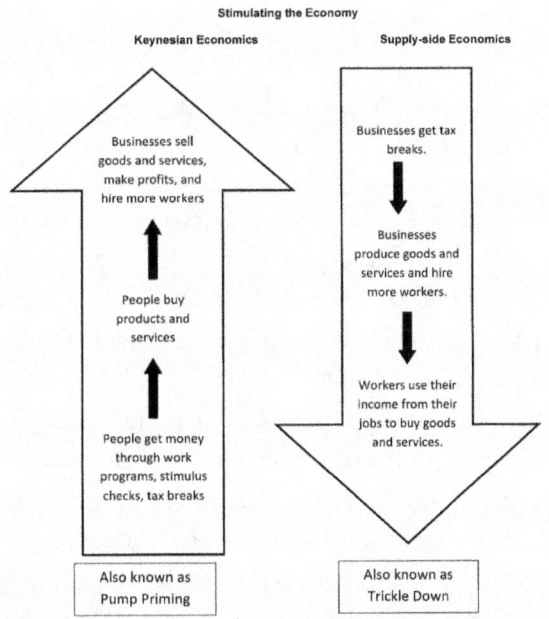

The "trickle down" view gives allegiance to the business cycle and its innate ability to deal with recessions and depressions in the regular economic activity. It strenuously opposes tax increases while seeking lower taxes to encourage investment in America's businesses. That being the case, companies will expand, and workers will be hired to produce the goods and services people want. Workers, in turn, will spend their income, and this will cause even more workers to be employed. In short, prosperity will trickle down and prosperity will reign—this conservative view animated President Hoover and the business community.

But what happens if the business cycle doesn't self-correct? What happens if the "trickle" is too limited or non-existent? What was the alternative to the "trickle-down" theory?

President Roosevelt accepted the Keynesian notion of "pump priming." What was this? It was common for farmers to start a dry pump by pouring a little water into the pump to generate a heavy flow. The New Dealers would apply this idea to the bleak unemployment situation. Federal money would be injected into the "economic pump" to jumpstart the economy. Two questions quickly emerged. How much cash would be needed and for how long? The Keynesians insisted on a deluge. Knowing full well that deficit spending was necessary to pull off this hat trick, the conservative streak in the president required something less than white water rapids.

In practice, it worked this way. Tax breaks were offered to businesses to encourage expansion. Stimulus checks were given to people on relief. Large government projects hired the jobless. In such cases, greater consumption should increase, and the GNP would expand. Provide people with money by "pumping" money into the economic system. That money will be spent, and businesses will grow to meet increased demand. Because of this, more workers will be hired. As noted earlier, in pushing against the business cycle, how much public money would be needed to prime the pump? And how will the money be spent? Lastly, how much indebtedness is the federal government willing to take on? Must every dollar borrowed be repaid with interest? In answering these questions, the New Dealers created programs to spur the economy and alleviate human suffering.

It would all begin with FDR calling Congress into an emergency session. There was no time to wait.

More Priming for the Pump!

FERA

On May 12, 1933, President Roosevelt asked Congress for an appropriation of $500 million for "a direct assault on unemployment." Loans and grants would be made to the states to put people back to work. The legislation created the Federal Emergency Relief Administration (FERA) under the direction of Harry Hopkins. His name was nearly as synonymous with the New Deal as Roosevelt's. He had led a similar program in New York State when Roosevelt was governor. He was an expert on social work and welfare issues. He believed the federal government would hire and put the unemployed to work. FDR agreed to this proposal from his trusted advisor. The government would get into the public works business.

Three goals were established for the FERA: first, it must be effective in putting people to work; second, it must provide work for those already on the relief rolls; and third, it must include a variety of programs aimed at the same end: reducing unemployment. Though government jobs were more expensive than the dole, they were psychologically more beneficial to the unemployed. One could keep one's self-respect. That was always important to the president. Assistance would be provided, but you would work for it. There would be no direct cash handouts unless there were unusual circumstances.

PUTTING PEOPLE BACK TO WORK

Though the FERA provided jobs mainly for men who were defined as breadwinners, women were also hired thanks to the persistence of Eleanor Roosevelt, the president's wife, and Ellen Sullivan Woodward, the director of the Federal Women's Division from 1933 to 1935. Jobs were created under the auspices of the Civilian Works Administration (CWA) against fierce conservative resistance. Generally speaking, the public did not perceive women as the "head of a household." There was concern about what kind of jobs would be available to women and what would be appropriate for them. Work was acceptable if it was "socially acceptable." Women were hired as clerical workers. They worked on projects such as sanitation services, highway and park beautification programs, and renovation of public buildings. They also dealt with public records, surveys, and museum projects. Many women were hired to sew. Over the life of the CWA, over 4 million garments were made and distributed to those in need. Scrap material was used to make toys for children. The women referred to themselves as "Santa's Helpers."

ELEANOR AND ELLEN AND WORK

CWA

This program was established on November 8, 1933. In its short span, it would last until March 31, 1934. The Civilian Works Administration was a temporary effort to put 2.6 million men to work as a bitter, harsh winter approached. Ultimately, over 4 million men were engaged in construction work, building 250,000 miles of roads, 12 million feet of sewer pipe, 40,000 schools, 150,000 privies, and 3,700 playgrounds across the country. Though successful, the program was scrapped because of the costs. The federal government spent $200 million monthly to put four million men to work. Another concern was the fear that a permanent dependent class was being created. Continuing high unemployment, however, would ultimately force Roosevelt's hand. A new jobs program was needed.

The demand for jobs with the CWA far outstripped its resources. For example, in Connecticut, over 1500 men registered for work, but only 480 men were hired. Preference was given to veterans with dependents. Since the federal program was administered at the local level, political favoritism could determine who got a job. This was especially true when it came to unemployed Blacks in some communities. For those who did have a CWA job, it meant all the difference in the world.

HIRNG THE IDLE

WPA

In January 1935, Congress created the Works Progress Administration (WPA). Harry Hopkins led the program. Over 1.5 million workers got a government job at a "security wage," which was twice the level of welfare payments, but well below union scales for the same work. Hopkins' mandate was to put millions to work as quickly as possible. He opted for labor-intensive tasks. Critics cried foul, claiming the agency wasted money on makeshift and inefficient projects. Supporters argued that wasn't the case, since the WPA improved or constructed 2,500 hospitals, 5,900 schools, 1,000 airport fields, and nearly 13,000 playgrounds. By 1941, the WPA pumped over $11 billion into the economy.

A WPA ROAD PROJECT

It should be noted that Hopkins appointed a series of Black advisors to design work to assist Blacks. In the first year of operation, the program hired 200,000 Blacks. That number increased each year. The WPA constructed Black schools and community centers. It opened domestic service training centers and conducted adult education classes. In the rural South Black men and women "flocked to literacy classes, which enabled them to learn to real and supplement the poor education they had received in deeply underfunded schools, or even to attend school for the first time in their lives." By the end of the 1930's Black illiteracy fell by 10%. However, despite the presence of "racial advisors," the WPA failed to address structural racism. That was beyond its purview and certainly beyond its power. By way of example, the WPA limited Black women's employment opportunities to domestic service training programs, while permitting white women to be trained for clerical work, gardening, and nursing.

REACHING OUT TO BLACKS

One unique aspect of the WPA is its cultural programs. Approximately 5% of the WPA budget went to the arts. This effort was collectively known as Federal Project Number One. Artists were hired to catalog, photograph, paint, and record everything happening during the Great Depression. For example, photojournalists were assigned to the Farm Security Agency (FSA) to create a pictorial record of America and its people. Artists and writers were employed under the auspices of the WPA to work with the Federal Writers Project to develop a series of state guides to entice people to visit other spots on the map. Folklortists were sent into the backcountry in search of "tall tales." Oral historians were dispatched to collect slave narratives; others, including highly trained musicians, compiled a fantastic collection of America's folk music. Under the WPA, there was a Theatre Project. It produced stage shows for the general public at ticket costs that didn't break the bank. The Arts Project decorated the nation's libraries and post offices with murals of "muscular workmen, bountiful wheat fields, and massive machinery." They portrayed an America not yet achieved. In that sense, they were aspirational. You can still see them in post offices and other public buildings. The WPA programs provided thousands of artists, actors, and writers with work. And not to be forgotten, these efforts established the precedent of federal support for the arts and humanities.

MURALS FOR AMERICA

HONORING THE AMERICAN DREAM

A 1939 Gallup Poll provided curious answers to this question: "What did you like most or least about the New Deal programs?" Curiously, the answer to both questions was the WPA. May critics lambasted men moving piles of leaves from one side of the street to another, or digging a ditch and then refilling it in a repetition of wasted effort and public funds. Labor unions were especially harsh. They protested the WPA's refusal to pay wages equal to those in the private sector. The program was always criticized for being inefficient. Construction costs were typically three to four times the cost of private work. And, of course, that was not only true, it was intentional. The WPA strenuously avoided cost-saving machinery to hire more workers. Hire 20 men to do what one man on a tractor could do. An unlikely supporter of the WPA was a future president of the United States, Ronald Reagan, a staunch conservative. In his recollection of the WPA, he said:

Some people have called it a boondoggle. But having lived through that era and seen it, no, it was probably one of the most practical social programs in those New Deal days.

The WPA was called socialistic, un-American, and expensive beyond the government's ability to fund. Of course, the greatest criticism came from the affluent, certainly from those who didn't worry about a meal.

PUSH BACK

PWA

The Public Works Administration (PWA) was involved with large-scale public works projects. It was headed by Harold Ickes, a trusted official close to the president. The PWA was created by the National Recovery Act of June 1933. The program initially aimed to spend $3.3 billion in the first year. That equaled about $10 per person in the United States. The long-term goal was to pay over 6 billion. The program did not directly hire the jobless. Instead, the federal government contracted with private companies to do the work. Contracted companies would employ as necessary. The projects included dams, canals, tunnels, bridges, naval vessels, schools, and hospitals. In addition, a considerable amount of funding went into street and highway projects. Over 11,400 road projects consumed some 33% of all PWA funds. The projects consumed over ½ of all the concrete used in the country, and one-third of all the steel. The main infrastructure program was a classic example of "pump priming" to increase consumption by putting cash (wages) in the hands of workers.

The dams built were of particular importance to specific regions and the country. The Grand Coulee Dam was built in Washington State. It was a concrete gravity dam on the Columbia River. The dam provided hydroelectric power for the northwest, flood control in the Columbia Basin, water for irrigation, and recreation on Roosevelt Lake, a massive body of water impounded by the dam. The Fort Peck Dam on the Missouri

River in Montana is the largest of six dams. The dam was 21,026 feet in length and over 250 feet in height. It was the largest hydraulically filled dam in the country. Fort Peck Lake was the fifth-largest artificial lake in the United States. The lake has a 1,520-mile shoreline, which is longer than the length of California's coast. As with the Coulee Dam, the dam on the Missouri provided for hydroelectric power, irrigation, flood control, and recreation.

FORT PECK DAM | GRAND COULEE DAM

The alphabetical programs introduced by the New Deal were, in some respects, revolutionary for the country. The power of the federal government to influence the economy through Keynesian policies put people back to work. What the programs couldn't do was guarantee their implementation at the local level equitably for all citizens. All too often, that proved to be the case for Blacks and other minorities. The letter that follows, by example, was written to President Roosevelt. The author was anonymous and remains so to this day. The issues he raised, however, were at the heart of how Blacks were treated, regardless of the best of intentions by the New Dealers. The writer resided in Reidsville, Georgia. The letter is dated October 18, 1935.

Dear Mr. President

Would you please direct the people in charge of the relief work in Georgia to issue the provisions and other supplies to our suffering colored people? I am sorry to worry you about this, Mr. President, but hard as it is, I believe the relief officials here are using almost everything you send for themselves and their friends. They give out the relief supplies here on Wednesday of this week, and give us black folks, each one, nothing but a few cans of pickle meat, and to white folks, they give blankets, bolts of cloth, and things like that. I don't want to take up too much of your time, Mr. President. Still, I will give you one example of how the relief is working down here with Nancy Hendries' own lands, stockholder in the Bank in his town, and she is being supplied with Blankets, cloth, and gets a supply of canned goods regularly. This is only one case, but I could tell you many.

Please help us, Mr. President, because we can't help ourselves, and we know you are the president and a good Christian man. We are praying for you. Yours honestly, I can't sign my name, Mr. President. They will beat me up and run me away from here, and this is my home.

There is no record that President Roosevelt ever saw this letter or that its contents were brought to his attention. Sufficient evidence exists, however, that the New Dealers were aware of the problems faced by Blacks throughout the country. Local control of programs limited the administration's power to end racial discrimination in its many forms. However, could more have been done to assist Blacks? Probably. What could have been done remained an elusive question.

Without a federal remedy, it fell on the Black community to fend for itself. It was not ill-prepared to do this. While the Great Depression was a new experience for white America, this was not true of Blacks, who had always lived an economically challenging life. The lesson was clear. To a great extent, Blacks had to take care of themselves. One woman who took up this task was Mrs. Fanny B. Peck. She organized what was called the Housewives League of Detroit. Black women banded together to actively struggle against discriminatory hiring practices and outrageous food prices in their community. Founded in 1930, they wanted Blacks to patronize only white stores that treated all people fairly and equitably. The slogan of this grassroots movement was: "Don't buy where you can't work." Where necessary, the group boycotted white businesses, including the meat-packing plants in the Detroit area. The many chapters of the Housewives League promoted an entrepreneurial culture focused on the startup of Black businesses in the community. With a membership of over 10,000, the group's larger effort was to feed and house Blacks in distress—the Housewives League disbanded by 1945.

FANNY B. PECK AND THE HOMEMAKERS
LEAGUE OF DETROIT

Taken in total, the New Deal program cited did not erase embedded racism in society. Pointedly, that was not their task. First and foremost, the New Dealers wanted to put people back to work and improve the economy. At most, they were into evolutionary "social experimentation," not revolutionary change.

Those opposing the New Deal never ceased in their criticism of the programs. The cost was too great, the Conservatives cried! The projects were a "boondoggle," Republicans clamored. Central planning was socialistic and a threat to the private sector economy, the National Chamber of Commerce proclaimed. Roosevelt's New Deal was unconstitutional since he was usurping Congress's traditional role as if he were a despot, the reactionaries screamed to the sky. Of course, the Democrats challenged these charges, essentially saying an emergency demanded an extraordinary response and constant experimentation and revision to determine what works. The goal was to put people back to work and feed and house the destitute and impoverished. That's all that mattered. Those were the cards Roosevelt played.

PRIMING THE PUMP WITH INITIALS

Priming the pump was more than an abstraction theorized by the Keynesians. It is accepted that government exists to assist the public, particularly during a severe economic downturn. Where the New Dealers could help the Black community, they would, though that assistance always seemed to fall short of equal benefits for Blacks. One song of the period captured this reality and the pain of Blacks in the Great Depression. It was called *Collector Man Blues*.

Hey, hey, somebody knocking at my door,
Hey, hey, somebody knocking at my door,
Says it may be collector, baby,
I sure don't know.

They will try to tear your house down, Lord,
And this is what he will say,
Says, "I have to have some money,

'cause you didn't give me anything last payday.

Folks, one thing that I sure can't stand,
Folks, one thing that I sure can't stand.
Your children can't even play for holin','
"Daddy, here comes that collector man!"

I say, folks don't buy nothin', Lord,
on the installment plan,
I say, folks don't purchase nothin', Lord,
on the installment plan,
And you will not be worried, Lord,
by no collector man.

I've begged and borrowed til,
My friends don't want me around,
I'll take old man Depression,
and leave this no-good town,
Depression's here.
They tell me it's everywhere
So I'm goin' back to Florida,
And see if the Depression's there.

Oh, how it would help,
If I could explain,
but Depression as me,
It's a out to drive me insane.

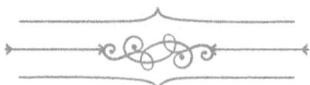

CHAPTER 22 – THE INFORMAL CABINET

On July 2, 1932, President-elect Franklin D. Roosevelt pledged himself to a New Deal for the American people. Speaking at the National Democratic Convention in Chicago, he declared in his acceptance speech:

Let us all here assembled constitute ourselves prophets of a new order of competence and of courage. This is more than a political campaign; it is a call to arms. Given me your help, not to win votes alone, but to win this crusade to restore America to its own people.

These are dramatic and inspiring words, but what would they mean once FDR was in the White House? What would the new order be? Restoring America to its own people… What did this really mean? As with any occupant of the White House, pledges and promises made in the heat of a presidential campaign must eventually become policies. Given the complexity and enormity of the incoming president's socio-economic problems, it was absurd to believe that one man alone had the knowledge and background to deal with such challenges on his own. He would need the advice and input of political pros, government bureaucrats, lobbyists, and his Cabinet. The new president was well aware of this. He also realized he needed "out of the box" views that challenged the status quo and conventional thinking to deal with the unprecedented challenges wrought by the Great Depression.

Sam Rosenman was Roosevelt's law partner, legal advisor, and speechwriter. He suggested the president look to the academic world, particularly the scholars at Columbia University in New York City. At the very least, they could provide him with the scholarly research necessary to underpin public policy. To that end, the president first recruited Raymond Morley, a political economist and an expert on criminal law and the justice system. Morley was the first of a group that became known as the "Brain Trust." This informal, non-elected group would meet regularly and advise the president as necessary. According to some historians, Morley coined the term New Deal, though there is debate about this. Morley's influence on the president was considerable. During the presidential campaign, he wrote the *Forgotten Man* speech that Roosevelt delivered on April 7, 1932. The speech focused on the jobless, the poor, and the American farmer. In part, the president said:

These unhappy times call for the building of plans that rest upon the forgotten, the unorganized, but the indispensible units of economic power for plans like those of 1917 that build from the bottom up and not from the top down, that put their faith once more in the forgotten man at the bottom of the economic ladder.

In referring to 1917, the president, by example, illustrated what the country could do in wartime if it had the political willingness to do so. Building from the bottom up was a Keynesian notion in opposition to the "trickle down" theory. The millions out of work, whether in cities or farms, needed assistance and would no longer be "forgotten."

Roosevelt (and Morley) reminded the radio audience that public expenditures alone would not completely solve the unemployment problem. As he said:

But it is clear that even if we could raise many billions of dollars and find definitely useful public works to spend these billions on, even all that money would not given employment to the seven million or ten million people who are out of work. Let us admit frankly that it would be only a stopgap. A real economic cure must go to the killing of the bacteria in the system rather than the treatment of external symptoms.

In time, Morley recruited two Columbia University colleagues, Rexford G. Tugwell and Adolf A. Berle, Jr., and a social worker from New York, Francis Perkins, the first woman in a presidential cabinet. Collectively, they would with others be known as New Dealers. Unlike previous cabinets staffed with wealthy patricians, prosperous businessmen, and party loyalists, the New Dealers were "Ivy League" intellectuals. As a group, they believed the government had a duty to intervene in the nation's economic life to improve the quality of American life. They were Progressive with a pragmatic edge. They were willing to experiment with new approaches to the White House's problems. They were also unified in their opposition to the laissez-faire orthodoxy and the narrow use of federal power advocated by Hoover and the Republican Party. They felt the government had responsibilities beyond balancing the budget and maintaining a strong defense. Collectively, the New Dealers wanted to reduce the concentrated power of corporations by vigorously enforcing antitrust laws. They differed, however, as to how to do this. Some wanted to see cooperation between business, labor, and the government. Others wanted deep centralized planning forged by the national government. Ultimately, it was up to Roosevelt to decide policy.

RAYMOND MORLEY | FRANCES
PERKINS | REXFORD TUGWELL

President Roosevelt asked Frances Perkins to join his cabinet in 1933. As already noted, she was the first woman to do so. The president had good reason to choose her. As governor of New York (1929-1932), he appointed her the New York state industrial commissioner. She supervised an agency of some 1800 employees. She put New York at the forefront of progressive reforms through her work. She fought for a minimum wage and unemployment insurance laws. In addition, she reduced the workweek for women to 48 hours and fought vigorously to end child labor in the state. When FDR went to Washington, he wanted her in his administration. She obliged. As the Secretary of Labor, she continued implementing progressive policies, including assisting in writing the legislation for Social Security and the Civilian Conservation Corps (CCC). She was also involved in establishing the She-She-She Camps (SSSC). These camps for young women, as a counterpart to the CCC, focused on unemployed men. The camps for women sought to ameliorate what women were experiencing during the Great Depression. One feminist writer described the situation of jobless women, saying:

...once out of work, women will go for weeks verging on starvation, crowding in some hole, going through the streets ashamed, sitting in libraries, parks, going for days without speaking to a living soul like some exiled beast.

Mrs. Roosevelt was especially appalled by the plight of young women. By 1933 there were almost two million women seeking jobs. She said of these women:

As a group women have been neglected in comparison with others, and throughout the Depression have had the hardest time of all.

Many of the jobless women seldom showed up at breadlines. Many were too often forced to live in subway tunnels and into a "tramping" lifestyle. In many cases, they foraged for subsistence outside the cities, hoping to survive in rural areas. The First Lady prompted Secretary Perkins to do something. Camp TERA (Temporary Emergency Relief Assistance) was the outcome of that effort. It was located in Bear Mountain, New York State. The camp opened on June 10, 1933, with 17 young women from

New York. In Camp TERA, the young women were taught a variety of skills. By 1934, there were also 28 She-She-She camps in 26 states. Enrolled women received $25 per month; $15 from that salary was deducted. That money was used for room and board.

THE FIRST LADY AT A TERA CAMP

In many respects, Mrs. Roosevelt's support of the TERA camps was tied to her desire to uplift the rights and protections of women in the workforce. In this, she found an able supporter in Frances Perkins. It was an ongoing challenge. The New Deal focused on unemployed men, the "breadwinner" in the family, in contrast to single, youthful women.

Rexford G. Tugwell was a Professor of Economics at Columbia University. Before being recruited by Raymond Morley, he had written extensively on the Great Depression. He wanted to focus on the 3Rs with other New Dealers:" relief, recovery, and reform. Stated another way, food, jobs, and regulatory change are needed to avoid another economic collapse. Tugwell was considered an advocate of significant governmental planning in the absence of the private sector, which seemed frozen in place, buried in a Neanderthal status quo. Without question, he was an "experimentalist" and certainly willing to depart from the past. Because of his willingness to expand the role of the federal government, he was denounced as "Rex the Red" by conservatives. Those opposed to state planning considered his ideas socialist. The political barbs did not seem to affect his philosophy of government.

As the Assistant Secretary of Agriculture, Tugwell helped to design the Agricultural Adjustment Act (AAA) to save American farmers from dreadful overproduction and declining prices. The key to his thinking was the "domestic allotment system." Farmers would be paid to reduce production by 30% voluntarily. The laws of supply and demand would now work to the farmer's advantage. If the supply was too plentiful, as had been the case, prices fell. In reverse, farm income should increase by reducing the supply of agricultural products. The legislation tried to protect sharecroppers and tenant farmers when land was removed from production. Landlords were required to share the payments they received when taking land out of production. Poor farmers were supposed to be compensated. Where local administration was prevalent, enforcement was not always practiced. The entire program was funded with a tax on processing companies that used farm commodities. The Department of Agriculture would manage the production of key crops by adjusting the subsidies for "non-production." This was encompassed in the Soil Conservation and Domestic Allotment Act, enacted on February 29, 1936.

The focus on soil conservation was in response to many factors, including the Dust Bowl, which had ripped away the topsoil, distributing it to the four corners of the country in huge dust clouds. It was also in response to the poor use, if not overuse, of the land that was encouraged by the government during World War I. Now, the effort was to improve the fertility of the land and to end the ruinous exploitation of the land.

ASSISTING AMERICAN FARMERS

Tugwell also had a vision of what we know as suburbia. This was a bold housing experiment, which many saw as the most radical of all the

New Deal programs. Confronting a housing shortage and an economy decimated by vast unemployment, and urban areas deteriorating, Tugwell wanted to build four "greenbelt towns" as an example of how suburban development might occur. The federal government went into the housing construction business as the chief force behind a planned community. Greenbelt, Maryland, was an example of this effort to prepare low-cost housing run by the federal government. Greenbelt was located in Prince George's County, only 8 miles north of Washington, D.C.. The community was built under the auspices of the Resettlement Administration in 1935-1936. The housing project provided work for the unemployed. It also provided housing for low-income workers, who rented units from the federal government. The community served as a model for future town planning.

In the case of Greenbelt 850, housing units were built initially. What made the Greenbelt community unique was the "inside out" planning. Two independent "circulation systems" were designed to allow automobiles and pedestrians to function harmoniously. Pathways for pedestrians wound through the community. This provided access to the interior residential streets, commercial areas, and parks. Major streets with heavy auto traffic were built with underpasses. Those walking or riding a bicycle never had to encounter Fords and Buicks, in contrast to high-density urban areas, which was quite something.

The workforce that built Greenbelt was comprised of both white and Black workers. However, only white families were able to apply for residency. Initially, Tugwell wanted to include a portion of the project's land for Blacks. Those plans were quickly jettisoned. An integrated community was considered too controversial for Prince George's County, which was deeply segregated in the 1930s. That being the case, the town was segregated based on race. Approximately 5,000 white families applied for housing. Applicants had to be married and earn between $800 and $2200 annually. The husband had to be employed. These factors alone made it difficult for Blacks to apply. Integration would have to wait until the post-World War II period.

SEGREGATED LOW-COST HOUSING |
BLACKS BUILDING GREENBELT

There is no question that the "Brain Trust" was influential in designing many New Deal programs. President Roosevelt depended on these academics to provide him with proposals in the tradition of Progressivism. They supported Keynesian economic theory and challenged the notion of an "invisible hand" that self-corrects recessions in the business cycle. Tugwell stated their case eloquently and the experimental programs they recommended.

The cat is out of the bag. There is no invisible hand. There never was... We must now supply a tangible and visible guiding hand to do the task that mythical, nonexistent, invisible agency was supposed to perform, but never did.

In other words, the New Deal would be the government's "visible hand." The chart below illustrates the themes of that effort.

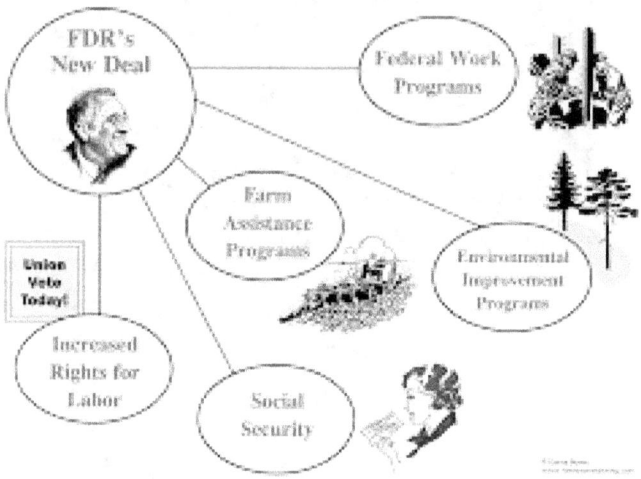

THE NEW DEAL

CHAPTER 23 – THE OTHER CABINET

The Roosevelt Administration coveted Black votes that had historically gone to the Republicans since Reconstruction. Many Blacks voted for the new president in 1932, but how would they vote in 1936? Could the Democrats gain the majority of the Black vote to ensure a party victory in Washington and elsewhere? With that in mind, the New Dealers set out to include Blacks in the New Deal programs. Side by side with this political need was an ethical argument. All Americans should be treated equally, regardless of race, gender, or background. Encouraged by Black organizations, FDR appointed over 100 prominent Blacks to "race-related advisory positions within the federal government." These unelected advisors provided input on the unique problems Blacks faced in society. They touched upon the pronounced cultural, historical, and racial issues facing the Black population. To a degree, these advisors were successful in their efforts. By 1936, some 30% of all Blacks participated in a New Deal program.

Robert L. Vann was installed as the Assistant Attorney General in the Justice Department. Robert Weaver was an advisor to the Department of the Interior and the Public Works Administration. Mary McLeod Bethune was an advisor to the National Youth Administration. In time, these advisors and others formed an informal group known as the "Black Brain Trust." They were middle-class, college-trained, and professionals. They met regularly at the home of individual members. Though never publicly acknowledged by the president, this informal group advised the

New Dealers. The Black press coined the term with pride since there was now a talented group of advisors on the steps of the White House.

ROBERT L. VANN | MARY MCLEOD BETHUNE | ROBERT WEAVER

Were Southerners aware of this group? Without doubt, yes. Could they do anything about it? Not really, but that was with one proviso. Their advice couldn't disrupt the Southern sensitivities concerning racial conditions below the Mason-Dixon line. As one historian noted:

Many white people in the South were dogmatically opposed to Negroes participating on equality with white people in any beneficial measures; and they insist that the administration of relief and in the application of the minimum wage scale there must be an exception to the general rule when it comes to Negroes.

On the issue of a minimum wage, the *Macon Telegraph* editorialized in support of equal treatment of the races. Letters to the editor took a different stance. As one reader wrote:

Your speeches and editorial on the greater things promised the South in the new deal are fine, and every word is gospel, but when you talk about being fair and generous toward the Negro you are on an unpopular side, and you had better watch out.

Was the Black Brain Trust successful? Answering the question is not easy. On the one hand, the Black Cabinet was important to Black people because it signified "that the government was paying attention to them in ways that had never been the case before." On the other hand... The Black Cabinet wasn't able to redress all the racial inequities embedded in the New Deal policies. Still, their efforts to direct federally funded work and relief programs toward Blacks proved essential in the community's ability to weather the economic crisis.

The most prominent member of the Black Brain Trust was Mary McLeod Bethune. She was a teacher, civil rights activist, and an advocate for women's rights. Though she was astute politically, she often declared she was not a politician. She was, however, bipartisan in her work to assist women and children. During the Coolidge Administration, she was an advisor to the White House Conference on Child Welfare. She was also an advisor to Hoover's Conference of Child Health and Protection. In 1935, FDR tapped her to serve as a Special Advisor to the National Youth Administration. A year later, the president asked her to take a new position within the department. She was to assist young women between 16 and 24 in furthering their skills, education, and training. She was to give special attention to young women living in rural areas. Under her supervision, thirteen training centers were established near colleges and universities. These centers proved invaluable as the country prepared for war in the late 1930s. Women were taught industrial sewing, welding, and machinery patternmaking skills. All young women, both white and black, were paid the same. In the White House, she had a most influential supporter. That was Eleanor Roosevelt. The two were kindred spirits in their desire to assist women and children.

KINDED SPIRITS

Though she made a valiant effort, Bethune was unable to move the Administration on the issue of lynching. In a letter to President Roosevelt dated January 18, 1940, she spelled out her views, stating:

The National Council of Negro Women, representing five million women, would appreciate some public statement from you on the anti-lynching bill.

Bethune was adroit in her use of words, pushing only slightly with the term "appreciate." Asking for "some statement" was a door wide open, providing the president with various possible responses. Building on that, she said:

We have watched with interest your great humanitarian program and we are sure that you are vitally interested in all minority groups.

Here, Bethune was stacking the deck, flattering the president, and reminding him that he was (and should) be interested in those being lynched. Having laid the groundwork, she continued:

Despite this assurance, we feel that since there are interests which are opposed to the passing of this vital piece of legislation, that you, as President of the United States, could do the Negro group a service that would never be forgotten, if some word could be said on this matter.

At this point, Bethune got into the heart of the matter. Though there were Southerners opposed to the Anti-Lynching Bill, and a political risk was involved for the White House, at least a modicum of support would be helpful. Such assistance would never be forgotten (particularly in the upcoming presidential election). In a sense, she was putting the president in a tight spot. True, FDR no longer had to completely cater to the Southern "bloc" to get his New Deal programs passed. But it was also true that the president was considering running for reelection; that is, for an unprecedented "third term." He needed the Black vote to win a close election, as well as the vote of Southerners. At the same time, the president was turning his attention to America's need to rearm, given events in the Far East (Japan's war in China) and Nazi Germany's invasion of Poland. Rebuilding the military needed Congressional political support in a nation split between isolationists (stay out of war) and interventionists (assist China and Britain). Rebuilding the armed forces also required funding. To do this, the White House needed Southern votes. Though Bethune pointed out that the Anti-Lynching Bill was "essential," it paled before Roosevelt's concern for the nation's security. There would be no outward support for the bill that would antagonize the opposition.

The Black Brain Trust is now a footnote in American history. It left its mark in many ways. Black scholars, professionals, and political appointees would influence future presidents. Most importantly, it paved the way for the Civil Rights Movement of the 1950s.

THE BLACK BRAIN TRUST – ANNOYING AND PRESENT

CHAPTER 24 – THE TREE ARMY

On March 9, 1933, President Roosevelt called Congress into an Emergency Session. The crisis was, of course, joblessness. Too many Americans were out of work. Too many families were suffering. Within the unemployment ranks were two groups for which the president had significant concerns. Millions of high school and college men were on the streets looking for a job. There were also veterans of World War I who combed the streets seeking work. The two groups represented a potential social explosion. Something had to be done, and Roosevelt knew it. Five days after his inauguration, Congress passed a bill creating the Civilian Conservation Corps (CCC). On April 5, 1933, the president issued an Executive Order putting into motion the bill entitled The Relief of Unemployment Through the Performance of Useful Public Work and other Purposes.

In addressing the Congress about this program, the president said:

I propose to create a civilian conservation corps to be used in simple work, not interfering with normal employment, and confining itself to forestry, the prevention of soil erosion, flood control and similar projects. I call your attention to the fact that this type of work is of definite practical value, not only through the prevention of significant present financial loss, but also as a means of creating future national wealth.

Of all the New Deal programs, the public supported this legislation. It would last a decade and put 3,000,000 young men and veterans to work building and restoring the country's natural resources through flood control, reforestation, firefighting, and building state parks. Over 250,000 Blacks would be part of this effort. The recruits would be known as the "Tree Army."

THE TREE ARMY

Initially, there was opposition to the bill. Many in Congress felt they had not been consulted or had insufficient time before voting on the measure. Labor unions resisted, feeling the government workers would compete with those in the private sector. There was also concern that the $1.00 per day pay scale for CCC workers might set the standard for all workers. Many objected to the Army's role in transporting CCC recruits to military installations and later supervising the CCC camps. Conservatives felt the program would be wasteful and too great an extension of FDR's constitutional authority. They also questioned the ability of the federal government to administer the program that would reach into almost every state and run a budget deficit. Against all this, the program survived and prospered.

THE OPPOSITION

The president's argument for the CCC was spelled out as such:

It is my belief that what is being accomplished will conserve our natural resources, create future national wealth, and prove of moral and spiritual value not only to those of you who are taking part but also to the rest of the country.

In the end the president was given the authority to enact the program as he so fit and "under such rules and regulation as he may prescribe by using existing agencies." However, one stipulation was included. Oscar De Priest, the only Black in Congress, offered the following requirement: "That in employing citizens for this Act, no discrimination shall be made on account of race, color, or creed." His proposal did not include gender. Enforcing such an edict would be difficult in all parts of the country. That was understood. However, a 10% plan was adopted. That percentage of openings would be reserved for Blacks equally to their percentage of the general population.

The CCC would be administered through the cooperation of four existing departments. The Department of Labor was responsible for recruiting and selecting the enrollees, who had to be between 18 and 25. They had to come from families already receiving welfare. The Army was charged with transporting, feeding, and clothing the recruits. Clothing meant WWI unused uniforms. All the young men would be inoculated against smallpox and typhoid and then sent to a military camp for conditioning. The Departments of Agriculture and Interior were responsible for selecting the locations of the camps and determining the work projects. Together with the Army, they would set up the camps.

As noted earlier, the recruits would be paid $30.00 per month. About $25 had to be sent home to their families if they were on public assistance. There was no charge for the food, clothing, and housing. The pay scale also applied to veterans whom the Veterans Administration selected. Initially, 25,000 vets were selected. Ultimately, 250,000 were in the program, including 2,600 Bonus Marchers. Special camps were set up for the older vets with no age or marital status restrictions. Most of these men were about 30 or older and stayed in the camps longer than the younger recruits. The vet camps were run a little less formally. The canteens sold beer, and families could move into a nearby town.

THE VETS

Other problems had to be dealt with. Since large groups of young men would be brought into local areas already dealing with homelessness and a high jobless rate. There was concern that the locals would resent the influx of the recruits. That was always an ongoing concern. There was also another problem. The CCC had insufficient supervisors skilled in firefighting, reforestation, and flood control. Local experienced men (LEM) who were previously unemployed were hired to remedy this. They could live off-site with their families, and age wasn't a factor. Their pay was based on a different scale. Initially, 3,500 LEMs were hired. These men were employed at the local level. This, of course, opened the door to political patronage and discriminatory practices. That was the price to recruit the local men in the CCC.

Blacks played a significant role in the CCC. Over 250,000 Blacks were in the program's 150 segregated camps. In a real sense, they were "hidden figures" in the history of the CCC. Was the administration of the CCC discriminatory? At the local level, yes… Were Blacks offered opportunities to improve themselves? Without doubt, yes. Did Black recruits receive the same compensation? Again, yes. It should be noted that the CCC also provided educational opportunities for all recruits, Black and white alike. After a full day of physical labor, you could earn a high school degree and even take college-accredited classes. However, many of the forestry and conservation skills learned were not relevant in an urban setting. Once they left the camps, many Blacks returned to "Negro jobs," such as chauffeurs, cooks, and gardeners.

STUDYING | INTEGRATED

The all-Black camps met resistance if placed too near white communities. Because of this, they were placed in more remote areas to appease community concerns. Also, only white supervisors were put in charge of the camps. It was a rarity to find an integrated camp. Those that existed were in the northwest. This generally happened when there were too few Blacks for a separate camp.

The Director of the CCC was Robert Fechner. Before being picked by President Roosevelt to head the CCC, he was the vice-president of the International Association of Machinists. In that role, he had a reputation for "fairness, tact, and patience" in his union role. He also brought considerable organizational and administrative skills to the table. Though he had a union background, he resisted efforts to unionize the CCC recruits, pointing out that the government was doing "all it possibly could for the well-being of the enrollees." They were well fed. They were helping to support their families. They were getting an education. They were "contributing constructively to the conservation needs of the country." There was no need for a CCC union.

On the issue of race, Fechner presented a complicated picture. Though the Army wanted integrated camps, Fechner understood his times. In many parts of the country, Jim Crowism reigned, permitting segregation and discrimination. Integrated camps would only exacerbate racial tensions. In 1935, he issued an order to make the "complete segregation of colored and white enrollees the rule." In response to the NAACP about this action, he said:

I am satisfied that the negro enrollees themselves prefer to be in companies composed exclusively of their race. This segregation is not discrimination and cannot be so construed. The Negro companies are assigned to the same types of work, have identical equipment, and are served the same food, and have the same quarters as white enrollees.

FECHNER AND THE FIRST CAMP

Fechner's view was in line with the prevailing judicial theme of "separate but equal" first stated in 1890 (Plessy v. Ferguson). This, of course, was an accepted principle in the Southern camps. In Camp Dix in New Jersey, there was a different situation. Though the camp was integrated, Blacks and whites were split into two groups. The records of Black enrollees were stamped with a large "C." Separation of the races was "completely and rigidly maintained." Though regrettable for Black recruits, this situation was okay for men out of work. This was especially true when it came to food—a full stomach made up for a lot of racial stuff. A typical breakfast consisted of boiled eggs, corn flakes, milk, bread, butter, and coffee. For lunch, there were frankfurters, sauerkraut, potatoes, gravy, bread, coffee, and apple butter. Dinner was at least bologna, applesauce, potato salad, coffee, and cake.

SUCCESS IN ENROLLING YOUTH AND VETS

The Tree Army was immensely popular with the public. Young men were off the streets and working hard to improve the country while helping their families. They worked hard for their dollar per day. The work was temporary, and no dependent class was being created. Even many conservatives eventually applauded this progressive program. The accomplishments of the CCC were recognized. Approximately 1,501,662 tree seedlings were planted on bare, unproductive land to fight back against the ravages of the Dust Bowl. Some 3,470 fire towers and 97,000 miles of fire roads and trails were built. The CCC built 66,161 miles of telephone lines. Bridges were also constructed, some 41,303. Campaigns were against tree diseases such as white pine rust and tree-attacking insects. CCC records indicate that 7,930,912 person-days were spent on forest fire-fighting duty.

PLANTING TREES | FIGHTING FIRES

One young man's experience was typical of those in the CCC. His name was George T. Nixon. At 16, he was enrolled in the program and sent to Salisbury, Missouri. Most of his work dealt with reforestation on land devastated by the Dust Bowl, land erosion, and poor farming practices. He was part of a group that worked to improve ten acres. As he later said of this experience:

As this was a soil erosion camp, we aimed to prevent soil erosion in farmers' fields and meadows. Ditches were graded, bottom and banks rounded and dams constructed of osage orange hedge, as we called it, by driving a double line of posts across and in the banks. The space between, we filled with smaller pieces of hedge, limbs, branches, etc. It was then packed tightly and bound tight to the posts on either side with heavy wire.

Continuing his detailed description of improving the land he said:

In late autumn we dug up the little locust seedlings, tied them in bundles and dug trenches and heeled them in for protection from freezing during the winter months. During the winter we went to the nearby river bottoms where there were thickets of small willows. We cut these from ½ inch diameter into approximately two-foot lengths, tied them into bundles and stored them for the winter. In the spring we took the willows and the locusts to the ditches where

225

we built the dams and planted the locusts along the banks. Then while there was mud in the bottoms we drove or pushed the willow sticks into the bottom hoping they would sprout and grow into trees.

As always, we are left with a challenging question. Did racial policies impact the CCC? Certainly, that seems to be the case. The camps were segregated, and racial prejudice existed at the local level, especially in the South. That said, the New Dealers had limited control over implementing the program. The Administration provided the legislation, funding, and blueprint for the program's function. In that sense, the CCC was aspirational and inspirational from President Roosevelt's perspective. As he said at Camp Roosevelt, he spoke to the youthful "Tree Army:"

Opportunities for employment in work for which individually you are best suited are increasing daily and you should emerge from this experience splendidly equipped for the competitive fields of endeavor which always mark the industrial life of America.

Continuing, he echoed the mantra of all the New Deal programs:

I want to congratulate you on the opportunity you have and to express to you my appreciation for the hearty cooperation which you have given this movement which is so vital a step in the Nation's fight against the depression and to wish you a pleasant and constructively helpful stay in the woods.

AT CAMP ROOSEVELT

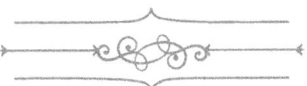

CHAPTER 25 – THE YOUNGEST VICTIMS

The impact of the Great Depression was far-ranging and brutal for many. This was particularly true of children and young people trying to continue their education, whether in high school or college. It wasn't unusual for young people to write to the White House. Those letters touched those who read them, including the First Lady. In 1934, she was quoted in the *New York Times*, saying:

I have moments of real terror when I think we might be losing this generation. We have got to bring these young people into the active life of the community and make them feel that they are necessary.

Mrs. Roosevelt had good reason to worry. During the first year of the Roosevelt Administration, she received over 300,000 letters from children and their elders. She would continue to receive hundreds of thousands of letters in the following years. The volume of mail was too great for any one person. The First Lady had a secretary in charge of the mail. She would read the mail and either reply or send it to another department for action. In addition, she would select some 50 letters each day for her boss to read. In some cases, Mrs. Roosevelt would dictate a response. The letters, especially from the young, provided a vivid image of personal tragedies across America, always heartbreaking. A ten-year-old girl wrote.

Please help us my mother is sick three year and was in the hospital three month and she came out but she is not better and my Father is peralised and cannot work and we are poor and the Coumunity fun gives us six dollars an we are six people four children three boy 15, 11, 12, an one girl 10, and to parents. We have no one to give us a Christmas presents please buy us a stove to cook and make good bread.

In the wealthiest, most prosperous country in the world, this child captured the enormity of one family's suffering, symbolic of so many more. One could only imagine what Mrs. Roosevelt would have felt had she read this letter.

A sixteen-year old girl from Texas wrote the White House (September 6, 1934). She addressed the letter to Dear Friend:

Well, I don't suppose you know who I am. Bit I'm a 16 year old mother-less girl that has to work hard for all she gets. I have a brother & a sister & daddy We are working at day labor for a living and don't get much of that t do. In the winter I could piece quilt s if I had any scraps. We are trying to keep off the relief this winter so we are keeping every penny we can to buy groceries this winter. Whether we have sufficient clothes or not. I though you might have some old clothes, coats, and shoes, or any kind of clothing you could send to us. I have read so much about your kindness I know if you have any you will send them. I would send money for postage but haven't any. Address to your loving friend.

Reading these letters today is painful. One finds it difficult to control his emotions, even as he reaches for a tissue. As the mother of four strong boys who had never missed a meal or lacked the latest fashions in the closet, Mrs. Roosevelt could only ask, "What in God's name is happening in the country?"

CHILDREN OF THE DEPRESSION

A twelve-year old girl addressed her letter to Dear President & Wife (August 23, 1934).

This is the first time I or Any of my people wrote Any president. And I am here to ask you for $8.00 to get me a winter coat. This may seem very strange for a girl 12 years old to do but my father is a poor honest Laundry man and he works on a percentage a week we have 10 in our family and my father does not have enough money to get him a bottle beer. He is a democrat and did all he could to have you voted. As little as I am I know just as much about depression as a grown person. I am 12 years old and am in the 8th grade curly hair Brunette & brown eyes & fair complexion & weigh 76 lbs. Hoping to hear from you soon I remain your true Democrat.

There is no record as to whether this youngster received a response. It's nice to think that $8.00 was found for a little girl in Barboursville, West Virginia. With millions in distress, not even the Roosevelts' personal checkbook could address all the needs the Postal Service brought to the White House. Two things were, however, abundantly clear. As little as she was, this little girl --- and millions more --- knew as much about the Depression as any grown person. Beyond that, the torrent of letters required an answer. The children were crying out for help.

On June 26, 1935, the president issued Executive Order 7086 to create the National Youth Administration (NYA) under the Emergency Relief Appropriation Act 1935. The focus of the legislation was to provide work and education for Americans between the ages of 16 and 25. As a group, they represented one-third of the entire working force. This was a New Deal effort to assist these young Americans during a tumultuous time. The key to the action was to keep them in school and keep them from dropping out. The annual budget was $580 million. Aubrey Willis Williams was picked to head the NYA, which also included a Division for Negro Affairs headed by Marcy McLeod Bethune. In explaining the need for his Executive Order, the president said:

I am determined that we shall do something for the Nation's unemployed youth because we can ill afford to lose the skill and energy of these young men and women. They must have their chancthae in school, their turn as apprentices and their opportunity for jobs --- a chance to work and earn for themselves.

Blending pragmatism and realism the president said:

I recognized that the final solution of this whole problem of unemployed youth will not be attained until there is a resumption of normal business activities and opportunities for private employment on a wide scale. I believe the National Youth Program will serve the most pressing and immediate needs of that portion of unemployed youth most seriously affected at this time.

As always, there was pushback from the conservative political element. Again, the old claim: the New Dealers are overreaching. The budget deficit will increase. The moral fiber of our youth will be weakened. The opposition was intense, but didn't have the votes to derail Roosevelt's program. Regarding the fiber of the young people... Later results indicated that NYA students stayed in school and did as well as others. A review of college grades reported that NYA students had higher grades than those outside the program. The president would say of those results, "We gave opportunities to young people who were strong, but it has left them indeed, if anything, stronger because of what they have done in connection with the NYA." The president also said:

As a matter of common knowledge, we do not have much to fear about this business of making softies of these young people who are eligible for work with the Youth Administration---they come from either from families on relief or in such obviously hard bitten circumstances that the daily provisioning of enough food, obtaining funds for the month's rent, and patching daily the clothes on their back, involves the whole family in the struggle.

Aubrey Willis Williams was a perfect fit for the NYA. He grew up in impoverished circumstances in Alabama. At six, he worked as a cash boy in a department store in Birmingham. His family of four sometimes lived on his $3.50 weekly wage. He struggled to stay in school by studying nights at a YMCA. He earned his way at Maryville College in Tennessee by painting signs. At the University of Cincinnati, he earned his keep by working in adult education. In time, he began a career in social work in Ohio and Wisconsin, eventually bringing his name to FDR. Williams would be the perfect candidate for an empathic president if empathy were required to run the NYA. Williams had known poverty. The Chief Executive had been cut down by polio.

AUBREY WILLIS AND THE NYA

On October 27, 1941, Williams confessed to Roosevelt what had been troubling him throughout his NYA tenure."

I must confess to all of you that I am thoroughly frightened. I think we are fighting with our backs to the wall all over this country.

That admission came even though the NYA had grown into a national youth development program or something close to that. The NYA was providing millions with jobs, job training, and remedial education.

Moreover, it instilled in youth the benefits of democracy at a time when "democracy was fighting for its life."

SAVING A GENERATION

How did the program work? College students were paid $30 to $40 monthly for "work study projects at their school. That meant they worked in libraries, in college laboratories, as research assistants, and as teaching aides. High school students received $10 to $20 monthly for part-time work, which included job training. Though the assistance was meager, it did keep millions of kids in school. It should be noted that all students were given the same grants. Young people could continue living at home while they attended school. Ultimately, 2,677,000 students remained in high school. Some 2,134,000 remained in college. Of the total, 1,000,000 were women. Both groups were involved in many construction projects. The statistics were imposing:

- Built or renovated 481,000 pieces of furniture.
- Repaired 1,000,000 toys.
- Salvaged or constructed 26,000 pieces of playground equipment.
- Constructed 125 schools and libraries.
- Built 74 warehouses.
- Constructed 2,000 handball and tennis courts.
- Built 5,149 athletic fields.
- Constructed 59 gymnasiums and dormitories.

Though the NYA was a federal program, it had 48 State Youth Divisions, plus youth Committees in cities and towns. As always, local involvement opened the door to unfair practices against Blacks. However, one of the NYA state directors was taking a different tack. Word was out that one director wasn't like the others. He was actually looking after Negroes and poor folks when most of the NYA weren't doing that. His name was Lyndon B. Johnson. Years later, he became the president of the United States. Once in the White House, LBJ continued his progressive policies with the War on Poverty, the Jobs Corps, and the Upward Bound Program.

TRAINING FOR ALL

Under the leadership of Mary McLeod Bethune, the Division of Negro Affairs provided NYA camps in some states, including Arkansas and Kentucky, to assist young Black women through literacy and occupational training. Those still in high school received up to $6.00 monthly in those states. Those out of school also received assistance once it was certified that their families were on relief. This group was employed in such projects as sewing, carpentry, construction, and repair work on schools and other public properties. Under Bethune's direction, every effort was made to provide facilities and training equivalent to those of the general population in an imperfect world.

For the first time, America's youth was beating back a paradox of the Great Depression. In many cases, you couldn't get a job because you lacked experience. Of course, to get experience, you needed to have a job. With over 1,750,000 youths entering the job market each year, the NYA provided both temporary jobs and job experience. It also included young women.

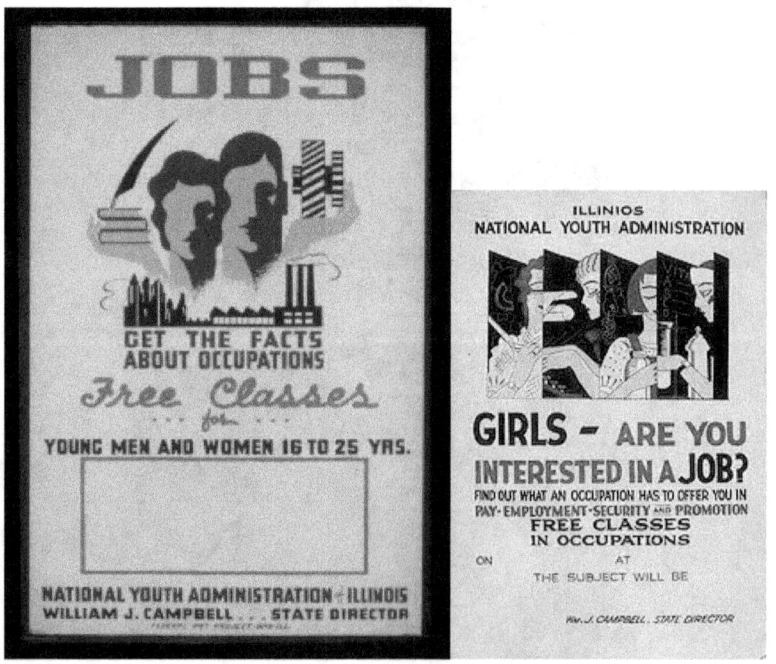

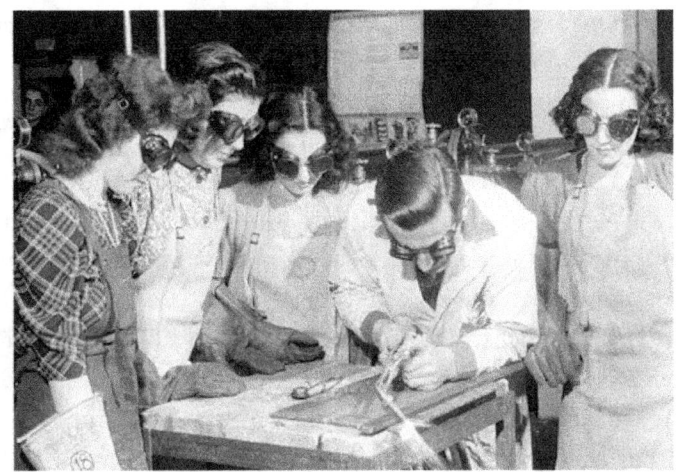

LEARNING NEW SKILLS

As with the CCC, the NYA was popular with the general public and especially with many young people. In 1940, a seventeen-year-old young man from Ohio wrote to Mrs. Roosevelt. He had hopes of attending college, but his family situation was desperate. He was representative of all the young people who wanted to pursue a post-high school education.

We are behind two months in our rent... There are 5 of us, mother, three boys and myself. I wouldn't be writing this, but I can't see ourselves evicted from our house. It would be all right if it was only me because I could take care of myself one way or another. My mother can't get work because she just recovered from tuberculosis and must rest. My little brothers shine shoes. They go out at night. The go most in beer gardens. Their little money helps. You might say, why don't we go on relief, well you just can't convince my mother on that. She said she would rather starve than get relief. I am working at a grocery store clerk at $8.00 a week. We could get along on this in summer but not in winter on account of the coal problem. I am wondering that maybe you could loan us about $35.00 or more, we could get on our feet again and once again hold up our heads. We would greatly appreciate this second start in life with all our hearts.

The young man from Cleveland added a postscript that must have touched anyone who read his letter.

I'll be praying every night for your loan. I'll give you $1.00 a month with interest until it is all paid up.

Was the loan ever made? There is no record. Did the NYA help this young man stay in school? Again, there is no evidence that this was the case. Did the young man find work in 1940? We can assume so. The industrial buildup for another global war was emerging. Soon, every man, woman, and teen would have a job, some at General Motors or Ford building trucks, jeeps, and tanks. Some would be at Boeing building winged birds to deliver bombs over Berlin, and later the B-29 that carried the war to Tokyo. And, of course, millions of young men would learn another occupation once they were drafted into the armed forces. Until that time, the young man from the Buckeye State would reflect the thoughts of many of his generation.

We all have faith in our president.

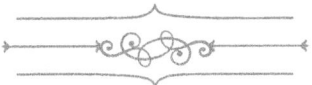

CHAPTER 26 – SAVING THE FARMER

Confronting the Roosevelt Administration was what appeared to be an intractable problem that had confounded the Hoover White House. The American farmer was in deep trouble, and the federal government seemed powerless to resolve the challenges facing those who tilled the soil and the consumers who needed their harvests of wheat, corn, cotton, and beef and pork products. The plight of agriculture was at once easily understood but difficult to remedy. In the simplest terms, the immutable laws of economics were at work. The yearly agricultural bounty exceeded demand. The imbalance drove down farm prices. For example, the cost of wheat in 1920 was $2.84 per bushel, and farmers made a reasonable profit. Even the poorest sharecroppers and tenant farmers could survive at that price. However, by 1932, a bushel of wheat sold for $ .30. At that price, farmers couldn't break even. This led to an unusual situation. The cost of growing wheat exceeded its market price. The same situation played out with cotton. In 1929, growers received $.37 per pound. This fell to $ .6 in 1931. Beef sold for $14.95 per hundredweight in 1920 and was now paid $5.78 in 1931. Farmers' gross income fell to 6.4 billion in 1932 from 16 billion in 1920. The picture was bleak for farmers with bankruptcies, evictions, and the loss of their livelihood. This was especially true for sharecroppers and tenant farmers already seeking a marginal subsistence. Something had to be done and done quickly. The New Dealers understood this.

The immediate economic goal was to restore the purchasing power of agricultural commodities or the fair exchange value of a commodity based upon price relative to the pre-depression period. Simply put, the farmers needed to make a fair profit after covering their expenses. Higher prices for their products would, therefore, be necessary. The question was how to bring this about without hurting the consumer?

The answer was the Agricultural Adjustment Act of 1933. The legislation created the Agricultural Adjustment Administration (AAA). This agency would seek to bolster agricultural prices by reducing surpluses resulting from overproduction. To do this, production adjustments would have to be made to influence prices and profits. This was, of course, counterintuitive to most people. Farmers were growing more to compensate for low prices, and now the government asked them to reduce their output. Consumers couldn't understand why people were hungry in the cities, and their government wanted to diminish production. In every sense, the AAA would be revolutionary, experimental, and controversial. The president alluded to this in support of the effort:

I tell you frankly that this is a new and untrod path. But I tell you with equal frankness that an unprecedented condition call for new means to rescue agriculture.

One historian stated the case as such:

Probably never in American history had so much social and legal inventiveness gone into a single legislative measure...

The Congress weighed in on the legislation, stating:

Congress declares its intent to protect the consumer's interest. This was to be done by readjusting farm production at a level that would not increase the percentage of consumer's retail expenditures above the percentage returned to the farmer before the depression.

The federal government was declaring war on the problems ravaging farmers nationwide. One political cartoonist fully captured the White House's intent.

How would the AAA work? The agency would secure the voluntary reduction in acreage in basic crops through agreements with producers. Those participating in the program would receive direct payments from the government. In theory, farm production would decline by controlling acreage production through cash incentives, leading to a better balance between supply and demand. To some extent, this had already happened before the AAA. Unable to recoup even the cost of production, many dairy farmers poured milk into the ground. Citrus growers poured kerosene on oranges to prevent their consumption. Pregnant sows and young pigs were sold. Corn was burned as fuel because it was so cheap. Livestock was slaughtered because feed prices outstripped what the meat market would pay. Though understandable from the farmer's perspective, these haphazard efforts did little to relieve the supply-demand problem. A more systematic and rational approach was needed that encouraged participation voluntarily. Washington was getting into a thicket, increasing what farmers were already doing.

Quickly, the press and the public cried unfair. Prompted by the demands of the AAA, farmers were plowing under millions of acres of already planted crops. Over six million young pigs were slaughtered to meet the AAA subsidy guidelines. For many, all this seemed blasphemous and wrongheaded. Why destroy a bountiful harvest while people were starving in the cities? The answer was straightforward from an economic point of view. The laws of supply and demand had to be balanced if the family farmer was to survive. The alternative was to nationalize agriculture, something that the president opposed.

To pay for the program's subsidies, the federal government placed a tax on companies that processed farm products. The AAA was using its broad powers to levy taxes on one industry to assist farmers, all based on the general welfare clause of the Constitution. To a degree, the program worked. There was some improvement in farm prices. Still, the AAA was not without controversy. Was the AAA trying to control or merely regulate an entire industry? Was the agency overstepping its power to tax by taxing one industry to subsidize another? All this came to a head in 1936. In United States v. Butler (297 US 1), the Supreme Court declared the AAA unconstitutional. The AAA could not levy a tax on food processors to assist farmers. Only the U.S. Congress can "lay taxes to the level necessary to carry out its other powers enumerated in Article 1 of the Constitution." In that context, the regulation of farming was deemed a state power. The federal government couldn't force the states to adopt the AAA program due to a lack of jurisdiction. As the Court stated:

A statutory plan to regulate and control agricultural production is a matter beyond he powers delegated to the federal government. Congress, through this program, was using unconstitutional means --- taxing and spending --- for an unconstitutional purpose --- regulating agricultural production.

The headlines captured the demise of the Agricultural Adjustment Act.

THE SUPREME COURT DECISION

The Court's decision raised and answered some perplexing questions. Who should support agriculture through regulations, Washington or the states? Had the federal government exercised too much power over farmers? Should flourmills and slaughterhouses have to pay a processor's tax? Those were the legal questions settled by the Court. On the other hand, moral and ethical problems plaguing the AAA. Was it right to destroy crops and cattle to raise prices while people in the cities were unemployed in the millions? Was it right to dump milk onto the ground while children lacked it? Were inherently morally challenging questions embedded in the capitalistic system, emphasizing the private sector and the need for profitability? In trying to sort through all this, the New Dealers would have to tinker and experiment to assist farmers.

An ugly side of the AAA was its implementation in the South. Contracts and subsidies were given to landowners to take land out of production. Initially, the legislation required landowners to pay the tenant farmers and sharecroppers on their land a portion of the money they received from the federal government. Southern Democrats, urged on by large landowners (the plantation class), pushed back against this requirement. The Department of Agriculture caved into the pressure. Prominent local white men served on the AAA's regional committees. They crafted policies that favored white farmers as land was taken out of production. The subsidies were sent directly to the landowners rather than those working the land. They were not shared. Moreover, sharecroppers and tenant farmers were squeezed off the land by eviction or not being rehired. With fewer acres plowed, fewer field hands were needed. Unstated was another issue. Since many farmers were Black and poor, local AAA control meant control over this segment of the population that continued to farm. An article in the *St. Louis Dispatch* in 1935 noted the situation.

Tenant demoralization from relief had either one or both of two meanings to the landlord. In the first place, it might have ben a fear that the tenant would escape from under his influence. It is probably not too much to say that the cropper system can only be maintained by the subordination of the tenant group. If the croppers were to become self-directing and take over his own affairs the system would necessarily crumble. In the second place, the landlords were influenced by the belief that when members of any group are given privileges to which they are unaccustomed, they are likely in their inexperience to abuse them for a time.

The experience of Black cotton farmers in Georgia exemplified the issue of control. By the 1930s, the state was dependent on cash-crop agriculture. That meant cotton. Every available acre was planted, leading to the soil being depleted of its nutrients and to erosion. The large landowners were not necessarily good stewards of the land. Profits had their place based on the availability of cheap Black labor. That meant AAA checks went to a powerful, dominant class determined to maintain the racial system in the state. Since approximately 40% of all Blacks farmed, they were disproportionately affected by policies that brooked no liberalization of Jim Crowism in the state. The New Dealers had almost no influence on altering this situation. Change would have to come from a different source.

The Southern Tenant Farmers Union (STFU) was founded as a civil rights organization to organize tenant farmers in the Southern states. It was formed in July 1934. Its goal was to assist sharecroppers and tenant farmers in getting better arrangements from the landowners. That meant at least two things: STFU members would share the AAA subsidies, and working conditions would be improved. In this regard, the STFU was among the few unions open to all races in the 1930s. The union promoted the goal of Blacks and whites working together to address their everyday problems. While the membership focused on non-violent activities, they were often met with harsh resistance from the landowners and local public officials. Leaders of the STFU were harassed. Many were physically attacked. Some were killed. In the face of defiance, progress was slow. The union was pushing against an entrenched system. That said, there were victories. In 1935, the STFU called for a strike in Georgia. Cotton pickers rejected a proposal to pay them forty cents per one hundred pounds. The union demanded one dollar. A few days after the strike began, the owners offered a compromise: 75 cents. It was the union's first victory.

FIGHTING BACK

The AAA was gone. The Supreme Court had seen to that. The problems the AAA had confronted still existed. What would the Roosevelt Administration now do? The answer came on February 29, 1936. On that day, the president signed the Soil Conservation and Domestic Allotment Act into law. The expressed purpose of the act was to encourage "the use of soil resources in such a manner as to preserve and improve fertility, promote economic use, and diminish the exploitation and unprofitable use of the national soil resources." Representative John Conover Nicholas (D-Oklahoma) argued on behalf of the legislation. His state had been hit harshly by the fierce dust storms of the 1930s. Regarding the state's soil, he said, "The country had been living in a fool's paradise with respect to the security of its most basic asset." Speaking for the White House, Rexford Tugwell praised the measure, saying, "It will pay farmers, for the first time, to be social-minded, to do something for all instead of for himself alone." Perhaps the most compelling support came from Hugh Hammond Bennett, a soil scientist and an advisor to the president."

What would be the feeling of this Nation should a foreign nation suddenly enter the United States and destroy 90,000 acres of land as erosion has been allowed to do in a single county?

He reminded all who would listen of the value of America's soil inheritance:

Out of the long list of nature's gifts to man, none is perhaps so utterly essential to human life as soil.

He also provided a stark warning:

To visualize the full enormity of land impairment and devastation brought about by this ruthless agent is beyond the possibility of the mind. An era of land wreckage destined to weigh heavily upon the welfare of the next generation.

Specifically, what would the Conservation and Domestic Allotment Act do? Farmers would be paid directly by the federal government, taking soil out of use by planting grasses and legumes to support the soil instead of commercial crops that exhaust their nutrients. The act classified commercial harvests like wheat as threatening the plains' soil. Farmers would be paid to weed their fields of surplus crops. There would be no tax on the processing companies to fund the program. The US mint would take care of that. The constitutional questions would be bypassed.

With a note to the past President Roosevelt, who spelled out the importance of the act as he signed the enabling legislation:

This legislation represents an attempt to develop, out of the far-reaching and partly emergency efforts under the Agricultural Adjustment Act, a long-time program for American agriculture.

He then spelled out the three primary objectives of the legislation. He said:

The first of these aims is conservation of the soil itself through the wise and proper land use. The second purpose is the reestablishment and maintenance of farm income at fair levels. The third major objective is the protection of consumers by assuring adequate supplies of food now and in the future.

As to the funding mechanism, the president pointed out:

There will be no contracts with farmers. The program does not control individual production of individual farm commodities. I am confident that the farmers, cooperating with the Government, will work hard within existing legal limitations to achieve the goals of the new law.

The reality of the challenges to preserve the soil was recognized by the president, as well as the need to feed America, while providing farmers with a predictable and fair income was emphasized by the president in his closing words:

I do not regard this farm act as a panacea or as a final plan. Rather I consider it a new basis to build and improve upon, as experience discloses its points of weaknesses and of strength. Aiming at justice for agriculture and self-interest for the Nation, the plan seeks to salvage and conserve the greatest values in human life and resources with which this Nation is endowed.

As with most New Deal programs, experimentation and innovation went hand in hand. The genius of the New Dealers was their willingness to deal with unprecedented challenges in unprecedented ways. They thoroughly understood that there were no legislative guarantees. All too often, they were sailing into uncharted waters, always cognizant of the need to maintain a private sector economic system while ironing out, to the degree possible, inequalities inherent in free enterprise, whether on the farm or in the nation's industrialized cities. Only one thing was clear. To the New Dealers, government was the engine by which those inequalities might be adjudicated at a cost. Keynesian economics demanded deficit spending. There were no freebies.

Were the New Dealers successful? As the following chart indicates, there was significant progress with respect to foreclosures and defaults.

Farm Foreclosures and Defaults, 1929–1945

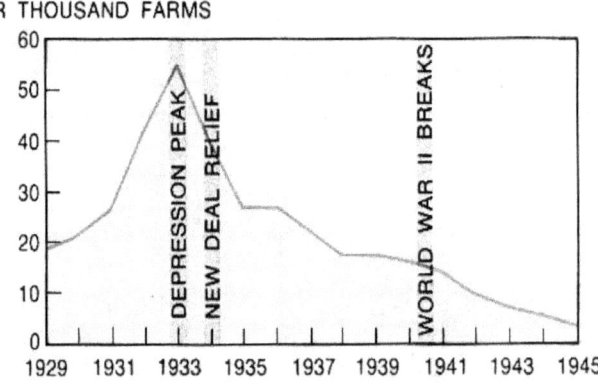

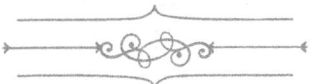

CHAPTER 27 – THE DUST BOWL

It started ominously on November 11, 1933. Bellowing strong winds swept across North Dakota, howling day and night. Much like a giant scoop, the winds stripped the topsoil from the farmlands, sending a cloud of dust high into the sky, and in time as far eastward as Chicago and eastward from there. The dust formed a darkish cloud, depositing 12 million pounds on the "City of Big Shoulders." Two days later, the dust reached Cleveland, Ohio, and New York City before reaching Washington, D.C. This would be the first of many dust clouds to blacken the skies and to leave once-prized soil, now only dust, falling like brownish snowflakes across the Great Plains. The clouds were called sand storms, "black rollers," black blizzards, or "dusters." The relentless onslaught of the dust would blacken Kansas, Oklahoma, Texas, New Mexico, Nebraska, and Colorado for almost a decade. The storms and the states they ravaged collectively became known as the Dust Bowl. They only added to the plight of farmers in the Great Plains already hammered by the Great Depression.

THE LAND DEVASTED

Like an alien force, the dust clouds harassed the land in preparation for one last malignant attack. It happened on Sunday, April 14, 1935. A mountain of blackness swept across the High Plains. It almost instantly turned a warm, sunny afternoon into a horribly pitched black world. It began around 4:00 p.m. A wall of blowing sand and dust "blasted into the eastern Oklahoma Panhandle and then spread itself across the state's western regions. The winds were in excess of 40 mph. The massive wall of blowing dust resembled a land-based tsunami. The blackness was so complete briefly that a person could see his own hands. Visibility was zero. Black Sunday had arrived.

BLACK SUNDAY

Robert E. Geiger was in Boise, Oklahoma. He was a reporter for the Associated Press and an eyewitness to Black Friday. He typed a story for the *Lubbock Evening Journal.* Edward Stanley was an editor for the Associated Press. He read Geiger's eyewitness report. In preparing the story for other newspapers and the radio audience, he coined the phrase Dust Bowl. The name stuck. Geiger's edited story described what had happened.

Spearman and Hansford County have been literally in a cloud of dust for the past week. Ever since Friday of last week, there hasn't been a day pass but what the county was besieged with a blast of wind and dirt. On rare occasions when the wind did subside for a period of hours, the air has been so filled with dust that the town appeared to be overhung by a fog cloud. Because of this long siege of dust with every building being filled with it, the air has become stifling to breathe and many people have developed sore throats and dust colds as a result.

THE SEIGE OF DUST

Most people couldn't comprehend what was happening. Some believed it was God's wrath because his children had gone astray. This was payback for our sins. Others, somewhat fatalistic, accepted the situation as merely the land recycling itself, undergoing some metamorphosis. In time, things would return to normal, or so they hoped. Pushing against these views were those in the Department of Agriculture who claimed and documented what was happening. The human mismanagement of the land caused the Dust Bowl.

The Great Plains had always been a harsh and inhospitable environment for those who ranched and farmed. This landscape is characterized by droughts, thunderstorms, blazing hot temperatures, and freezing winters. The soil was fertile but fragile. A tough grass root called sod covered the prairie and helped the soil retain moisture and support vegetation. Humans interfered with this natural situation. Overgrazing by cattle severely damaged the sod. Deep plowing left the land with little topsoil as the natural grasses were destroyed. There was nothing left to anchor the soil. Added to this, mechanized plows permitted large-scale plowing. The same crops were planted yearly on every acre: wheat, corn, and cotton. There was slight, if any, crop rotation. The land never had an opportunity to rest and replenish. By 1934, an estimated 35 million acres of cultivated land had been rendered useless for farming. Another 125 million acres were rapidly losing the topsoil. This was an area approximately the size of Texas.

Dodge City, Kansas, provided an example of what happened when the dust clouds descended on a town. During April 1935, the state recorded 14 straight days of dense dust. Visibility was less than 100 feet as the town was shrouded in semi-darkness. Travel in Dodge City was difficult and almost impossible in the rural areas. The downtown streets were covered with dust that was an inch thick. Piles of dust were a foot deep in some places, much like snow drifts. The town had to haul away loads of dust to wash the streets. On top of this, the dust in the air was making people sick. Many citizens had lungs full of dust. They experienced chest pains, coughing, breathing difficulties, and high fevers. Some had pneumonia. A few died from suffocation. Bad as it was in Dodge, it was worse on the farms. There was almost no place to hide from the dust.

Dust storms and droughts, combined with the misuse of the land, created a desolate landscape in the Great Plains. In 1935, Ernie Pyle, then a roving reporter, described what he saw in Kansas.

The land was flat as a billiard table. The horizon was far, far away. Following the horizon around, as you sometimes gaze out from a ship at sea, I saw not a solitary thing but bare earth, and a few lonely, empty farmhouses. As far as the eye could see there was not a tree, or a blade of grass, or a fence,

*or a field: not a flower or a stalk of corn, or a dog or cow, or a human bing ---
nothing at all, but gray raw earth and a few far houses and barns, sticking up
white cattle skeletons on the desert. There was nobody in the houses; the people
had given up and gone. It was death, if I have ever seen death.*

DEATH ON THE GREAT PLAINS

Many in the Great Plains decided it was time to leave. The Dust Bowl
had left 500,000 homeless. Unable to wrest a crop from the land, already
poor dirt farmers went broke. Some were evicted from the land that no
longer could support a sharecropper or tenant farmer. Others packed up
their meager belongings, piled into the old "jalopy" and headed westward
looking for work. Oklahoma lost about 440,000 people to this self-imposed
migration. Many reached the Golden State looking for a job in the rich San
Joaquin Valley. They were called "Okies," a derogatory term many held of
the migrants. Others were called "Arkies" with the same disdain.

THE GREAT MIGRATION

The migrants were not always welcomed with open arms in California. In his novel The *Grapes of Wrath,* John Steinbeck chronicled the anxiety many felt as the landless and homeless entered the state. Many feared for themselves, their property, and their own jobs. Deep hostility and prejudice towards the Okies emerged in the land of orange and lemon groves.

In the West there was panic when the migrants multiplied on the highways. Men of property were terrified for their property. Men who had never been hungry saw the eyes of the hungry. Men who had never wanted anything very much saw the flare of wasn't in the eyes of the migrants. And the men of the towns and of the soft suburban country gathered to defend themselves; and they reassured themselves that they were good and the invaders bad, as a man must do before he fights. They said, "These goddamned Okies are dirty and ignorant. They're degenerate, sexual maniacs. These goddamned Okies are thieves. They'll steal anything. They've got no sense of property rights."

In 1935, folk singer Woody Guthrie wrote a poignant song entitled "So Long, It's been Good to Know Yuh." In time, the lyrics were simply called "Dusty Old Dust." They expressed the pain of a world gone astray and the need to move on. They still haunt us today, and all those who must migrate, leaving behind all they know on a gamble that a better future lurked just behind the rainbow.

I've sung this song, but I'll sing it again
Of the place that I lived on the wild, windy plains
In the month called April, county called Gray
And here's what all of the people say

So long, it's been good to know yuh
So long, it's been good to know yuh
So long, it's been good to know yuh
This dusty old dust is a-gettin' my home
And I've got to be driftin' along.

A dust storm hit, an' it hit like thunder
It dusted us over, an' it covered us under
Blocked out the traffic an' blocked out the sun

Straight for home all the people did run, singin'

So long, it's been good to know yuh.

We talked of the end of the world, and then
We'd sing a song an' then sing it again
We'd sit for an hour an' not say a world
And then these words would be heard

So long, it's been good to know yuh.

History is often painful. Steinbeck and Guthrie understood this and tried to convey this understanding to those who would read and listen.

GUTHRIE AND STEINBECK

The Dust Bowl was only partially responsible for the plight of American farmers during the Great Depression. Farmers were already in deep economic trouble before the Wall Street Crash, though no group was hit harder than those who tilled the land. Some would say it began with World War I. Prodded by President Wilson, farmers were urged to expand production to feed an army in the field and many people in France, Belgium, and England. The need was great. Russia, a usual grain supplier, was battling the Kaiser's forces. Shipments of wheat in particular were curtailed due to the fighting. The world's supply of food was at risk. President Woodrow Wilson wanted America's farmers to enter the breach, which they did. Acreage expansion took place. Profits were made. Even the poorest farmers could make a living. And then the war ended on November 11, 1918, and European demand for American grain slackened. Prices dropped and profits dwindled. It was a classic case of oversupply and decreased demand. To compensate, farmers resorted to planting even more crops, believing that greater production, even at lower prices, might make up for the lost demand. The following chart indicates that every effort only led to decreased farm income.

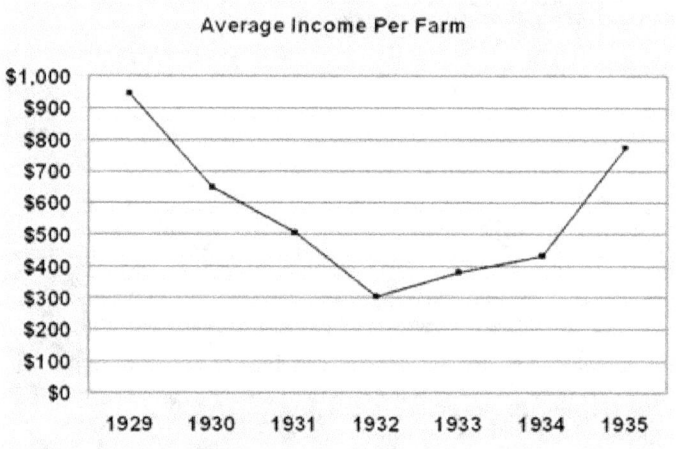

Average Income Per Farm

Farm income fell by two-thirds during the first three years of the Great Depression. A bushel of wheat sold for $2.94 in 1920. Wheat fell to $1.00 by 1929 before reaching the bottom in 1932- $.30 per bushel. Massive price drops also occurred with corn and cotton, as well as with pork bellies and cattle. All suffered from a paradox; greater production only decreased prices. A "glut" dictated all. Eventually, this led to indebtedness, bankruptcy, and eviction notices.

Farm Foreclosures and Defaults, 1929–1945

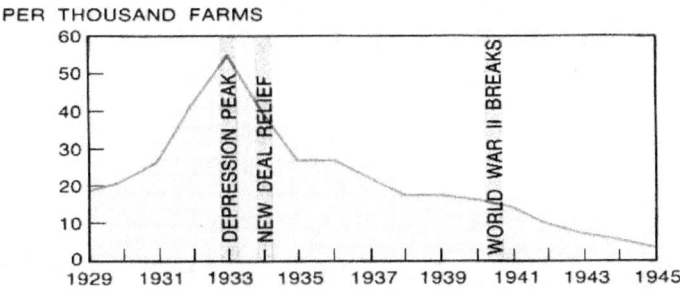

Other factors were also at work. The user of farm machinery encouraged greater planting. Stronger, if not better, fertilizers contributed to increased production. Improved varieties of wheat and corn played a role. And then there were cultural changes. People ate less bread. Rayon replaced cotton in clothing. Added to this were higher tariffs to keep out foreign goods and grain. This inevitably led to retaliatory tariffs, thereby reducing American exports. Though they made reasonable efforts to stop the downward plunge of farm income, the Hoover Administration could not stem the tide. It would be up to the new dealers to remedy the situation, if possible.

Dealing with the Dust Bowl was a significant challenge. To some extent, the Civilian Conservation Corps helped by planting trees across the landscape and taking other conservation steps. The Soil Conservation Act sought the same outcome by taking land out of production. The process of restoring the land would take decades.

CHAPTER 28 – THE GREAT RIVER

The Tennessee River begins its flow at the confluence of the Holston and French Broad Rivers near present-day Knoxville, Tennessee. It was once known as the Cherokee River in honor of the Cherokee Tribe that lived along its banks. The current name of the river is derived from the Cherokee town of Tanasi, which was located on the Tennessee side of the Appalachian Mountains. The river flows 652 miles and is the largest tributary of the Ohio River. From the Knoxville area, it snakes its way southward through east Tennessee into Chattanooga before crossing into Alabama. The river's ebbs and flows carry it through the Huntsville and Decatur area before it finally reaches Muscle Shoals. It will curve through a sliver of northeast Mississippi before returning to Tennessee. It then meanders northward until it reaches western Kentucky and flows into the Ohio River at Paducah. Its journey is done. The currents of the Tennessee River have flowed through the Tennessee Valley.

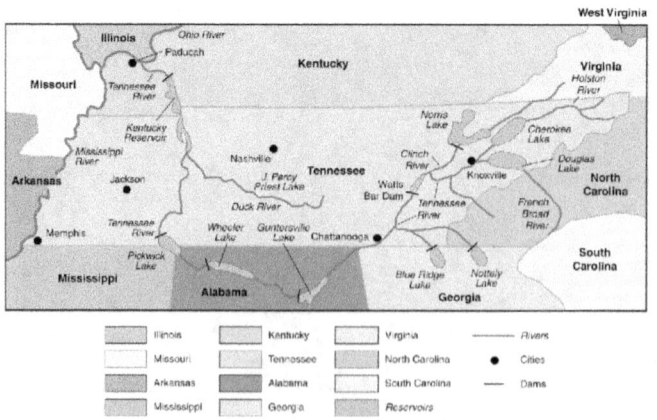

The Tennessee Valley was an area of 40,000 square miles. Within the valley were 2,000,000 people, divided between whites and Blacks based on a 2:1 ratio. It had a wealth of coal and phosphates. It had abundant plant and animal life. The Tennessee River provided for navigation, irrigation, and the personal needs of those near its turbulence. The area should have been prosperous. In 1933, it was not. Indeed, it was perhaps the poorest area of the country. The average income in the rural areas was $639 per year. Per capita income was only 45% of the national average. A significant number of families survived on far less. About 62% of the people in the valley farmed. This was twice the national average. Only 28% worked in manufacturing, trades, and services. This was half the national average. Much of the land was exhausted due to poor farming practices. The soil was depleted and eroded. Crop yields were declining each year, as was farm income. Approximately 10% of the existing forests are lost each year to fire. Electricity was available in some towns and larger urban areas. It was almost non-existent on farms. Much of the daily work had to be done by hand, not with machinery. There was no "juice" for a refrigerator, a radio, or a light to read by. And on top of all this 30% of the valley's population was afflicted with malaria. In every possible way, the Great Depression exacerbated distress in the region. This was even more so for Blacks.

For Senator George Norris of Nebraska, there was in the Tennessee Valley a mighty untamed river that inundated the land, destroying good farmland, carrying away homes and small towns at flood time, and yearly washing away God's good top soil, leaving the souls who till the land destitute. He meant to change all that.

FOLKS IN THE TENNESSEE VALLEY

According to Norris, new agricultural methods were needed, including terrace farming, strip cropping, and the use of fertilizer to improve crop productivity and farm income. What was required in the valley was a whole new approach to tilling the soil. It was apparent to him that the private sector could not create the circumstances by which this could happen. He also advocated for electrifying the area, pointing out that without power, there was no refrigeration to store milk, butter, and eggs. Without electricity, there was no light to read by. The radio had no power to hear music or learn the latest news. All that Norris sought to change.

The first effort to do this began in 1916 under President Woodrow Wilson, who signed the National Defense Act of that year. The legislation authorized the construction of a hydroelectric dam on the Tennessee River at Muscle Shoals. The justification for the dam was national defense. With abundant electricity, nitrates could be produced for ammunition for the Yanks headed to the Western Front. That need would be more than apparent with the coming of World War II.

By the 1930s, another need was recognized. Private utility companies, it was contended, were charging customers too much for electric power. Combining into "holding companies," the utilities exercised monopolistic power and indulged in unfair practices. Since 94% of all electricity generated was in the hands of private companies, which were essentially unregulated, there was a growing demand for the government to do something. That first effort beyond Wilson's tenure came at the behest of Senator George Norris of Nebraska. After first feuding with Henry Ford, who wanted to build a private sector dam at Muscle Shoals, Norris introduced the Muscle Shoals Bill in 1925. The Senate and House passed the legislation. President Hoover, however, vetoed it, claiming the bill was "socialistic." By 1932, Hoover was gone, and the New Dealers reigned. On May 18, 1933, President Roosevelt signed the Tennessee Valley Authority Act. In supporting the act, the president said:

If we are successful here, we can march on, step by step, in the like development of other great national territorial units within our borders.

The president argued for an experiment in social and economic planning, saying we need to:

Create a corporation clothed with the power of government but possessed of the flexibility and initiative of a private enterprise.

SIGNING THE TVA LEGISLATION
(NORRIS, THIRD FROM RIGHT)

With the legislation, the Administration was fulfilling a "three C" goal: conservation of natural resources, protection of the nation's forests and rivers, control of corporations and monopolistic business models concerning utilities, and antitrust legislation to challenge the concentration of power. Finally, consumer protection from unfair practices would be provided. It was hoped that the bilking of families would end in the Tennessee Valley and elsewhere.

Dams would be constructed and owned by the federal government. The Tennessee Valley Authority would receive no taxpayer funding. It would operate similarly to a private for-profit company. Knoxville, Tennessee, would serve as the headquarters for the project. In time, the TVA became the most significant public utility in the country and the sixth-largest power supplier. In doing so it would (a) provide and improve navigation on the Tennessee River; (b) make extensive efforts to control flooding; (c) generate electricity for the region; (d) assist in providing sufficient irrigation for family farms in the Valley; (d) stimulate the manufacture of fertilizer; and (e) encourage the development of recreational areas. Norris Dam was the first such structure built to realize these outcomes. It was named in honor of Senator Norris, who fought for the project over two decades.

NORRIS DAM AND THE SENATOR

Opposition to the TVA was strenuous and ongoing. Hoover's initial veto was to support private sector capitalism. Private utilities claimed there would be too much government control over the economy and society if the project and others like it were developed. They saw the TVA as a competitor with government jobs, paychecks, and possibly even lower charges for electricity. It all smelled of creeping socialism, they argued. To some degree, the opposition was right. The federal government would be in the utility business for the first time. It could determine what it costs to create a kilo of electricity for the first time. Until TVA, the government had to accept the numbers provided by the industry. Moreover, the cost of delivering fertilizer was known for the first time. The government wouldn't depend on figures from an industry driven by profits with little competition.

The most serious challenge to the TVA came in 1939. In a case brought before the United States Supreme Court (297 U.S. 288) by Commonwealth and Southern Corporation shareholders. The owners of preferred stock in the company sued to prevent the TVA from acquiring any of the company's property and equipment under a concluded contract. They also opposed TVA's selling of electricity to consumers. In particular, they objected to Wilson Dam being used for this purpose. All of this, they argued, was unconstitutional. Wendell Willkie, the lead attorney for Commonwealth and Southern, who once said of the TVA, "Every time somebody turns on a light in Tupelo, Mississippi, the entire country pays for it."

In its decision, the Supreme Court upheld the constitutionality of the Tennessee Valley Authority Act. The Congress had the authority to construct dams for national defense and to improve interstate commerce. As to the sale of electricity, the Court ruled in favor of the government. Based on Article IV, section 3 of the Constitution, the federal government could sell property it owned; in this case, excess electricity could be sold to consumers or other utilities. The Court stated:

The authority of Congress to dispose of electric energy generated at the Wilson Dam is not limited to a surplus necessarily created in the course of making munitions of war. There was no basis for concluding that the contract exceeded the federal power to dispose of property, and invaded rights reserved o the State or to the people.

The dam across the Tennessee River at Muscle Shoals, known as the Wilson Dam, was constructed pursuant to the National Defense Act of June 3. 1916, in the exercise of constitutional functions of the Federal Government, (a) as a means of assuring abundant energy for the manufacture of munitions in the event of war; (b) to improve the river's navigability.

The TVA was clearly constitutional and in the business of assisting millions in the affected states. It could build dams and sell electricity. However, the TVA was far more than a federal utility. Given the number of states involved, it was a grand experiment in social-economic planning that only the federal government could undertake.

The New Dealers always understood that the TVA would displace thousands of people in the Tennessee Valley. Land would be needed for the concrete or earthen dams, and even more land would be necessary for the reservoirs and lakes behind those structures. Of necessity, there would be a relocation challenge for those affected, which included the federal government appropriating their land. Eminent domain was the process by which this was done. The government had the power to take private property even if the owner didn't want to sell.

Under the Fifth Amendment, eminent domain must be exercised for some "public use," such as a road, bridge, or, in this case, a series of dams on the Tennessee River. Those losing their land must be compensated at a fair price. To ward off the government acquisition of personal property, it must be proven that no "proper public use" exists, or that the government hasn't offered the "just value" of the property. Many in the Tennessee Valley resisted the power of eminent domain and the intrusion of Washington into their lives.

RESISTANCE

Ultimately, over 125,000 residents were removed. That amounted to over 15,000 families. For many, the involuntary displacement fell most heavily on marginal farmers, tenant farmers, and sharecroppers, regardless of race. Many of the displaced were poor Blacks, and without the resources to challenge the federal government in what many later called a "Black diaspora." Entire towns and communities were disrupted and damaged by eminent domain. The tightly knit social fabric was torn asunder as people were dislodged from their churches, schools, and businesses. For the more prosperous landowners, the buyout of their property provided them with the capital to invest in their future. This was not true of the poorest farmers. As one historian explained the situation:

Over and above the class-based discrimination the TVA's relocation policies perpetuated existing racial discriminatory policies in the South. Like most New Deal programs the benefits were not evenly distributed. The agency maintained a policy of institutional racism.

Many in the administration of the TVA assumed that there was no significant Black community because they did not have leadership positions in local town government and other institutions. That view, of course, did not fully appreciate the discriminatory practices perpetuated by Jim Crowism that restricted Blacks from leadership roles. This led to a misunderstanding of the social situation by the all-white staff of the Family Removal Section of the TVA.

TVA workers assumed that, because Blacks were excluded from community leadership posts and from the white community, they did not have a community of their own and did not suffer from community disruption after relocation.

In building the Norris Dam and others, the New Dealers envisioned a fair hiring system that didn't discriminate against Blacks, who were supposed to be hired according to their population proportion. They were also supposed to receive the same wages. All this proved illusory at Norris Dam, where the TVA built the first dam on October 1, 1933. You had to pass a Civil Service Examination to qualify for the project. That, of course, assumed (1) you knew about the exam; (2) you were permitted access to the exam; and (3) you had a level of literacy to pass. Though Blacks comprised 7.1% of the general population in the 12 counties around the construction area, only 1.9% qualified. The exam took its toll. Where Blacks were hired, it was generally for lower-level positions such as janitorial work. There was little opportunity for advancement.

How should we understand the TVA in terms of race? Initially, in terms of displacement and jobs, it could be argued that racist policies and attitudes were present. In the long term, however, the TVA revitalized the Tennessee Valley, bringing a better life to everyone in the region through which the great river flowed. On January 15, 1940, President Roosevelt spoke to Congress on the overall benefits of the "experiment in social planning." He said:

The original legislation in 1933 was intended-in part as an experimental project --- to raise the standards of life by increasing social and economic advantages in a given area, in this case the whole of the watershed which runs into the Tennessee River and including portions of many states.

The original objective of the law included many other things (beyond producing electricity) such as the planting of water-retaining forests near the headwaters of the many rivers and streams, the terracing of farm hillsides, the building of small check-dams, the development of fertilizer, the diversification of crops and other soil building methods, the improvement of highways and other forms of transportation, the bringing in of small industries, and the extension of rural electric lines.

The president concluded his remarks by focusing on recreation wrought by the lakes behind each dam.

It is coming to be realized more and more that in the improvement of our American civilization, we cannot stop at hospitals and schools any more than we can confine ourselves to strictly economic subjects. Recreation in a broad sense is a definite factor in the improvement of the bodies and minds of our future citizens.

In many ways, the TVA was aspirational in that it looked to the future, where today's work would benefit all citizens. In that sense, the TVA was idealistic even as it dealt with the sharp realities of impoverishment and racial disparities that plagued the country, and the South in particular. It is important to remember that the New Dealers were not semi-deities cleansed of all biases and prejudices. They lived in an imperfect world. Overall, the lasting benefits of the TVA must stand on their own merits. This is what the president understood.

The president didn't need a defender of his views. However, he got one from the most famous reporter in America, known to all who read a daily newspaper. His name was Ernie Pyle. In 1935, this small, skinny man visited Norris Dam. He impressed everyone because of what he did. He walked right out onto the dam, which had no guardrails. He looked straight down 15 stories to the Clinch River below. He confessed that when he glanced down, "he got down on his knees and elbows, and took a death grip on a couple of steel rods sticking out of the cement, and then just peered over a little at a time." A few days later, he discussed the dam and the Tennessee Valley Authority in one of his columns. He pointed out:

TVA is one of those things that everybody knows exists, but few people (outside this valley) seem to make heads or tails of it. So I came down to give it the works. It was my ambition to be the first American to explore TVA so that a little child can understand it.

He went on to say:

TVA, as nearly as I can figure out, is an attempt to do the same thing to a whole section of the United States that a doctor does to a man who is all smashed up in an auto accident. And that is, fix him up.

He described the construction activity:

There is a terrific fascination about a growing dam. The height, the hundreds of men scampering all over it... there is a boom, boom, boom about it that gives me the same rush that I get at 42ⁿᵈ and Broadway.

Pyle often returned to the dam to inform his readers of the construction process.

Norris Dam has grown up since I saw it last. The dam is bare, and immobile, and lonely, just standing there. Norris Dam is what it should be: finished, unromantic and working. The lake is blue, and the water is clear, and there is hardly a ripple on the shores. There is no flood worry on the upper Cinch River.

Pyle concluded:

TVA is a good dream, and when you drive around here, it looks like a dream that has solid stuff in it.

President Roosevelt couldn't have asked for a better endorsement.

ERNIE PYLE AND THE DAM

As to Senator George Norris … As one historian wrote:

This is the giant whom the American people have at their service to obey their will, and perform their labors, and gladden their lives. This is the giant who was ready and willing at a time when the demands of war, involving a serious need for great electrical power, presented a grave crisis to t he American people. This is the giant who will brighten the lives and bring laughter to the lips of many generations of children in the old Southland where poverty and national neglect have brought sorrow. And this giant, striding across America, begetting stalwart sons of the river valleys, will fight the battle of the American people to realize the hopes of happiness to which all peoples aspire.

CHAPTER 29 – STRINGING THE LINE

They seemed to be everywhere in the Tennessee Valley. They were in the Post Office. Businesses had them in their windows. Some were nailed to telephone poles. Newspapers had photographs of them. And where the TVA had offices, there was an abundance of them. Posters! Posters! Posters!

TVA POSTERS

Even the political cartoonists commented on the vast change descending on the Tennessee Valley.

"GOSH"
Reprinted from the Indianapolis Times

ELECTRICITY

In addition to lively coverage of the changes, local newspapers peppered their stories with an array of photographs. High in the sky, men were shown stringing electrical wire, mile after mile, seemingly oblivious to all else. Other men gathered around a transformer, transfixed by the lever about to be pulled.

STRINGING THE LINES

TURNING ON THE JUICE

Of course, all the cartoons, posters, and photos had one thing in common. They were about an uncommon experiment bringing electricity to the Tennessee Valley in 1935. Approximately two-thirds of the country had electricity, namely in urban areas. For the most part, rural areas, ranches, and farms did not. The TVA meant to do something about that. On May 11, 1935, President Roosevelt issued Executive Order 2037 to create the Rural Electrification Administration (REA). Soon afterwards, Congress passed the necessary legislation. Since the private sector was both resistant and reluctant to do so, the federal government, now that the Norris Dam was completed, supported the installation of an electrical distribution system to serve rural areas and, in the process, put people to work.

A word about the Norris Dam… It was the first significant project of the TVA. Construction began on October 1, 1933. The dam was completed on March 4, 1936, for $36,000,000. It was 1860 feet long and 265 feet high. Norris Lake became the largest reservoir on any tributary of the Tennessee River. The lake had 33,840 acres of water surface and a shoreline of 809 miles. Most importantly, it could generate 126 megawatts of clean hydroelectric power and provide flood control. The first generator went online on July 28, 1936. The coal oil lamp was out, replaced by the light switch.

As to why the private utility companies were uninvolved… It all boiled down to money or what some might call more politely, "the return on investment." Private utility companies believed transmitting power to rural areas was not economically feasible. Part of the problem was highly technical. In the cities, a 2300-volt system was used. This was a relatively low voltage. Electricity would only be transmitted about four miles before the voltage dropped. Additional transmitters were necessary to push along the electricity. Bringing power to rural areas would demand more expensive transformers that used a 6900-volt distribution system. Electricity could be transmitted 40 miles. The private sector would not invest. Profitability and providing dividends to stockholders were of preeminent concern. That being the case, the New Dealers made the case for a federal program.

How to fund the federal program was a significant question. Initially, funds were going to be distributed to smaller, private companies. It was soon apparent that this was going to be very expensive. A different tactic was taken. Farmers had a long history with co-ops, initials that were shorthand for a cooperative. This business model was owned and operated for the benefit of its members, especially when an urgent need was identified. Farmers had banded together for grain and dairy cooperatives. Now they would do the same for electricity. Farmers, ranchers, and small towns organized themselves into local cooperatives. Initial funding came from the federal government at a low interest rate, usually 2 to 3%. In addition, electricity generated by the Norris Dam was sold to the co-ops at a wholesale price, which was generally paid far less than what private companies wanted to charge.

The next step was for the REA to string lines from Norris Dam to rural areas in the Tennessee Valley. The government provided engineers to assist the ops in doing this. Using the bulk buying power of the REA, the cost of the materials involved was negotiated. Consequently, the equipment cost undercut what the private sector would have paid. Where private companies estimated the transmission costs to be $2,000 per mile, the op-ops did the same job for $625 per mile. REA crews traveled throughout the Valley. Trained electricians wired houses, barns, and stores so that the power could be used. Each home, for example, had a ceiling-mounted fixture installed in each room. A single switch at the door controlled the light. One outlet was installed in each room. The effort was an instant hit. By 1940, only a few years later, over half of all farms had access to electricity. One op-op took notice, parceling a humorous but serious monument to the past.

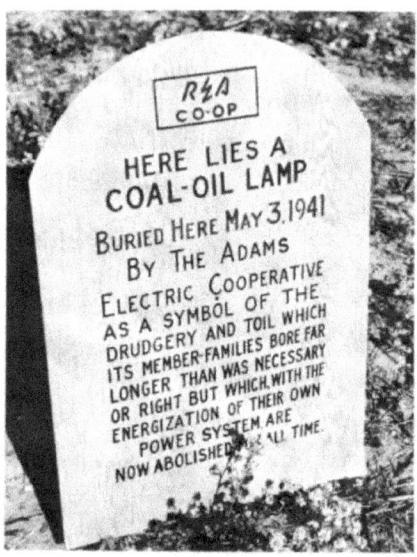

SATIRE

The TVA and the REA were larger-than-life projects but not untypical of American ingenuity. The Homestead Act of 1862 comes to mind. Signed by President Abraham Lincoln in the midst of the Civil War, it granted the adult head of a family 160 acres of surveyed public land in the West. Only a minimal fee was necessary, but the family had to live on the property for five years.

The construction of the Transcontinental Railroad was another massive project the nation embarked upon. On May 10, 1869, trains from the East and West met at Promontory Point in Utah. In doing so, they revolutionized travel. The country was now "one," a land mass connected by steel rail and the sweat of those who laid the lines. Similarly, the Panama Canal connected two oceans, the Pacific and the Atlantic, thereby permitting shipping traffic through the Isthmus. In more recent times, the building of the Interstate Highway during the Dwight D. Eisenhower Administration in the 1950s connected all corners of the country, this time by concrete and four lanes of auto and truck traffic. Of course, President John F. Kennedy's pledge in the 1960s to land a man on the moon showed again the nation's ability to take on challenging but exciting tasks.

HOMESTEAD ACT AND LINKING THE NATION

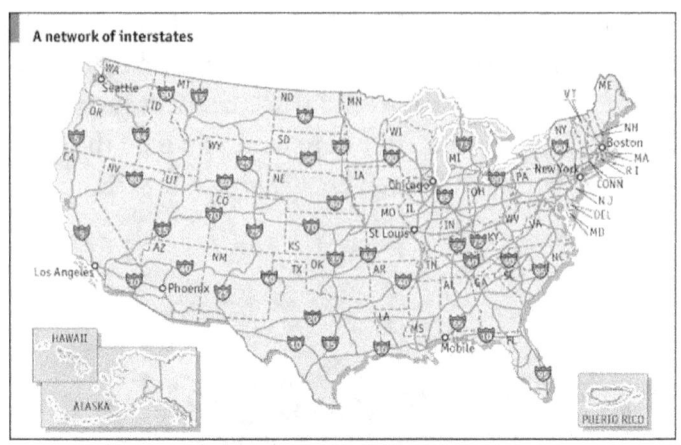

A network of interstates

INTERSTATE HIGHWAYS AND THE CANAL

MOON LANDING

In speaking in support of government involvement and action, President Lincoln said on July 4, 1861:

... to *elevate the condition of men; to lift artificial weights from all shoulders; to clear the paths of laudable pursuit of all; to afford all an unfettered start and fair chance in the race of life.*

The New Dealers' goal through the Tennessee Valley Authority and its sister-ship, the Rural Electrification Act, was to benefit all citizens regardless of their background. In that sense, as with all the New Deal programs, the goal was aspirational.

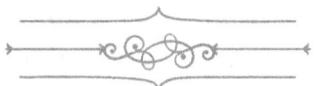

CHAPTER 30 – THE
WORKER REBELLION

FDR had dealt with the farmer. Now the New Dealers had to turn their attention to industrial workers in the cities where violent confrontations were increasingly occurring between assembly line employees and employers. The situation facing the Roosevelt Administration was this. In 1932, there were about 3.5 million workers in labor unions. This was down from 5 million in 1920. Most of those in unions were confined to such industries as construction, railroads, and local truck delivery companies. Major industries such as steel and auto were not unionized. Across the country, there was an effort to change this, leading to bitter labor-management warfare.

Generally speaking, workers wanted (a) pay raises; (b) better working conditions; (c) an emphasis on safety; (d) ending arbitrary decisions to hire or fire employees; (e) ending company unions; (f) ending open shop rules; (g) some assistance when injuries occurred on the job, and (f) some improvement in an existing pension program. To this end, there were 27,000 work stoppages between 1930 and 1941, resulting in the loss of 172 million labor days. Unfortunately, there were also 90 known deaths. During much of this period, no federal laws recognized the right of labor to organize and negotiate a labor contract through collective bargaining. The same was true of most states. Without such legislation, labor took its demands to the streets.

The West Coast Waterfront Strike

On May 9, 1934, every West Coast port dockworker left the job. They were members of the International Longshoremen and Warehouse Union (ILWU) led by a fiery leader, Harry Bridges. Their strike would last for 83 days and include "Bloody Thursday" and the San Francisco General Strike, which stopped almost all work in the city for four days before a settlement was finally reached, resulting in the unionization of longshoremen.

The ILWU was trying to replace what were called "company unions," often referred to as a "yellow union." Such unions were recognized as not being freely elected by the employees, over which an employer exerted significant control. As such, it was not an independent union free of management. For the dockers, such a union was seen as a management tool, not as a friend of the guy on the docks. As to how this worked... Longshoremen were required to go through a hiring hall operated by a company union where a "blue book" was kept. This referred to the color of the membership book that listed workers the company considered acceptable.

The ILWU was also opposed to an "open shop." Where a labor contract was agreed to, such a shop did not require workers to join the union as a condition for being hired, nor did a worker have to support the union with membership fees. Such a situation diluted the power of a union and was opposed for good reason. Individuals not in the union received the benefits of a contract but did not have to participate in the struggle to gain those benefits.

STRIKING LONGSHORE WORKERS

Once the strike began, it immediately took a violent turn. Vigilantes were hired to beat the strikers. These "thugs" seemed immune to law enforcement. Supported by the local police and political establishment, they took the law into their own hands. In addition, the employers hired strikebreakers to replace the workers on strike. They were housed on moored ships or placed in walled compounds. Police escorted the strikebreakers or "scabs" to work. On May 15, 1934, strikers attacked the compounds. In response, the police fired into a crowd of men, killing two strikers and wounding many others. Similar clashes occurred along the West Coast in Portland, Oregon, and Seattle, Washington. The spreading violence slowed down or stopped the movement of goods out of these ports.

On July 5, 1934, the whole business exploded. Various accounts suggested the following. The employers tried to open the port of San Francisco. The police assisted, firing tear gas canisters into a crowd of strikers. Mounted police then charged the workers, who responded by throwing rocks and canisters at them. Later in the day, some strikers surrounded a police car. They attempted to tip it over. In response, the police officers started shooting… Three men were wounded. Two of the three died. The strikers immediately cordoned off the area where the shooting took place. They laid flowers and wreaths. The spot became "synonymous with the memory of the two slain men and "Bloody Thursday." The following day, a funeral procession took place on Market Street. It stretched more than a mile with thousands of strikers, families, and sympathizers participating.

VIOLENCE IN THE STREETS OF SAN FRANCISCO

BURYING THE DEAD

By the end of the day, strikers were calling for a general strike, and dozens of local unions agreed to participate. On July 16, 1934, the general strike began with over 150,000 workers refusing to work. For the next four days, the city was essentially shut down. Soon afterwards, arbitration was ensured, and eventually, a deal was cut. The dockers received a raise to $.95 per hour and recognition as a union. The violence ended.

THE GENERAL STRIKE

The Textile Strike

The United States textile workers' strike of 1934 was the largest textile strike in labor history. For many, the job action was known as "The Uprising of '34." Over 400,000 textile workers participated in the strike, including workers in New England, the Mid-Atlantic States, and the South. The background to the workout goes back to at least the 1920s. What was once an industry concentrated in New England had migrated southward. By 1933, more than 70% of cotton and woolen textiles were produced in the South. The mill plants in the South were more modern. The pool of workers available to the companies included dispossessed farmers and laborers willing to work for the lowest possible wages. That meant working for about 40% less than their counterparts in the North. Unfortunately, the industry was strictly segregated; almost all the workers were white. Blacks accounted for approximately 2% of textile workers.

By the 1930s, an intractable problem faced the industry, the same one that had besieged agriculture: overproduction. The boom times of World War I were over. The government's demand for cotton products dried up. Foreign competition bit into the American domestic market. The industry could not regulate itself and thereby regulated competition to drive down production. As with the farmers, the textile companies tried to increase production to compensate for diminished demand. This led to unreasonable demands on the mill workers, many of whom were women. The number one culprit was to squeeze more work out of the employees. The "stretch-out" method was used on the assembly line. Each worker was assigned to an increased number of looms. Break times were limited, and in some factories, they were reduced in time. Workers were now paid by piece rates rather than daily. More supervisors were hired to keep workers from "slowing down, talking, or leaving work."

By 1934, the United Textile Workers (UTW) had had enough. On August 13, 1934, it called for a special convention in New York City. A list of demands was drawn up. They included (a) a thirty-hour workweek; (b) minimum wages ranging from $13.00 to $30.00 per week; (c) elimination of the stretch-out rule; (d) reinstatement of workers fired for their union activities; and (e) recognition of the UTW to represent the employees. An overwhelming membership vote would call for a strike if the demands were unmet. The demands were unmet, and the strike began on September 1, 1934. So-called "flying squadrons" carried the union's views to workers nationwide; much like an uncontrolled fire, thousands left the mill. Within a week, over 400,000 textile workers left the looms.

ON STRIKE AT THE MILLS

As expected, the mill owners fought back. They persuaded local authorities to swear in special deputies, sometimes their employees or residents opposed to the strike. In some cases, private guards were hired to police the areas around the plants. As predictable as the sun coming up each day, this led to violence between the guards and the picketers. The governors of two states also got into the fray on behalf of the companies. Governor Blackwood of South Carolina deputized "mayors, sheriffs, peace officers, and every good citizen" to maintain order, which meant opposing the strikers. In addition, he called out the National Guard with orders to "shoot to kill any picketers who tried to enter the mills." In North Carolina, Governor Ehringhaus followed his example. Throughout the country, strikers were violently opposed by the companies backed by the local police and the National Guard. It was inevitable that many strikers would be killed. The worst occurred on September 6, 1934, at Honea Path, South Carolina. Seven picketers were killed and over thirty others were wounded in what was described as the Chiquola Mill Massacre.

STANDOFF

It would be nice to think the strike accomplished its goals. That, however, was not the case. Especially in the South, local government officials refused to provide even a modicum of assistance to the strikers. Though the union promised to feed the striking workers, it could not. Ultimately, the strikers slowly drifted back to work, and the mills operated with a skeleton staff. Adding to the distress, the White House supported a commission's recommendations to hear the workers' complaints and prevent the companies from discriminating against strikers. The recommendations did not include recognition of the UTW. Other demands were not forced on the industry. It was a total and complete defeat for the union.

The Minneapolis General Strike of 1934

On May 16, 1934, the Teamster Union began a strike in the Twin Cities against trucking companies operating mainly in Minneapolis, an important distribution hub for the Midwest. The strike was immediately effective. Nearly all commercial traffic was shut down. One exception was made for farmers. They could bring their produce into the city, but they had to deliver everything directly to grocers rather than to the market area, which was shut down by the union.

What were the Teamsters demanding? First and foremost, the union wanted to be recognized as the bargaining unit for the truckers. They also wanted significant pay increases and shorter work hours. They also wanted the union to represent the "inside workers" employed in distribution centers who were not drivers. They also wanted to end arbitrary hiring and firing practices.

Resistance to the strike was immediate and violent. On May 19, 1934, the Minneapolis Police Department and private guards beat a large number of strikers who were preventing strikebreakers from unloading a truck. On May 21st, the police and several hundred newly deputized members of the Citizen Alliance attempted to reopen the central marketing area in the city. The Alliance was a company organization with one purpose: to break the strike. A violent confrontation took place between the picketers and the police. Armed with clubs of all types, additional strikers poured into the area, intent upon supporting the union. The ensuing fighting was physical, but no shots were fired at the strikers.

Soon, other unions supported the Teamsters, leading to a general strike. At that point, the Governor of Minnesota mobilized the National Guard but stopped short of deploying them. Governor Floyd B. Olson didn't want to alienate the Teamsters in his desire to end the strike. On May 25, 1934, the employers and the union reached an agreement on a contract that recognized the Teamsters as the bargaining unit for the workers. It also included the reinstatement of all strikers and a non-discriminatory clause. Overwhelmingly, the union members approved the contract. That should have been the end of the General Strike.

The Teamsters thought the contract included "inside workers" such as warehouse employees (drivers and loaders). When the companies reneged on this provision, the strike was renewed. It would lead to "Bloody Friday," July 20, 1934. On that day, the fifty-armed police opened fire with shotguns to stop strikers from shutting down a delivery truck. An eyewitness to the confrontation described what happened when strikers tried to aid their fallen comrades,

They flowed directly into buckshot fire… And the cops let them have it as they picked up their wounded. Lines of living, solid men fell, broke, wavering…

In the end, two men were killed and sixty-seven were wounded. The violence continued unabated. On July 26[th,] the Governor declared martial law after more strikers were killed. Four thousand troops were deployed in the city. Curfews were established, and security patrols roamed through the town.

The union leaders were arrested after the troops took over the Teamsters' headquarters. The next day, they were released, but the Governor had made his point. Troops would be used to keep the peace. In response, the Teamsters called for another General Strike. To ward this off, a federal mediator proposed a settlement that granted most of the union's demands. Company resistance ended. A contract was signed. The bloody strike was finally over.

The Kohler Strike of 1934

The Kohler Company is located in Sheboygan, Wisconsin. The company was known as a producer of fine plumbing products and enamelware. Management had aggressively fought all efforts to establish a union. The company created a workers' association to forestall the creation of an independent union. This in-house, management-controlled entity only handled minor shop floor grievances. It intentionally never negotiated contracts with the workers, who were forced to accept any company offer. In 1933, the workers applied for union membership within the American Federation of Labor, which was granted. On June 22, 1934, the union presented executives at Kohler with a 14-point proposal. The first business item was the union recognition to represent the workers. All other concerns could be worked out through collective bargaining. Four days later, Kohler announced a shutdown of the entire plant indefinitely. The lockout came without warning, leaving the employees without an income. The company's message was clear. The head of the company was Walter J. Kohler, Sr. He was determined to show who ran the enterprise and that "he could not be bargained with."

As in other strikes, violence quickly spread as picketers clashed with special deputies hired by the company. Only July 27, the deputies attacked those on strike with guns and tear gas. The pretext for the assault was that the company was experiencing vandalism. Two workers were killed and 47 others were wounded, men, women, and children. Two days later, the 250 members of the National Guard drove into town at the behest of Walter Kohler and the local sheriff. A semblance of order was restored. The strike ended unsuccessfully with the company demanding and maintaining an "open shop" stance until 1954, when the company finally recognized the United Auto Workers (UAW).

In 1960, the National Labor Relations Board held that the Kohler Company had not bargained in good faith after a 1954 strike occurred. The company was forced to reinstate 1700 workers. It took another two years and additional lawsuits by both sides to finally reach a contractual settlement. In 1965, the company agreed to pay $3 million in back wages to 1400 former employees and hand over $1.5 million in pension fund contributions to the union. The UAW now represented the workers and ended the longest major strike in American history. The photos that follow remind us of what took place.

THE NATIONAL GUARD ARRIVES

KOHLER ENTERS HIS PLANT

THE STRIKE CONTINUES

The labor strife of the early 1930s raised many questions, some financial, others social, and certainly a few ethical concerns. Does a company have the right to hire and fire employees? The obvious answer is yes, but there is some small print. Can a company discriminate in doing this? Can it act arbitrarily? Also, does a company have the right to set a pay scale? Of course, but does it have the legal right to set up a two or three-tiered pay scale? Does a company need to make a profit and to share such profits with shareholders and investors? Again, the answer is obvious. A business is in the industry to make money. As to the employees... Do they have the right to organize for better pay, working conditions, and a legal process by which employees are hired or dismissed? There can be no doubt about this. Labor has a right to withhold its labor. Are workers merely cogs in a corporation, what we might call tenant farmers in industrial jobs? Should workers be subject to abuse by management in whatever form it might take? Does a negotiated contract through collective bargaining provide labor and management with a process to reduce labor tension? Questions and more questions, many not always easily answered.

For the most part, the New Dealers tried to avoid these intense labor disputes, limiting themselves to recommending that both sides come together and that violence be avoided. In the back rooms of the White House, however, an ongoing effort was taking place to write legislation that would move beyond recommendations and pleas. Of necessity, such legislation would need the support of Congress as well as the president's signature. Until it was ready, labor strife would occur. To a degree, then, labor was on its own.

There is a parable about a pencil. One man asked, "Why do I need to join a union? I can bargain by myself." The answer was, "Yes, you can do that, but like a single pencil, you can be broken." The man responded, "Suppose I join with a few other guys. Would that help?" "Of course came the answer, but even a few pencils can be snapped in half." "Well," asked the man, "what's the answer?" "My friend, the answer is in numbers. The more pencils that gather together, the more difficult it is to break them."

In Flint, Michigan, in 1935, the parable of the pencils would be challenged by the behemoth of American business: the automobile industry. That clash would settle the struggle between management and employees for once and for all.

CHAPTER 31 – THE SIT–IN

For many, having a job during the Great Depression was a blessing, regardless of the pay and the conditions under which they worked. Certainly, you could gripe: "I hate this." "No pay raise again." "Always the demand to work harder." "Turn out product." Of course, if you griped out loud, your supervisor might say, "Joe, there are a hundred guys out there who want your job, so suck it up." In response, there wasn't much Joe could say. He was the breadwinner. His wife and children depended on his sometimes less-than-modest paycheck. No, Joe had to bite his tongue; he had to quell his passions and frustrations of being locked to a job where the company seemed to be taking advantage of him, seemingly unconcerned about whether he lived or died. He was just a cog in a giant machine that could easily replace him. That was Joe's lot, and there seemed to be no end to this dreadful life and little future for his children.

Of course, Joe wasn't alone in this predicament. Thousands and thousands were caught up in this bind each day they reported to work at General Motors Plant #4 in Flint, Michigan.

Before the stock market crash, General Motors employed over 200,000 workers in its various plants. By 1932, this massive company had reduced its workforce by 39,000. Cars weren't flying off the shelf. The workforce had to be trimmed, and salaries had to be reduced. The average annual salary was 1,195 dollars and has been stagnating. The federal government estimated that a family of four needed at least $1,434 to survive. Guys like Joe had to make do, even as the supervisors demanded intense speed-ups in production, which left men so exhausted they couldn't even eat their lunches. The production line was unsafe because of brutal working conditions and an absence of reasonable safety rules. Joe and his buddies needed help. It didn't come from the government. It came from the United Auto Workers (UAW) and the men who joined this union.

Under the leadership of Walter Reuther, the UAW had been trying to organize employees at General Motors. The union had been formed in 1935. It found that it was a dangerous and challenging endeavor to attract members. This was especially true of Plant #4 in Flint. Flint was a company town beholden to GM. The local government and police department were always looking for "organizers." Outsiders were scrutinized. An extensive spy network in the plant ferreted out those sympathetic to the union. Workers couldn't discuss the UAW on the assembly line or in the lunchroom. Guys like Joe had to watch their step. You never knew who was a friend. That being the case, the UAW met with workers in their homes, quietly behind closed shades. As members signed up with the union, their names were kept secret.

In late 1936, the union made a crucial decision. It was ready to challenge GM by striking the most valuable plant, Plant #4, which produced motors for all the company's various vehicles, especially Chevrolet. The plant was the "heart and soul" of production. Cripple this production and you cripple GM. The UAW wasn't meant to strike so soon, but was in a box. Two brothers had been fired at the Cleveland Fisher Body plant, and the workers decided to attack. The UAW supported the Cleveland workers and expanded the strike to include all GM plants.

In Flint, that meant a new strike tactic. The workers entered the plant, turned off the machinery, and sat down. This was an unconventional strategy. There would be no union picketing outside the plant on the cold sidewalks. There would be no picket lines to discourage strikebreakers from entering the plant. Management couldn't bring in strikebreakers. The strikers occupied the plant. Bad weather wasn't a problem. Joe and his buddies were inside. They were somewhat immune to outside pressures and the hostilities of the community. Inside the plant, the workers elected an informal government to maintain order. The number one rule was to avoid damaging the machinery. There was to be no property damage. This was a "sit-down strike."

THE SIT-IN STRIKE

The job action lasted for 44 days. Ultimately, the UAW was recognized as the bargaining agent for the workers on the line. GM consented to the immediate rehiring of workers who were on strike. All workers would receive a 5% increase in salary. It is imperative that the UAW union members can wear UAW buttons on the job. They could also discuss union activities at lunch or on their breaks. The UAW now had legitimacy. The victory led to an immediate drive to sign up new UAW members. Within a few weeks, over 100,000 men were in the union. Within a year, membership reached 500,000. Other related industries, including Goodyear, Packard, and Goodrich, quickly followed suit.

It is a little-known fact that women played a significant role in the Flint 'sit-down" strike. The central figure here was Genora Johnson. This determined and passionate union activist and later civil rights fighter was born in Kalamazoo, Michigan. However, she was raised in Flint, where her family had roots in the town's founding. She received an excellent private school education. In time, she found employment at the Briggs

Manufacturing Company. There, she became a Chief Steward of UAW Local 212. This was in an all-women's department in the company's central plant.

As the story goes… Due to her outspoken union activities, she was severely beaten with a lead pipe while alone in her home. Many concluded the company had hired Mafia members to do this. She then married a GM worker named Kermit Johnson, who worked in the Flint factory.

GENORA JOHNSON

Once the "sit-in" strikers occupied GM's Plant #4, Johnson organized women to support their husbands, fathers, brothers, and good friends. In time, she was noted as the leader of the Women's Emergency Brigade. She was appalled by GM's retaliatory actions against the men. GM cuts off the heat at the plant during especially harsh weather. Following this, the company turned off electricity and attempted to keep food supplies from reaching the men. When this didn't dispel the occupiers of the plant, tear gas was used to drive them out. In response to these actions, Johnson organized women to picket outside the plant and to funnel food to the workers inside the plant. Many women wore red berets and armbands with EB inscribed on them. In time, they would carry wooden clubs under their long coats to fend off the police and strikebreakers. Militant and passionate, the ladies of Flint went to war.

THE WOMEN PROTEST

In her own words, Johnson expressed the stakes and how women would fight.

We will form a line around the men; if the police want to fire, they'll have to fire on us.

This was no idle threat. After GM fired tear gas into the plant, the women, spurred on by Johnson, used their clubs to break windows so the striking men could breathe. In doing so, they had to face off against the police.

Speaking to the women of Flint, she said:

If the police are cowards enough to shoot down defenseless men, they're cowards enough to shoot down women. Women of the city of Flint, break through these police lines, and come down here and stand with your husbands and you brothers, your sons and your sweethearts.

Refusing to be fearful of the police and thugs hired by GM she challenged women to engage in the fight, saying:

We have to have a military formation of the women. If the cops start firing into the men, the women can take the front line ranks. Let them dare to shoot women!"

As women joined the Brigade Johnson reminded them that this wasn't for the faint of heart.

You can't get hysterical if your sister beside you drops down on a pool of blood. We can't be bothered having to take care of two people, if one is injured and another is going to go hysterical. Do not sign up for the Women's Brigade, take your role in the strike kitchen, take your role in the first aid station in the Ladies' Auxiliary.

The response to Johnson's call was immediate and dramatic. The women came forth, young and old, to assist the men in Plant #4. One of those who first signed up was a woman in her seventies. Johnson reminded her that this "would be difficult for her." The older woman responded, "You can't keep me out. My sons work in that factory. My husband worked in that factory before he died, and I have grandsons there." Johnson had no choice but to acquiesce.

The *Flint Journal* wrote about the women. The paper called the Brigade the "Rolling Pin Brigade" and quoted Johnson:

We will be ready in the future to have women at the scene of trouble within 10 minutes. If there is a fight, we'll get into it… police bullets don't frighten me.

THE WOMEN'S AUXILIARY

One member of the Emergency Brigade described her experience as such:

We saw that there was such a need for women who would gladly give the life, because that is what they asked us to do. We faced tear gas, we faced rocks, we faced police, we faced National Guard, and General Motors' goons and everybody else.

The Sit-Down Strike started on December 30, 1936, and lasted until February 11, 1937. Both the men and women could be proud of their victory.

CELEBRATING VICTORY

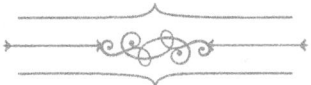

CHAPTER 32 – DEALING WITH LABOR

The New Dealers were in a bind, and they knew it. The shadow of continuing labor strife threatened the efforts to pull the country out of the Great Depression. Something, as always, had to be done.

On the one hand, the business community needed to be considered in proposing and implementing new legislation concerning "job actions" that often led to violent confrontations between management and employees. Generally speaking, businesses tended to be conservative, Republican, and staunch status quo supporters. In practice, what did this mean? Corporate America and small businesses wanted the least amount of federal regulation and, where they existed, only the most limited enforcement. This included hiring and firing practices, working conditions, wage settlements, and safety factors. Put, businesses frowned on any policy that infringed on their independence of action and their profitability. Understandably, employers mounted a furious and continuing opposition to labor unions.

On the other hand, labor tended to support the Democratic Party and those regulations that supported workers. Wages and working conditions ranked high, as did protections from arbitrary hiring and firing practices meant to keep workers in line. Protection of pension funds was critical, as was the right to organize and negotiate a contract through collective bargaining. Government involvement was seen as necessary and beneficial, not an unnecessary intrusion. Labor's view was that business was entitled to make a profit. Investors were entitled to a fair return on their money.

Management had a right to generous salaries. Equally so, labor desired an equal right to a livable wage. From this perspective, all parties --- management, investors, companies, and unions --- were partners, each benefitting from the contribution and collaboration of others. Again, from labor's vantage point, there was no company without the men and women who produced the goods and services that consumers desired to purchase.

The challenge to the New Dealers was to find a balance point that benefited all parties, assuming that this elusive goal was possible in a world where political considerations were necessary. Labor was a significant voting bloc. Democrats could ill afford to lose this vote. Given the upsurge in labor confrontations and the increasing violence, the Democratic Party reached out to one of its own, Senator Robert F. Wagner from New York State. He had built a career in Congress as a forward-looking progressive, always seeking to cleanse the ills of an industrialized nation through carefully thought-out reforms. To say the least, he was viewed suspiciously by business interests and favorably by labor. He was determined to unite these dispirited groups into a fragile relationship imposed by Washington. As a major advisor to FDR and an accepted member of the president's "brain trust," he supported the Social Security Act in 1935 and the Housing Act of 1937. His one great political regret was his failure to pass an anti-lynching law. In 1936, a valiant effort was made, proposing legislation that would hold public law officials responsible for protecting those in their custody. The president, always cognizant of the "Solid South," refused to give strong public support for the legislation. The 1936 presidential election was on the horizon. Political expediency was necessary for reelection. Southern votes were crucial.

In 1935, at Senator Wagner's urging, the National Labor Relations Act (NLRA) was submitted to Congress. In time, it would be known as the Wagner Act. After considerable debate, the 74th Congress passed the bill. President Roosevelt signed it on July 5, 1935. Through this action, the federal government became a full-fledged partner in the nation's labor disputes, as it had never done before in America's history. The act aimed to "correct the inequality of bargaining power" between employers and employees." The focus of the legislation was to encourage:

... the practice and procedure of collective bargaining and by protecting the exercise by workers of full freedom of association, self-organization, and designation of representatives of their own choosing, for the purpose of negotiating the terms and conditions of their employment or other mutual aid or protection.

SENATOR ROBERT WAGNER

The Wagner Act established the National Labor Relations Board (NLRB). It was charged with prosecuting violations of labor laws specified by the new legislation. It was also tasked with overseeing the process by which employees decided which entity would represent them through collective bargaining. The act also established the rules governing the collective bargaining process. The right to strike was now guaranteed by law.

Nothing in this subchapter, except as specifically provided for herein, shall be construed so as either to interfere with or impede or diminish in any way the right to strike, or to affect the limitations or qualifications on that right.

The NLRB banned the "company union," much to the delight of both the CIO and the AFL. The oppressive, hostile, almost dictatorial control of employees, at least in law, was over. Companies would no longer relegate workers to a near-industrial sharecropper status, earning barely survival wages. Companies could no longer ask employees about their union loyalty, sympathy, or involvement. Companies could no longer threaten to close a plant if employees wanted a union. Workers could no longer be terminated because of their union involvement. That day was over. Unions were now able to confront management openly and legally. Through complex and often protracted negotiations, unions now had their place in the sun.

The rise of labor unions in the 1930s did not exclude Hollywood. In the land of movie stars and homes overlooking the Pacific Ocean, a new union was born in 1938, the Screen Cartoonists' Guild (SCG). By 1941, it had signed contracts with every major studio with one exception. Walt Disney was reluctant to negotiate an agreement, if not totally resistant. It was true that Disney's cartoonists had the best pay and working conditions in the industry. The studio, however, was not immune to labor discontent. In 1941, SCG called for a Disney animators' strike to shut down Walt Disney Productions and disrupt film production. The strike would last for five weeks. More than 200 members of the studio staff went on strike during the production of Dumbo. According to many, the strikers maintained a "carnival atmosphere on the picket line, using humor and artistic skills in producing signs. The unionized staff at Technicolor and the United Auto Workers supported the strikers. The League of Women Shoppers advocacy group picketed theaters exhibiting Disney films.

Disney was a non-unionized workplace where inequities of pay and privilege existed. The company reacted to the job action by firing many of its animators. Eventually, the company was pressured into recognizing the SCG. This was in response to the National Labor Relations Board's request to Walt Disney to sign a union contract. He agreed. A contract was signed that included rehiring those workers who had been fired. With this agreement, Hollywood went union.

LABOR ACT AT DISNEY PRODUCTIONS

On April 1, 1941, the Ford Motor Company finally recognized the United Auto Workers (UAW) as the bargaining agent for Ford's employees. Ford was the last auto company to accept collective bargaining. General Motors and Chrysler had already done so. The contract stated that Ford would be a "closed shop." All employees had to be union members. A "dues check-off" provision allowed union dues to be deducted directly from a member's pay. The money would be sent directly to the union. The settlement at Ford came after a ten-day "wildcat strike" that blocked entry to the River Rouge plant in Dearborn, Michigan. This was the largest industrial complex in the world. It was also where the company's Service

Department spied on workers and committed violent acts against those advocating unionism. At its peak, the Service Department had 3,000 spies and thugs. The *New York Times* described this force as "the largest private quasi-military organization in existence."

Though Henry Ford, the company's principal owner, paid his workers the best wages in the industry and promoted the notions of "high wage, high productivity, and high consumption," he was dead set against the UAW. In 1932, Ford's Service Members and Dearborn police fired on unemployed demonstrators, killing four and wounding others. History records the event as the Ford Hunger Strike. In 1937, Ford's Service members attacked UAW official Walter Reuther and a dozen union supporters, mostly women, seeking to pass out flyers. This event was known as the Battle of the Overpass. In both cases, the Ford Company tried to destroy any photographic evidence of the confrontations. Surviving photographs, however, were published nationally as "evidence of Ford's brutality." Publication of the photos swayed public opinion in favor of the union.

Walter Reuther described what happened at the Overpass:

Seven times, they raised me off the concrete and slammed me down on it. They pinned my arms. I was punched and kicked and dragged by my feet to the stairway, thrown down a flight of steps, picked up, slammed down on the platform, and kicked down the second flight. On the ground, they beat and kicked me some more.

REUTHER ATTACKED | FORD THUGS AT WORK

Several compromises were necessary with the conservative elements in Congress to pass the Wagner Act. The legislation did not apply to agricultural and domestic workers, many of whom were Black. The influence of the Southern senators was evident here. The act did not cover supervisors. All government workers, federal and state, were exempted. Shutting down government facilities was not going to happen. Also, two essential forms of transportation were left out of the act: railroad workers and airline employees.

As expected, the Wagner Act was bitterly opposed by the Republican Party. It was denounced as "socialistic," something akin to communist practices in the Soviet Union. It was portrayed as taking away freedoms from everyday Americans. Every possible legal effort was utilized to stop the implementation of the act. Injunctions were filed in the courts. Judicial appeals were made and litigated. Eventually, the whole business went before the US Supreme Court. On April 12, 1937, in NLRB vs. Jones Laughlin Steel Corporation, the constitutionality of the Wagner Act was upheld.

Background to the case:

The complaint alleged that Jones had wrongfully terminated several workers based on their leadership in the local labor union. After a hearing, the NLRB determined Jones had discriminated against the employees. The board ordered the company to rehire the workers and pay them back wages.

In a majority opinion written by Chief Justice Charles E. Hughes, the majority found that companies cannot discriminate against employees for exercising their fundamental right to unionize.

Rule of law: Congress can regulate interstate activities that directly or indirectly affect interstate commerce.

Victory—The Court ruled in favor of the NLRB, claiming that the Commerce Clause allowed the government to regulate interstate commerce. Because Jones and Laughlin Steel Corporation were conducting unfair labor practices, they violated the Act.

#105

Speaking on behalf of the legislation, Senator Wagner stated:

There is no scintilla of truth in the widely spread propaganda that this bill would tend to create a so-called "labor dictatorship." It does not encourage national unionism, favor any particular union, or force or even counsel any employee to join any union if he prefers to deal directly or individually with his employers. It seeks merely to make the worker a free man in the economic and political fields.

Concerning people of color... The Wagner Act did not include specific measures to protect the rights of racial minorities in the workplace. Inclusion of such provisions would have jeopardized the passage of the legislation. Discriminatory practices were not outlawed in unions. The AFL did not grant membership to Blacks. The CIO did include Blacks, but engaged in internal discriminatory practices. The most preferable jobs went to whites even when Blacks were equally competent. Seniority in the union was difficult for Blacks to achieve. At the worksite, companies still discriminated against Blacks, the Wagner Act notwithstanding. There were no nondiscrimination clauses in negotiated contracts.

Without question, the NLRB was pro-labor. It was not neutral. It was an overt legislative effort to force companies to accept the realities of unions. Beyond that, unions and management must play by accepted rules. To do this demanded impartiality. Assuming the NLRB functioned as designed, labor strife and violence would be reduced. Though future events proved that this was not always the case, the unionization of workers was a New Deal success, consolidating as it did labor's support for the Democratic Party.

Alluding to the possible legacy of the Wagner Act, its author said:

The enactment of this measure will clarify the industrial atmosphere and reduce the likelihood of another conflagration of strife such as we witnessed last summer. It will stabilize and improve business by laying the foundations for the amity and fair dealing upon which permanent progress must rest.

Years later, Martin L. King addressed the legacy question.

The labor movement was the principal force that transformed misery and despair into hop and progress. Out of its bold struggles, economic and social reform gave birth to unemployment insurance, old-age pensions, government relief for the destitute and, above all, new wage levels that meant not mere survival but a tolerable life. The Captains of Industry did not lead this transformation; they resisted it until they were overcome. When in the thirties the wave of union organization crested over the nation, it carried to secure shores not only itself, but the whole society.

CHAPTER 33– DEALING WITH WOMEN

The New Deal was first about unemployed men and finding a way to return them to work. The "numbers" made that paramount. Though women were jobless, their numbers, compared to men, were almost insignificant on a policy level. At a time when men were understood as the "breadwinners" and the "head of households," unemployment, cresting at nearly 25% was destroying families, leaving a large percentage of the general population destitute. The New Dealers understood the painful implications of joblessness. With three or four family members dependent on a single salary, the fabric of family life was at risk.

Applying Keynesian "countercyclical" policies was appropriate to spur the economy and boost the nation's GNP. But again, that meant policies that focused on men. The math was uncompromising. By the millions, men were out of work. Male jobs had been hit hardest by the economic collapse—industrial, assembly line work, manufacturing, mining, working in steel mills and auto plants, and other forms of tough, physical work.

By comparison, women had suffered fewer layoffs because most worked in the service industry as clerks, telephone operators, nurses, teachers, maids, cooks, cleaners, and domestic workers. While these jobs were not depression-proof, they did have a degree of resistance to a declining GNP.

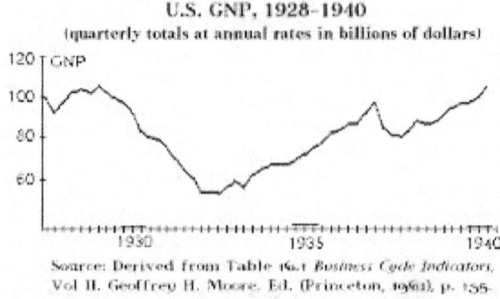

U.S. GNP, 1928–1940
(quarterly totals at annual rates in billions of dollars)

Source: Derived from Table 16.1 *Business Cycle Indicators*, Vol II. Geoffrey H. Moore, Ed. (Princeton, 1961), p. 135.

The New Dealers were quite aware of joblessness within the ranks of women. They consciously determined to focus on putting men back to work. Assistance for women would be limited, almost as an afterthought when designing relief and work policies.. The conventional wisdom was that a woman's "paid work" was only marginally important to the economy. At the time Wall Street "crashed," most married women only took jobs for what was called "pin money" or because of a personal interest. This being the case, it only seemed natural that they should be paid less. They would also have fewer protections in the workplace. This view was extended to single women. In 1930, approximately 10.5 million women were working. By 1940, that number would swell to 13 million as the nation prepared for war. Assisting women proved to be a challenge for the Roosevelt Administration. This was particularly true of married women who were the "head of the household," the sole breadwinner, where divorce or death, if not the loss of a job, had made this so.

And then there was the question of barring women from jobs. Beginning in the 1880s, there was a long history of opposition to hiring married women. Informal but powerful rules were in place to bar women from jobs and reserve work opportunities for men. In the case of unmarried women without families to support, where jobs were available, they came with the lowest pay and the least prestigious positions. To a degree, keeping women out of the workplace had general support. In a *Fortune Magazine* poll in 1936, only 15% of the respondents indicated that a woman should work. As the depression hardened, opposition to women working increased. Married women, as the argument went, shouldn't take a job away from a man or from a single woman. The bias increased when it came to married couples working.

BIAS IN THE WORKPLACE

In Wisconsin in 1935, a resolution was passed by the state legislature. The resolution stated, "When married women with working husbands get jobs, they become the 'calling card for the disintegration of family life." Going on the resolution said:

The large number of husbands and wives working for the state raises a serious moral question, as this committee feels that the practice of birth control is encouraged, and the selfishness that arises from the income of employment of husband and wife bids fair to break down civilization and a healthy atmosphere.

In 1933, the federal government got involved in barring married women. The Economic Act of that year forced women working for the federal government, if married, to resign from their position (Section 213). The avowed purpose was to make more jobs for men. Women were also forced to use their husbands' names. They couldn't avoid detection by using their maiden name. This led, in many cases, to women marrying in secret. No wedding announcement or party. Some 25 states had similar provisions. Intentionally, women were excluded based on gender, not experience, competency, or educational background. They were also excluded without considering the need to support their families or themselves. The federal government assisted one group at the expense of another.

NO MARRIED WOMEN

Beyond barring women, single or married, from gainful employment, gender discrimination was present in at least two New Deal programs. As noted earlier, the Civilian Conservation Corps (CCC) focused on putting high school and college-age men to work. In particular, urban males were hired to do construction work while living in government-established camps where they received the benefits of free square meals each day and a solid roof over their youthful heads. Recall that the wage payment was $30.00 monthly, with almost all of that sent home to families on relief. In the few camps for women, only an allowance was provided, not a wage. The men could stay in the CCC for up to two years. The women in the CCC were restricted to one month, during which they received training in hygiene and housekeeping. Over 2.5 million men were enrolled in the CCC compared to only 6,500 women. In response to this, the woman quipped, "As is often the case, the boys get the breaks. The girls get neglected."

Another example of gender discrimination was the Works Progress Administration (WPA). Millions of men were involved in construction projects. Initially, there were few tasks for women. In time, empty warehouses were transformed into sewing centers. Some 200,000 women were hired to make the needed mattresses, clothes, and blankets. Others were involved in canning fruit and vegetables. Based on their educational skills, some were placed in teaching positions or to work in libraries. A few even led adult education programs. Those talented in the arts were employed as artists and writers. Regarding equal treatment, women were asked to take a back seat.

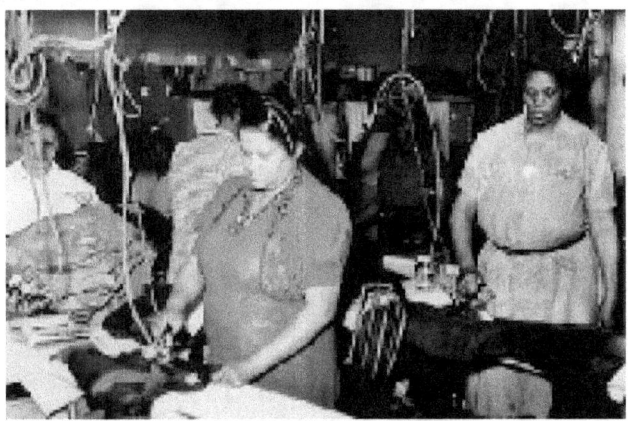

PUTTING WOMEN TO WORK

WPA jobs for women did have supporters. As one woman said:

Every time a woman is removed from the demoralizing ranks of the jobless, removed from the humiliation of a breadline, and given work to do, a home somewhere becomes more secure.

The situation for African-American women during the Great Depression was particularly bleak. Already chained to a history of hard, demanding agricultural work, epitomized by sharecropping and tenant farming, they were accustomed to a difficult life. The collapse of the stock market and the ensuing depression did not catch Blacks by surprise. This had been their economic experience for years. The advent of New Deal programs, relief, and work did little to assist Blacks compared to whites.

Again, as earlier seemed, these programs were implemented at the local level where racial biases could determine who would be assisted and to what degree.

If there was a more than informal "brain trust" of mainly male academic advisors to assist President Roosevelt and his formal cabinet, there was also the "Black brain trust" influencing policy at the edges. One other group also advised the president. These were talented women tabbed by the president to work in the government. They were not merely spear-carriers for FDR. In their appointed positions, they developed and initiated policies that focused on women. They constituted an influential "female trust group" with the backing of the Administration.

Mary Dewson

One such appointment was Mary Dewson. She was an avowed feminist and political activist, and a lifetime supporter of progressive policies and the Democratic Party. She was born in Quincy, Massachusetts, on February 18, 1874. She was the youngest of six children and was very athletic. Unconcerned about her appearance or the social need to play with dolls, she preferred to play baseball and tennis; that is, she liked the "boy's toys. She attended Wellesley College, graduating in 1897 with a degree in Sociology and a future as a social worker.

MARY DEWSON AT WORK

After college, she worked for the Women's Educational and Industrial Union. While doing so, she met Mrs. Roosevelt at the Women's Club of New York City. The "First Lady" influenced her to participate in the Democratic Party. This she did. In time, she became the head of the Women's Division of the Democratic National Committee. In that role, she created the "Reporters Plan." She had thousands of women spread information about the New Deal Legislation. To that end, she had to educate the women so they could explain Roosevelt's policies to those less informed. In the process of doing this, she involved women in the 1932 presidential campaign. The future president took notice of her efforts, as he had earlier when she campaigned for Al Smith in 1928 and for Roosevelt in his New York State gubernatorial campaigns in 1930 and 1932.

President Roosevelt then asked her to serve on the Advisory Council of the President's Committee on Economic Security. The recommendations of the Council were later incorporated into the Social Security Act of 1935. It was her position that at least one woman should be appointed to the Social Security Board, which initially was only composed of men. In 1937, the president appointed her the first woman on the board. Once on the Board, she advocated for expanded coverage to include domestic workers, farm laborers, widows, and dependent children. Not many of these goals were accomplished while she was on the Board. That notwithstanding, FDR referred to her as his "Little General" for her persistence and dedication in fighting for what she believed.

Josephine Roche

This Roosevelt appointee brought a variety of experiences to Washington. She was a humanitarian, industrialist, social activist, and a sharp politician who knew how to get things done. Josephine Roche was born in Nebraska on December 2, 1886, to an affluent family. Before matriculating at Vassar College, she attended a private girls' school, where she had a double major in economics and the classics. She was also an excellent athlete, as noted by her participation in basketball and track clubs. She was known by her peers as "cheerful and happy in the prospect of having almost more to do that day than she could accomplish." Though her father was a conservative and violently anti-union, Roche felt no such compunction. She embraced the liberal social and economic ideas flourishing on the Vassar campus. She saw the benefits of trade unionism and the need for minimum working hours and reasonable wages. She felt people should have a decent standard of living.

She later attended Columbia University in New York City where she earned a degree in Social Work. For a time, she was involved in various social causes in the City before moving on to Denver, Colorado, where she studied in depth cost-of-living issues. It was also where she became Denver's first female police officer. That was in 1912. She was an inspector of Amusements. She supervised public dance halls, cafes, and the "Red Light" district; in many cases, that meant taking girls back to their families. She proved to be zealous in persecuting crimes related to prostitution. After a relatively short time, she was forced out of the job by more lenient folks in the "Mile High City."

Taking an interest in her, President Woodrow Wilson appointed Roche a Special Agent of England and the United States for the Commission for Relief of Belgium in World War I. Moving on, she worked as the Director of the Girls Department in Denver's

Juvenile Court. From 1918 through 1923, she was involved with the Foreign Language Information Service (FLIS). This agency provided legal assistance, news, and information to immigrants in their native languages. In 1923, she moved to Washington as Director of the Editorial and Special Studies Department of the Children's Bureau. Later, she moved back to Denver and became active in Colorado's Progressive Party. There she worked to end child labor, especially in the sugar cane industry.

ROCHE, A SUPPORTER OF UNIONS

This work was interrupted by her father's death in 1927. From him, she inherited his coal company, the Rocky Mountain Fuel Company. The business and the mineworkers were engaged in a bitter strike over higher wages and better working conditions. Across the state, almost 90% of the mine owners were dealing with striking miners. In responding to this situation, and as the CEO of her father's company, she went against the prevailing winds in the industry. She issued what was then considered a revolutionary statement. She said:

The men employed in the mines are as much an essential factor in the industry as the capital invested and have the right to act upon equal terms with the investor to determine working and living conditions.

She supported the unionization of her workforce by working with the United Mine Workers of America (UMWA). She rehired striking workers, raised pay, eliminated company scripts, and instituted workers' compensation insurance. Lastly, she hired workers to sell union coal.

In 1934, she entered the Democratic Party primary for governor. She coined the phrase "Roosevelt and Roche." He won and she lost. She supported Al Smith in the 1928 presidential election and Roosevelt's two terms in the New York State House. Her efforts were recognized by FDR, and in 1934, he appointed her the Assistant Secretary of the Treasury. She quickly became known as the "baby member" of the Brain Trust. She held that post until 1937. While in Washington, she was involved in the committees pulling together the Social Security Act of 1936. She also promoted and pushed for a national health program in 1938, 1939, 1940, and 1943. To her regret, she could not defeat the conservative coalition opposing her plans. Many politicians labeled the plan "socialistic." Private insurance companies considered such a program too radical. The American Medical Association fought her tooth and nail. She reciprocated in kind but to no avail. Her vision would have to wait another time.

Florence E. Allen

President Roosevelt nominated Florence Allen to a seat on the US Court of Appeals for the Sixth Circuit. The US Senate confirmed her nomination on March 15, 1954, in the face of stiff opposition. The tide turned in her favor from an unlikely source. Supreme Court Justice Will Stephenson was initially opposed to her nomination. He wasn't sure he wanted to share the bench with her or any female. As he examined Allen's background and her rulings, he had a change of heart. He came to Washington and spoke on her half, stating, "There is no Court too big for Judge Allen." This view was proven later in her judicial career when she presided over a three-judge panel in the case of Tennessee Electric Power Company v. Tennessee Valley Authority. The panel ruled in favor of the government. It had the "constitutional authority to build dams and reservoirs and to regulate interstate commerce on interstate waterways like the Tennessee River."

In receiving this honor, she became only the second woman to serve in the federal judiciary. Who was this woman selected by the president? She was the first woman assistant county prosecutor in the United States, the first woman elected to a judicial office in Ohio, and the first woman elected to the Ohio Supreme Court. Those titles and "firsts" appealed to the White House.

JUDGE ALLEN

Allen was born in Salt Lake City on March 23, 1884. Her father was a professor and linguist at Western Reserve University in Cleveland. There, he taught Greek and Latin to his students, but also to his daughter. As with language, Allen had a strong love for poetry and music. She eventually enrolled in Western Reserve, receiving an MA in political science. Following this, she earned a law degree from New York University School of Law. Initially, she found it challenging to maintain a law practice. Many of her male colleagues refused to take her seriously. During this period, she did legal work for the Legal Aid Society. This provided her with the experiences of the "other half" of society. She also became active in the Women's Suffrage Party. In many ways, this seemed only natural for this highly educated woman, and because as a child she had actually heard Susan B. Anthony speak.

In 1920, she was the first woman elected as a Common Pleas judge in Ohio. In that capacity, she would hear over 900 cases. Two years later, she was elected to the Supreme Court of Ohio. She was reelected in 1928. She noted in her diary that the men on the court exhibited "uneasiness" due to her gender. She overcame this by asserting herself competently in dealing with cases ranging from labor disputes, public taxes, and questions related to public education. During that period, she was a proponent of jury service for women when many states did not allow this. Along these lines, she was quoted as saying:

When women of intelligence recognize their share in and their responsibility for the courts, a power moral backing is secured for the administration of justice.

Those following her career suggested that the president consider her for the US Supreme Court. This included Mrs. Roosevelt, who said, "If the President of the United States should decide to nominate a woman for the Supreme Court, it should be Judge Allen." It almost happened. In 1939, Supreme Court Justice Louis D. Brandeis was about to retire. Allen's supporters went to bat for her. In the end, Roosevelt nominated William O. Douglas. This pattern of gender exclusion continued. Every time there was a vacancy, Allen's name came up, and each time a man received the nomination.

In the post-war period, Allen turned her attention to world peace. Her message was simple. Relying on the United Nations to keep the peace was insufficient. In her mind, it was essential for individual citizens to keep demanding that each country, large or small, respect the rule of law. She said:

There cannot be justice unless there is a rebirth of moral principle among the nations. There cannot be a rebirth of moral principle unless the conscience of the peoples becomes articulate.

Her philosophy of government and the role of active citizens was summarized as follows:

Liberty cannot be caged into a charter or handed on ready made to the next generation. Each generation must recreate liberty for its own times. Whether or not we establish freedom rest with ourselves.

Clara Mortenson Beyer

Still another member of Roosevelt's unofficial "female brain trust" was Clare Beyer. Her public career focused on labor economics and the rights of workers. She pioneered working for a minimum wage, first in Washington, D.C., and later throughout the country. Her academic background trained her for this focus. She graduated from the University of California at Berkley with an MA in economics. Later, she taught at Bryn Mawr College, where she influenced her students to join picket lines and investigate Philadelphia sweatshops. Not bad for a young woman born on April 13, 1892, in Lake Country, California, a few miles north of San Francisco. Due to her father's death, she and her mother were forced to work as fruit pickers and as domestic laborers. There is no question that these experiences shaped her views about the fair treatment of workers regardless of their field of endeavor.

While teaching at Bryn Mawr, she attended a lecture by Felix Frankfurter, a visiting Harvard professor and a future justice of the Supreme Court. Apparently, they hit it off. He invited Beyer to work in Washington on the War Labor Policies Board. She agreed and did so during World War I. After the Armistice, she was named Secretary of the Minimum Wage Board of the District of Columbia. Congress had just passed a minimum wage law for the federal district. Her assignment was to study prevailing wages paid to women who were working. She determined that 10% of the women in the city received less than $9.00 per week, and 75% received less than $16.00. Eventually, a minimum wage of $16.50 was set, making it one of the highest in the country.

Other assignments came her way. She was appointed the Director of the Department of Labor Children's Bureau. In 1934, she became the Assistant Director of the Division of Labor Standards. She would serve until 1937. In that capacity, she focused on such issues as apprenticeship programs and vocational education policies for immigrant workers. In time, she became a close friend of Frances Perkins, the Secretary of Labor. The two were involved in developing the provisions of the Social Security Act of 1935. Her work continued in establishing the Fair Labor Standards Act of 1938, which set minimum wage and maximum hours standards nationwide. This was no easy task. Organized labor was concerned that a minimum wage law would lower pay overall. To allay this fear, she lobbied William Green, the American Federation of Labor president. She gained his support, and Congress passed the legislation. When the act was challenged in the courts, she helped prepare the government's successful defense before the Supreme Court. Perkins and Beyer were quite a team.

PERKINS AND BEYER

The common thread uniting these women was their stance on suffrage and the need for women to participate in making New Deal policy. They found a favorable response in the Roosevelt Administration.

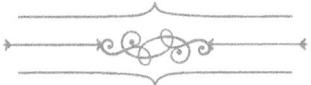

CHAPTER 34 – TWO STRONG WOMEN

They called her "Judge Lucy, though she described herself as a lawyer, politician, and feminist, and not always in that order. She was also seen as a radical in her day for stating that women should have the same access to college, a career, and promotions as society offered men. To that end and in response to harsh criticism, she said, "I glory in being a feminist."

Lucy Somerville Howorth was born in Greenville, Mississippi, on July 1, 1895, to a progressive family in its politics. Her father was an open-minded civil engineer who discussed the day's political issues with his family. Her mother was a temperance and suffrage leader. No to alcohol and yes to the vote… The family emphasized that the young Lucy liked the proverbial fish to water. She said, "My greatest here in life was realizing I could read." In 1912, she enrolled in Randolph-Macon Woman's College in Virginia, where she soon became a leading advocate for suffrage as a member of the Equal Rights Club.

A FIGHTER FOR EQUAL RIGHTS

She majored in psychology and taught for one year at the college. In 1918, she matriculated at Columbia University in New York City for graduate work in psychology. She took time off from her academic pursuits during World War I to work in a war plant. While there, she saw how supervisors terribly mistreated women. The experience left a lasting impression on her.

After the war, Judge Lucy was hired by the Young Women's Christian Association as a research assistant after the Armistice. In that capacity, she reported extensively on the working conditions of women in the textile industry. Again, this experience only hardened her view that women needed protection in the workplace and the ballot to make their voice heard. Coming from an affluent family and a somewhat privileged life, she was forced to confront another world. She said, "It was in New York that I learned to be a whole human being."

In 1919, she changed her major from psychology to law. She applied to the Columbia School of Law and was denied admission because she was a woman. That humiliating experience profoundly affected her. Undaunted, however, she applied for and was admitted to the University of Mississippi in 1920. At the same time, she was, as an aside, present in the gallery to watch the Tennessee legislature ratify the 19th The amendment gave women the right to vote. Two years later, she finished law school. She was tops in her class. Again, as an aside, she expressed a different opinion from the University president. He had banned the teaching of Darwin's Theory of Evolution. She took him to task.

SUFFRAGE

Howorth found it difficult to practice law. Little work came to her, perhaps because she was a woman and not taken seriously. Her legal future brightened when she was appointed the Commissioner (magistrate) of a US District Court. In this role, she had jurisdiction to hear various federal cases, including civil and criminal matters. That's when she became "Judge Lucy."

In 1923, she was caught up in a most unusual situation. Her mother, Nellie Nugent Somerville, became the first woman to serve in the Mississippi House of Representatives. 1931 Lucy Howorth was elected to the House, becoming the only mother/daughter state legislators. Together, they posted a progressive agenda, including gaining state control over the oil industry, creating more state parks, and pushing for a State Game and Fish Commission. This led to an unusual law. The younger Somerville wanted individuals to be able to raise and sell game and fish caught on their private property. Over time, this led to the Mississippi Delta becoming the catfish capital of the country.

In 1932, she worked for the election of FDR. Her efforts caught the attention of the administration. In 1934, she was named to the Board of Appeals of the Veterans Administration. She was the first of three women assigned to this agency. Much of their effort was to provide relief to "vets." She would hold this position until 1943. That year, an administrative rule declared that only veterans could serve on the Board. The three women were terminated. Undeterred by this, Howorth turned her attention to the American Association of University Women (AAUW). She was elected the Chairman of the AAUW Committee on the Economic and Legal Status of Women. In this role, she spoke up for promotional opportunities for women in government and the private sector. She also wanted greater recognition of women in the sciences. She confronted the quota systems that kept women from professional and graduate schools. She also sought advancement status for women in the military. In 1949, her greatest accomplishment occurred when AAUW membership was extended to Black women. All this was in tune with her philosophy of life: "Organizations open doors for women. Advances for women do not happen by accident."

They called her the woman who broke glass ceilings. Nellie Tayloe Ross was the 14th governor of Wyoming, the first female governor of any US state, and the 28th and first female Director of the US Mint. In these endeavors, it is still possible to hear the glass shattering.

THE FIRST WOMAN GOVERNOR

THE WOMAN WHO MADE GOOD

Businesslike—Able—Courageous. She Has Earned Re-election

Ross was born in St. Joseph, Missouri, on November 29. 1876. After graduating from high school, she completed a two-year teacher-training program in college. She then taught kindergarten for two years before meeting and marrying William Bradford Ross, a young attorney aspiring for political office. Her husband was from the progressive wing of the Democratic Party. That meant he stood for lower interest rates to help farmers and ranchers. He wanted lower railroad rates so farmers could sell their crops at a fair price. He also believed the average family needed protection from greedy corporations. Overall, he was a progressive in the tradition of Teddy Roosevelt and Woodrow Wilson. Though he lost many early elections, he finally won one in 1922. He was elected Governor of Wyoming. Two years later, he was dead, the victim of an appendectomy gone wrong. His wife was left devastated. Within a few days, she was asked to run in a special election to replace her husband.

Ross was most reluctant to do so. She had always supported her husband in his efforts to win public office. In doing this, she had learned a great deal about the "sharp elbows" needed in a campaign. Running for office would be more than just providing her husband with support and advice. She wasn't sure she was up to it. She said, "As long as my husband lived, it never entered my head or his that I would find any vocation outside our home." That was one side of the coin. The other was this. She was ambitious, and she was progressive. If she ran, she needed to tread lightly. Again, as she said:

I understood ambition was a quality she'd have to disguise. It just wasn't seemly for a woman to look ambitious."

She finally decided to run, entering the race 45 minutes before the deadline to file. The election was one month away. She refused to campaign. She left that to surrogates who took the fight to the Republicans in the "Equality State." In 1869, the Wyoming Territory was the first government in the world to grant women the permanent right to vote. In 1894, Estelle Reel was the first woman ever elected to a statewide office in the country, doing so in the "Cowboy State." And a month later, Ross became the first female governor in the United States. True to her husband's progressive stance, she promoted banking reform, tax cuts, and legislation to protect miners, children, and women workers in the state. Two years later, she ran for reelection and lost. Once more, she refused to campaign or to end her support for prohibition.

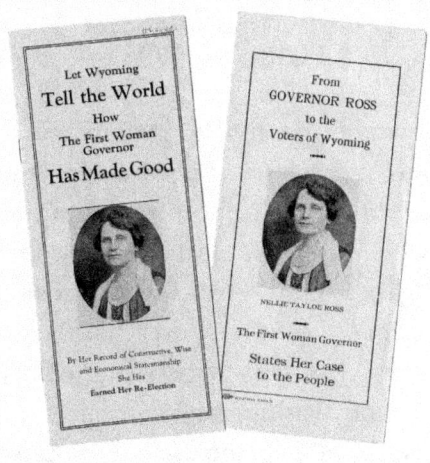

CAMPAIGNING

In 1928, she actively supported Al Smith in his race against Herbert Hoover. Smith lost. She didn't. She served on the Democratic National Committee (DNC) and was the Director of the DNC's Women's Division. In 1932, she worked hard for the election of Franklin Roosevelt. In response, the new president appointed her the Director of the Mint. That was on May 3, 1933. She was the first woman to hold this position. She did so for the next twenty years. Taking over the Mint in the midst of the Great Depression was no easy chore. One of her Wyoming colleagues pointed out, however:

Governor Ross has shown her ability to meet new situations masterfully and I am convinced that she could cut this new path for a woman with distinctions and without any fuss.

FDR AND ROSS

Time would prove the appraisal correct. When she took over at the Mint, there were staff shortages, outdated equipment, and questionable hiring practices. The Mint was in no position to meet the needs of an expanding economy once the New Deal policies took effect. The demand for coins would increase as GNP grew. Over her tenure, she rectified the Mint's problems. In time, she oversaw over 4,000 employees and ran the Mint for two or three shifts while supervising Mints in San Francisco, Denver, Philadelphia, and Washington, DC. She was also responsible for two US Assay Offices in Seattle and New York City. Members of both political parties agreed she ran the Mint efficiently and with a responsible approach to managing the funds the government appropriated for the Mint's operation. Ross's role also included keeping a watchful eye over the Silver Depository at West Point, New York, and the Gold Depository at Fort Knox, Kentucky. During World War II, the Mint's medal department was greatly expanded under her watch to provide military combat awards. And during the war, there was the question of pennies. People were hoarding them in glass jars and piggy banks, a legacy of tougher times. Pennies were made of copper, and the war effort needed this vital mineral. She spearheaded the Mint's efforts to get people to turn in their pennies by buying war bonds and stamps.

Once she retired from the Mint in 1953 she continued to advocate for progressive policies and especially for equality in the treatment of women in the society.

WYOMING HONORS ROSS

CHAPTER 35 – THE DYNAMO

On August 27, 1935, the New Deal did something extraordinary and revolutionary. The Emergency Relief Appropriation Act of 1935 provided funds to the Works Progress Administration (WPA), which sponsored something that had never been done in the United States. An effort would be made to assist unemployed artists, actors, directors, playwrights, and theater workers. The program would be called Federal Project Number One (FPNO). The project would run for about four years before being eliminated by a conservative faction in Congress, which saw the whole effort as socialistic, if not something directly out of Moscow. The fact that the program was fully integrated did not play well in some parts of the South. While it existed, millions of Americans would see live theatre for the first time nationwide. Well over 10,000 artists were employed, and hundreds of plays were produced. All this was done on a budget of about $27,000,000 over the lifetime of FPNO. That was about 0.5% of the WPA's budget of 4.8 billion. At that price, Project Number One was almost a steal. So why end it on June 30, 1839?

One considered review of the program stated the following:

Although the Federal Theatre is far from perfect, it has kept an average of ten thousand people employed on work that has helped to lift the dead weight from the lives of millions of Americans. It has been the best friend the theatre as an institution has ever had in this country.

To a large extent, the program's success depended on who would lead it. That being the case, the FPNO was most fortunate. It was found in a barely five-foot-tall Irish gal who loved the theatre. Her name was Halle Flanagan. At a time when a theater ticket cost $1.10 to $2.10 and a Hollywood movie required $.25, the program opened the doors to live performances at no cost to millions who had never seen a stage play. That was Flanagan. Provide entertainment for the public and relief for artists. As she said:

For the first time in the relief experiments in this country the preservation of the skill of the worker, and hence the preservation of his self-respect, became important.

FLANAGAN AND THE ARTS

Flanagan was born in Redfield, South Dakota, on August 27, 1889. She attended Grinnell College, where she majored in German and Philosophy. She stated the guidelines she would follow at graduation: "College women who go out into the world having gained knowledge, with no love for humanity, have failed." She was determined not to fail. Following graduation, she went to Vassar College, where she eventually became the Director of English Speech, a fancy title for the developing Drama Department, separate from the English Department. While at Vassar, she received a coveted Guggenheim Foundation Award for one year to study theatre in Europe. She was the first woman to receive this award. Upon returning from the continent, inspired by what she saw, she wrote a book entitled *Shifting Scenes of the European Theater* (1928). While her book sales were limited, one New Dealer and former Grinnell College graduate read it. His name was Harry Hopkins. Against stiff opposition in the Roosevelt Administration, he selected Flanagan to head Project One. He didn't want someone from the commercial world of theatre. He wanted an academic. In choosing her, he reminded her of this "whirlwind of energy" that:

This is a tough job we're asking you to do. I don't know why I still hang to the idea that unemployed actors get just as hungry as anybody else.

Hopkins also reminded Flanagan what he wanted in the program: "… a free, adult, uncensored theatre."

Flanagan immediately developed the concept of regional theatres. Plays would be staged in every corner of the country, where common interests would be focused. These interests included geography, language, traditions, culture, and the occupations of the locals. Four main regional centers were operated: Los Angeles, Boston, Chicago, and New Orleans. This was in line with Flanagan's vision:

The far-reaching purpose is the establishment of theatres so vital to community life that they will continue to function after the program of the Federal Project is completed.

Within a year, 15,000 people were hired. They were paid $23.86 per week. They earned their money. They gave up to six weekly performances with only four hours to rehearse daily. Over 200 legitimate theaters were used for the productions. Plays were also performed in parks, schools, churches, clubs, factories, and on closed streets. Approximately 65% of the productions were free to the public. Where tickets were for sale, the price of admission was modest. Though some revenue was generated, the primary purpose was to hire the unemployed. Flanagan allotted to this, saying:

In any consideration of the cost of the Federal Theatre, it should be borne in mind that he funds were allotted according to the terms of the Relief Act of 1935, to pay wages to unemployed people. Therefore, when the Federal

Theatre was criticized for spending money, it was criticized for doing what it was set up to do.

Controversy seemed to follow the program, especially regarding *the Living Newspapers*. Playwrights turned researchers checked the local papers for interesting and important current events. They then turned the daily newspaper into what were called *Living Newspapers*. Almost always, they focused on "hot-button issues," such as housing inequity, syphilis testing, the Tennessee Valley Authority, and farm policy. One example was the play, *Triple-A Plowed Under*. This play focused on the Agricultural Adjustment Act of 1933 and the plight of Dust Bowl farmers. The play took the AAA to task for how tenant farmers and sharecroppers were treated. The play's theme was that farmers and laborers should work together to avoid the "middleman" who had his own commercial interests in mind. One vignette in the play centered on farm foreclosures. Others focused on the deliberate destruction of crops to reduce the supply of farm commodities. Those of a conservative bent saw farmers' organizations as socialist and dangerous.

Another play that rankled some was called *The Revolt of the Beavers*. This play was written for children. It tells the story of two children transported to "Beaverland," where they were forced to work endlessly by a cruel Beaver Chief who sits back and reaps the benefits. In time, the children are involved in a revolt against the Beaver Chief led by a beaver named Oakleaf. The revolt tries to end the exploitation of the beavers. The fantasy fable came under immediate attack by the House Un-American Committee for promoting Communist ideas.

ARTISTIC CHALLENGES TO THE STATUS QUO

Project One and Flanagan really got into hot water with the adaptation of Sinclair Lewis' work, *It Can't Happen Here.* Published as a political novel in 1935, the plot line envisions an American politician named Senator Berzelus "Buzz" Windrip who gains control of the federal government and becomes a dictator. The plot, of course, is an allusion to Adolf Hitler in Germany, General Franco in Spain, and Benito Mussolini in Italy, three fascist demagogues who fomented fear and distrust while promising to "fix" everything once in power. The fictional Windrip appeals to patriotism, loyalty, and traditional American values while denouncing his political enemies. The revolt of the autocratic and reactionary right is opposed by a fictional journalist named Doremus Jessup, but to no avail. Windrip defeats FDR in the Democratic primary in 1936 and defeats a fictional Republican opponent, Senator Walt Trowbridge, in the November election. The play opened on the same day across the country. It challenged the notion that a fascist takeover could never happen in the good old USA. The play was offered in different languages, including Spanish and Yiddish, and played for 260 weeks. Regarding the play, the *New York Times* critic, Brooks Atkinson, said: Thousands of Americans who do not know what a Fascist dictatorship would mean now have an opportunity to find out." As expected, the political left and right had a field day discussing the play's message.

A WARNING FROM SINCLAIR LEWIS

Controversy followed Flanagan in another area. She was intent on demanding diversity and showcasing underrepresented artists. Succinctly, that meant integration. Blacks and white artists would be on the same stage. As a justification, Flanagan pointed to the WPA's guidelines against racial prejudice: "There shall be representation in all national planning." There would be no discrimination in Federal Project One. Her approach to race, as expected, angered many conservatives from the South. The use of all-Black productions disturbed many people. Always swimming against the tide, Flanagan created a Negro Theatre Unit (NTU) in New York City and then expanded it to a total of seventeen cities. The NTU was split into two parts. There was the "Contemporary Branch" that focused on Black issues. The "Classic Branch" performed classic drama. In doing so, over 1,000 Blacks were hired. The NTU in Harlem became the most famous with its productions in the Lafayette Theatre.

In 1936, the NTU produced a blockbuster. It was entitled *Voodoo Macbeth*. The director was Orson Welles. The twenty-year-old Wells reproduced and reinterpreted William Shakespeare's play. The setting for the drama was moved from Scotland to a fictional Caribbean island that reminded people of 18th-century Haiti and Haitian "vodou" that replaced medieval Scottish witchcraft. The cast of *Macbeth* numbered 150. However, only four were professional actors. Rehearsals took six months before Wells was satisfied that the production was ready for a live audience. As the story goes, Wells had initial problems asserting authority over the Black cast and crew. He won them over with his warmth and energy. He also ensured plenty of food and drink at the rehearsals.

Voodoo Macbeth opened at the Lafayette Theatre in Harlem on April 14, 1936. A free preview before opening day brought out crowds. Over 3,000 people could not be seated. The theatre was already full. Talking about opening night years later, Wells said:

> *There were five blocks in which all traffic was stopped. You couldn't get near the theatre in Harlem. Everybody who was anybody in the black or white world was there. And when the play ended, there were so many curtain calls that finally they left the curtain open, and the audience came up to congratulate the actors. That was magical.*

Voodoo Macbeth played for ten sold-out weeks. In time, it toured venues across the country, including Texas, where an integrated crowd watched the show. That was a most unusual experience for Dallas at that time. Wherever the play was performed, it gave many Americans their first opportunity to see a professional performance by Black actors.

ORSON WELLS' MACBETH

OPENING PERFORMANCE

Again, the House Un-American Committee, led by Representative Martin Dies, challenged Flannigan's efforts. In response to all her political critics, she said:

They were afraid of the Project, but not for the reasons they mentioned on the floor of Congress. There were afraid of the Federal Theatre because it was educating the people of its vast new audience to know more about such vital issues of the day as housing, agriculture, and labor. They were afraid --- and rightly so --- of thinking people.

TESTIFYING

In the end, Hallie Flannigan's response was the living legacy of Federal Project No. I.

CHAPTER 36 – THE BROWN CANDOR

The New Dealers, though focused on pulling the country out of the Great Depression, were not immune to what was happening in the world beyond America's shores. This was particularly true of Blacks who were closely watching events in East Africa, adjacent to Somalia and the "Horn of Africa." Their focus was on Ethiopia and its capital, Addis Ababa, and the impending invasion of the last African country that had not been colonized by European imperialism. On August 3, 1935, some 25,000 Blacks and whites gathered on Lenox Avenue in Harlem to protest Italy's plans to invade Ethiopia. The protesters included Black laborers, religious groups, intellectuals, and Communists opposed to fascism in Rome and Berlin. They had lobbied Congress and the White House to pressure Italy's leader, Benito Mussolini, to avoid invading one of the oldest African countries. Especially for Blacks, they saw in Mussolini's attempt to recreate a new Roman Empire in Africa something akin to the slave system undone by the American Civil War. The saw in Rome's attempt to control the Mediterranean under the guise of "Mare Nostrum," our sea, an attempt to oppress people of color in Africa. No distinction was possible between Jim Crowism in the US and the enslavement of an independent, free African people. The Black protests on Lennox Ave reverberated with Blacks demonstrating in Jamaica, Barbados, and Trinidad.

ETHIOPIA AND MUSSOLINI

Why was Italy about to invade an ancient center of Christianity and a country of special significance to Blacks because of the "Black Diaspora?" Rome's argument was reminiscent of other imperialistic powers. Additional colonial territory was needed to consolidate her control of nearby Somalia and Eritrea. The Italian economy needed to be stimulated. A war, it was thought, would do that. Italy's high unemployment rate needed to be lowered. Another colonial possession might provide an outlet for the country's excess population. Ethiopia's raw materials and markets would also fall under the sway of Rome. Hovering in the shadows were two other explanations. Italy had invaded Ethiopia before, and in the Battle of Adwa in 1896, Italian troops had been humiliated by spear-throwing natives. It was time to erase that shameful loss.

BATTLE OF ADWA

A successful second war would expunge that historical outrage. Then, there was the view that Italy was an agent of white rescue. As early as 1927, Mussolini had warned Italians that "white people could face extinction since black and yellow people were at our doors." He claimed that non-whites would end "the hegemony of white civilization." Defeating Ethiopia would implement Italy's fascist vision of "total racial domination."

Italy invaded Ethiopia on October 3, 1935, and declared victory on May 8, 1936. It was a brutal campaign. A modern industrial nation attacked a third-world country still emerging from a tribal past. Italy deployed a million men for the invasion. Only 25% of the Ethiopian military had advanced training and weapons. The disparity of arms and training was seen in Haile Selassie's order for mobilization.

All men and boys able to carry a spear go to Addis Ababa. Every married man will bring his wife o cook and wash for him. Every unmarried man will bring any unmarried woman he can find to cook and wash for him. Women with babies, the blind, and those too aged and infirm to carry a spear excused. Anyone found at home after receiving this order will be hanged.

Atrocities followed in the wake of the Italian army. Low-flying modern planes bombed villages. However, illegal mustard gas bombs were dropped on the natives and soldiers alike. A European doctor with the Red Cross described the gas attacks:

... an oily liquid, dropping like fine rain and covering a huge area with thousands of droplets, each of which, when it touched the tissues, made a small burn, turning a few hours later into a blister. Thousands of soldiers were affected by severe lesions.

Red Cross facilities were destroyed. Concentration camps were built. Though the Ethiopians fought valiantly, it was no contest. Over 380,000 deaths were directly attributable to the war. Another 300,000 people died of privations due to the destruction of villages and farms. And the world essentially stood by and did nothing.

Paris signed a Franco-Italian assistance and peace agreement on January 7, 1935. Already concerned by the rise of Nazi Germany, the agreement seemed in France's interest. The French wanted to maintain this agreement. Criticizing Mussolini and the attack on Ethiopia might jeopardize the relationship. Britain also saw the merit in following suit. In no way did either country want Italy to turn to Berlin in some form of alliance. This appeasement policy was a "blank check" for Rome. There would be no real opposition from London and Paris. This was also true of the League of Nations, of which Ethiopia was a member. The international body passed resolutions condemning the attack. Sanctions were discussed and passed. Oil, in theory, would not be shipped to Italy, and the use of the Suez Canal would be closed to Italian shipping. The sanctions were evaded, and the vital waterway remained open. Ethiopia was isolated.

In June 1936, Haile Selassie went before the League of Nations to state Ethiopia's case. He began by saying:

I am here today to claim that justice, which is due to my people, and the assistance promised to it eight months ago when fifty nations asserted that aggression has been committed in violation of international treaties.

Continuing, he said:

There is no precedent for a Head of State himself speaking in this assembly. But there is also no precedent for a people being victim of such injustice and being at present threatened by abandonment to its aggressor.

He also pointed out the atrocities afflicting his country.

Special sprayers were installed on board aircraft so that they could vaporize, over vast areas of territory, a fine, death-dealing rain. Groups of nine, fifteen, eighteen aircraft followed one another so that the fog issuing from them formed a continuous sheet. It was thus that, as from the end of January, 1936, soldiers, women, children, cattle, rivers, lakes, and pastures were drenched continually with this deadly rain. In order to kill off systematically all living creatures

Speaking clearly and decisively, he concluded his speech.

It is to defend a people struggling for its age-old independence that the head of the Ethiopian Empire has come to Geneva to fulfill this supreme duty, after having himself fought at the head of his armies. What reply shall I take back to my people?

BEFORE THE LEAGUE

The Administration focused on repairing the damaged economic system in the United States. After the Senate rejected the Treaty of Versailles in 1919, Washington never joined the League of Nations. Leaving behind the idealism of Woodrow Wilson, the country was now "Back to Normalcy," with it a series of neutrality laws to hinder involvement in another conflict. The spirit of isolationism was in reaction to the slaughter of the Great War and "Flanders Field." Beyond that, the US had no colonies in Africa. Guam, Cuba, and the Philippines were in the Pacific. Commercial trade with Ethiopia was minuscule. With domestic pressure building up and 1936 being a presidential election year, the president was forced to take a stand. He did so on February 29, 1936.

By the Resolution approved August 31, 1935, a definite step was taken toward enabling this country to maintain its neutrality and avoid being drawn into wars involving other Nations. It provided that in the event of the Executive proclaiming the existence of such a war, an embargo would be attach to the exportation of arms, ammunition, and implements of war destined to any belligerent country. It also authorized the Executive to warn citizens of this country against traveling as passengers on the vessels of any belligerent except at their own risk.

The president's message was crystal clear, regardless of Roosevelt's personal views or the State Department's concerns about appeasement. Ethiopia would receive no assistance from America. Moreover, it was illegal, at least on paper, for US citizens to fight for a foreign power. But that, however, didn't mean Americans couldn't fight with each other. On October 3, 1935, as Italian soldiers poured into Ethiopia, Blacks and Italian Americans brawled in Brooklyn at PS 178. They fought each other with shouts, picks, and pipes. Shortly afterwards, a riot occurred at King Julius General Market on Lenox and 118th Street. This led to the New York Police Department deploying an additional 1200 officers on "war duty." The same situation was occurring in other eastern cities.

Most Italian-Americans admired and supported Mussolini. El Duce had celebrity status in New York City. He wrote a monthly column in newspapers owned by William Randolph Hearst and even made the cover of *Time Magazine.* Mayor Florello LaGardia presented the Italian Consul General with a check for $100,000, money raised by donations from thousands of Italians.

JULY 20, 1936 | JANUARY 6, 1936

African Americans took a different and unique stance. After Italy invaded Ethiopia, a young man from Gulfport, Mississippi, challenged the Roosevelt Administration. His name was John Charles Robinson. In time, he would acquire a nickname, "The Brown Candor." In January 1935, he announced his intention to volunteer to fight in Ethiopia. He did so at a meeting of Black business owners and community leaders. Dr. Malaku Baven, Haile Selassie's cousin, was at the meeting. Impressed by Robinson's impassioned statement and his background as a flyer, he contacted the monarch with a recommendation to hire this Black-American. In April 1935, the monarch wired an official invitation. Robinson was headed to Africa. Before leaving, he encouraged other Blacks to do so. Around the country, others responded to his pleas.

VOLUNTEERING FOR AFRICA

Who was John Charles Robinson? He was born in Carrabelle, Florida 1903, though he spent his early life in Gulfport, Mississippi. He attended Gulfport Colored High School, where he showed an aptitude for machinery and mechanics. Because of racist laws in the state barring high school attendance beyond the 9th grade, he had to leave school. He was, however, able to study mechanical science at Tuskegee Institute. He was also enrolled in literature, history, and composition courses there. From there, he tried to enroll in the Curtiss-Wright School of Aviation in Chicago. Unable to do so, he worked at the school as a janitor. As the story goes, a faculty member recognized his potential and assisted him in becoming the first Black student at the school. He would graduate at the top of his class as a master mechanic in 1931.

What motivated Robinson to assist Ethiopia? He was a flyer, but he had no opportunities to do so in our military or for domestic air carriers. Indeed, the military explicitly denied Blacks from the service. He was also aware of the lynching problem in America and saw in Italy's aggression the lynching of Black people. Ultimately, he wanted to fly for the last independent African nation.

ROBINSON

Once in Ethiopia, he was named commander of the Ethiopian Air Force, which amounted to 20 Potez 25 biplanes that were weaponless. He used the planes judiciously for reconnaissance and supply. In time, he received considerable attention in the Negro Press, especially the Chicago Defender, and through the Trans-radio Press Service. In 1936, he returned to the States and became a catalyst for Blacks in the armed forces, eventually leading to the famed Tuskegee Airmen. He returned to Ethiopia after its liberation in 1943 by the Allies. Once there, he started a pilot training school and played a role in creating Ethiopian Airlines. He died in Addis Ababa on March 27, 1954.

For many African-Americans, the invasion of Ethiopia was personal. White Europeans were again oppressing Africans. What they could do, they would do to aid Ethiopia. Certainly, that was true of John Charles Robinson.

THE BROWN CONDOR

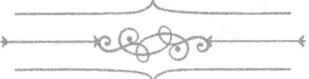

CHAPTER 37 – A ROOF
OVER MY HEAD

In January 1941, President Roosevelt delivered his annual "State of the Union Message." In doing so, he enunciated "The Four Freedoms." The first was freedom of speech. Those listening, regardless of political persuasion, realized the importance of this constitutional right. Every citizen had the right to critique their government without fear of reprisal. It was as simple as that, but sadly lacking in authoritarian-type governments in Germany, Japan, and Italy in the months leading up to Pearl Harbor. The second freedom was freedom of religion. Everyone understood what that meant. You had the right to worship as you chose. Roosevelt declared it so, and the First Amendment to the Constitution backed him up. Again, as Americans understood, this "right" was absent where Fascists controlled police power and exerted control by intimidation and fear. The third freedom was freedom from fear, whether economic in nature or from an oppressive government. The last freedom was freedom from want. Most people understand that this meant a "healthy, peaceful life" emphasizing security and contentment, at least economically. Did you have a job? Was there food on the table? Were a few bucks available for winter clothes for the kids and perhaps a new coat for the wife? And most importantly, was there a roof over your head? In a tremendous sense, this last freedom was called into question by the Great Depression.

FDR MONUMENT IN WASHINGTON

On June 27, 1934, many years earlier, the Roosevelt Administration pushed a revolutionary piece of legislation through Congress. It was called the Wagner-Steagall Housing Act, sometimes better known as the "Better Housing Program." The Act created the Federal Housing Administration, known popularly by the public as FHA, and the Federal Savings and Loan Insurance Corporation (FSLIC). The goals of the FHA were straightforward: (a) making housing more affordable; (b) making mortgages as affordable as possible; and (c) stopping the flood of bank foreclosures and the eviction of homeowners. The main goal of the FSLIC was to protect banks and depositors with a program similar to the FDIC. Together, this bucketful of initials, it was hoped, would create a new foundation for home construction and the mortgage industry.

The housing market in 1932 was in chaos. Half of all mortgages were in arrears. Approximately 1,000 homeowners were becoming delinquent per day. There was a substantial decline in home construction and homeownership as unemployment went through the roof. Banks were "calling" in their outstanding loans because those without a job couldn't meet their mortgage obligations. Following foreclosures, banks acquired depressed properties, the collateral backing the loan. The situation was, to a degree, caused by banking practices. Most home mortgages were of short duration, from three to five years. There were no amortization features. There were often heavy balloon payments due when the mortgage came due, requiring a lump-sum payment. It was almost impossible to refinance a property. As to new homebuyers… They had to make down payments of 40 to 50% of the property's value. Succinctly, it was difficult to keep your home if unemployed and challenging to buy a home because of the down payment factor and high interest rates.

Figure 1

Nonfarm Real Estate Mortgage Foreclosure Rate, 1926–1941

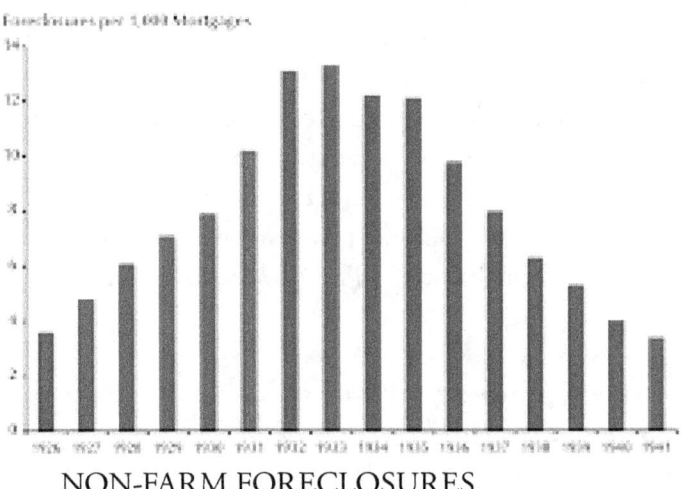

NON-FARM FORECLOSURES

The New Dealers wanted to restart the construction and mortgage industries. That meant banks had to make loans. The federal government had to accept some "risk" to induce the banks to lend funds. The FHA would provide insurance for mortgages from private lenders for various properties, including houses, apartments, and hospitals. The idea was to safeguard the banks from financial loss due to mortgage defaults. The FHA would compensate the lender for the outstanding principal balance. In theory, this would incentivize the banks to originate more loans. Because the risk factor was diminished, the down payments could be reduced to 10% and the mortgage repayment period could be extended to 10 or more years. If all worked out, the housing industry would be stimulated as banks originated more loans and consumers took advantage of lower interest rates. In particular, the New Dealers wanted to see first-time buyers with moderate incomes purchasing a new home. Over time, this proved to be the case, even as adjustments were made to the program.

The New Dealers desired that the FHA and the FSLIC would be "color-blind." That is, all citizens would benefit. There would be no racial or gender discrimination. This was not to be. Built into the two programs was "institutional racism." About that, there is no debate.

The FHA provided the banks with an *Underwriting Manual* to determine what a property was worth and the ability of an individual to repay the loan. Appraisers would be hired to do this. They were instructed to allocate funding to projects "with the highest appraisal values." The FHA required two benchmarks to be considered. The first was the relative economic stability of the property. In the appraisal process, this accounted for 40% of the total. The second benchmark was "protection from adverse influences." This requirement was worth 20%. Precisely what was meant by an "adverse influence?" The *Underwriting Manual* was quite explicit about this.

If a neighborhood is to retain stability it is necessary that properties shall continue to be occupied by the same social and racial classes. A change in social and racial occupancy generally leads to instability and a reduction in values.

Part II   **UNDERWRITING MANUAL**
233-235

social groups are present, to the end that an intelligent prediction may be made regarding the possibility or probability of the location being invaded by such groups. If a neighborhood is to retain stability it is necessary that properties shall continue to be occupied by the same social and racial classes. A change in social or racial occupancy generally leads to instability and a reduction in values. The pro-

Again, what was an adverse influence? The *Manual* spelled it out as "the infiltration by inharmonious racial or nationality groups." The inharmonious groups were Blacks, Asians, Hispanics, and other non-white groups. As a result, the FHA, since federal subsidies for home ownership went almost entirely to white people, promoted racial segregation. To accomplish this, the appraisers adopted a procedure known as "redlining." Red lines were drawn around Black communities on maps. These areas were deemed "hazardous" to any new construction for whites. A rating scale was used to determine how severe the "hazard" was. The scale was A through D. An A rating was the least risky and had a homogenous white population. A D-rating had the most risk and defined Black areas. As described by academics, relining was:

A discriminatory practice consists of the systematic denial of services such as mortgages, insurance loans, and other financial services to residents of specific areas based on their race or ethnicity.

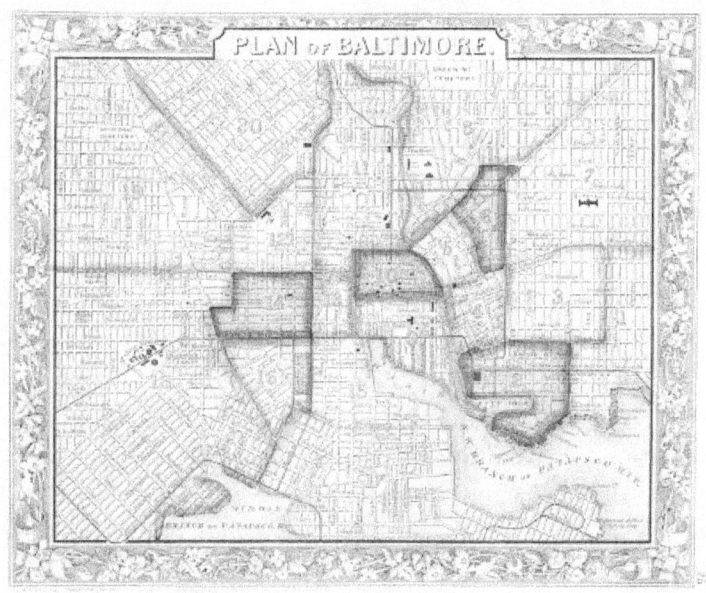

REDLINING IN BALTIMORE

Without doubt, whether consciously or inadvertently, the FHA was fostering practices founded in the South where Jim Crow laws existed to maintain racial segregation in schools and housing. However, in less overt ways, the same results existed in northern states based on de facto practices based on zoning laws, the costs of purchasing a home, and a desire by groups to remain apart. The value of property also entered the picture. The prevailing view in the real estate industry supported this bias.

Redlining practices were sometimes justified on the grounds that the black or minority neighborhoods were poorly maintained and hence homes in them were bad investments. As for the new suburbs, the justification was that if African-Americans bought homes at or near them, the property values of the homes would decline, putting loans at risk---an assertion that had little empirical evidence behind it.

Contractors and bankers abided by the FHA requirements, sometimes in the most unusual ways. In 1940, a contractor wanted to build a housing development near a Black area. The FHA denied insurance to the project. In response, the builder constructed a half-mile-long, six-foot-high concrete wall between the proposed site and the Black homes. The project, now deemed "less risky" by the FHA, received a go-ahead. In some cases, roads and highways were constructed in such a way as to keep different groups apart. Though not under the auspices of the FHA, "existing patterns of segregation were carefully and deliberately engineered and socially engineered by the government."

Of course, one question does arise. What do you do with a Black family that has the funds to purchase a home in a white neighborhood? If the family did move in, the FHA refused to insure future mortgages, even to whites in that community, because the whole area was threatened with integration. To avoid this, many whites had housing deeds that stated outright that the house could only be sold to white people in accordance with FHA requirements. In such cases, the stipulation included a refusal to sell to Jews.

As an aside… In 1957, professional baseball moved from the East Coast to California. The Brooklyn Dodgers landed in Los Angeles. The New York Giants found a home in San Francisco. It was a love affair in both cities. You no longer had to listen to the radio or watch a grainy picture on television. You could see your heroes in person. As expected, the transported players took up residences in their adopted cities. In San Francisco, Willie Mays went looking for a home. It all should have been so easy. The star of the Giants living down the street... Fantastic. A future Hall of Famer playing ball with your kids... What could be better? With cash in hand and a celebrity status, Mays and his wife found a lovely home in an exclusive area called Miraloma Park. The home located at 175 Miraloma Drive was precisely what they wanted, all 3,200 square feet. The home developer seemed delighted to sell to Mays and backed out of the deal. He justified his action, saying, "claiming that his business would suffer if it became known that he had sold a property to a Black man." According to the *San Francisco Chronicle,* "what followed was an embarrassment to a city known for free thinking, in a state and a nation that still did not ban racial discrimination in housing."

Into the fray stepped Mayor George Christopher. Due to Mays' public stature and the adroit arm-twisting of City Hall, an agreement was worked out. The developer reversed positions and sold the home to Mays for $37,500, $5,000 more than the original sale price. Mays accepted the higher cost and moved into his home in an exclusive white neighborhood.

SIGNING THE FINAL PAPERS | WILLIE MAYS

Could the New Dealers have done more to ban racial discrimination in the housing market? Given the nature of housing patterns in the 1930s and the tight control the Southern "block" had on legislation, probably not. The federal government could provide funding through the FHA, but implementation was at the local level, where housing patterns were firmly in place. As with most New Deal programs, the purpose was to provide economic relief for the largest number of people; that is, to assist the white majority population, first and foremost. In the area of housing, the FHA accomplished this task.

The underlying idea behind the program was that by providing insurance to lenders, more individuals would ultimately qualify for mortgages and buy homes. And it worked. Once mortgage lenders knew the government would guarantee their loans, it enabled them to offer more generous terms, like requiring just 20% down and repayment terms of 20 to 30 years. The FHA was successful in stabilizing and then stimulating the national housing markets and extending housing credit to Americans for whom homeownership had once been out of reach.

As a matter of record, over 12,000,000 people were assisted by the FHA during the 1930s. New homes were built, older homes were modernized, and the construction industry thrived. The flip side was that minorities rarely benefited from the FHA programs. Non white-Americans were not eligible to receive insured loans or move into areas that they helped to subsidize through their taxes. The implication of this was significant. Homeownership was a "strong predictor" of educational and economic opportunities. Home appreciation led to equity enhancement over time as the mortgage balance declines. The tax code also assisted the homeowner. Taxes and mortgage interest were income tax deductions as opposed to those renting "temporary space" in an apartment. In the end, the FHA policies, at least until later reforms, led to a "wealth gap" between white and minority communities. Clearly, the FHA was a classic example of institutional racism for which the Roosevelt Administration bears some responsibility.

CHAPTER 38 – NATIONAL PLANNING

A sense of urgency and experimentation colored the first "One Hundred Days" of the Roosevelt Administration. The economy was in a crisis mode. Past efforts by Hoover had failed to stem the economic collapse. Given this, the New Dealers went out on a legislative limb, trying for the first time in American history to regulate on a national level production, wages, and prices during peacetime. On June 16, 1933, Congress passed the National Industrial Recovery Act (NIRA). In time, the public would come to the proposal as the NRA --- the National Recovery Administration. The legislation authorized the president to set production levels in many industries and prices for products and services. The avowed purpose of the new law was to "spark business growth and to improve labor conditions. Almost immediately, the NIRA was challenged by difficult questions.

Would private sector businesses support this government intrusion into the country's capitalistic economy?

Would the unions support the legislation?

Would the farming community get behind the NIRA?

Would it be possible to get cooperative action among businesses to achieve fair and rational competition?

Would "big business" seek advantages over "small companies" in writing the national regulations, and would this inadvertently promote monopolies?

Would it be possible to limit the concentration of wealth and economic inequality through national planning?

Was it possible to stop unrestrained competition through government regulations?

Could the federal government enforce a standard workweek, shorter working hours, and better working conditions?

Would the NIRA actually spur economic recovery?

And most crucially, would such legislation be constitutional?

QUESTIONS

The enacted law was divided into two Titles. Title I was devoted to industrial recovery. It authorized the creation of industrial Codes of fair competition. An essential element was Section 7(a), which permitted collective bargaining rights before the eventual passage of the Wagner Act. Section 7(b) allowed the regulation of working standards, including maximum hours of work, minimum rates of pay, and efforts to enhance working conditions. This did not always work out as planned. Participating industries and labor complained and found loopholes in the legislation, which were used to violate minimum wage and child labor laws.

Title II established the Public Works Administration (WPA) and deficit spending to put people back to work (see Chapter 21).

Under Title I, some 500 industries signed on by midsummer 1933. Over 22,000,000 workers were covered. Approximately 4,500 business practices were prohibited. Some 557 basic and 189 supplemental industry codes were adopted over two years. This amounted to 10,000 pages of governmental involvement in the nation's economy. A federal bureaucracy on steroids was being created. The public face of the Act was the *Blue Eagle* symbol. This insignia was displayed in shop windows across America. It indicated the business was participating in the program, including burlesque theaters in New York City. The show's managers agreed to a code limiting the number of times the strippers would undress each day.

A woman hangs a National Recovery Administration (NRA) eagle emblem in a restaurant window, 1934

From its initiation, the NIRA had critics. In an effort to avoid charges of Socialism, the program allowed each industry to "draw up a code setting production quotas, limiting hours of operation, or restricting construction of new factories." Assuming the president approved a code, there was now pressure on included businesses to comply. In the end, however, there was still enormous pushback against the program. Most of this occurred in the courts, with injunctions and appeals finally reaching the Supreme Court. On May 27, 1935, in the "sick chicken case," the Court ruled the NRA unconstitutional. This judicial decision had implications for other New Deal policies, eventually leading to a "court packing proposal" from the Roosevelt Administration. What follows is a summary of the case that unhinged the NIRA.

Schechter Poultry Corporation v. United States

Argued before the Supreme Court May 2-3, 1935.

Case decided on May 27, 1935

Facts in the Case

The National Industrial Recovery Act, enacted by Congress, allowed the president to regulate specific industries. This would be done by distributing authority to develop codes of conduct among business groups and boards in these industries. The legislation did not provide standards for the president or the business groups in implementing its objectives. The Schechter Poultry Corporation was indicted for violating a business code governing the poultry industry in New York City. The company was convicted of violating the Live Poultry Code. The company appealed the conviction, arguing that the NRA was unconstitutional and in violation of the "non-delegation doctrine." Under this principle, Congress cannot delegate its legislative powers or lawmaking ability to other entities. This prohibition typically "involves Congress delegating its powers to administrative agencies or private organizations." This position is stated in Article 1, Section 1 of the Constitution.

All legislative Powers herein granted shall be vested in a Congress of the United States, consisting of a Senate and House of Representatives...

Background to the Case

The Live Poultry Code fixed the maximum hours a poultry employee could work. It also imposed a minimum wage for such workers. Finally, it banned specific methods of "unfair competition. The Schechter Company bought live poultry from New York City and Philadelphia sources. It then sold slaughtered poultry to retailers and butchers in Brooklyn. The government claimed that unfit chickens were sold and that the Schechter brothers were selling chickens individually. Further, the government argued that the company avoided inspections by local poultry regulators and that records were falsified concerning poultry sold to agents without a license to purchase poultry. This led to a conviction in a federal court for the sale to a butcher of an unfit chicken. Because of this, the whole business was described as the "sick chicken case" in the New York newspapers.

The company was charged with violating "straight killing" codes established by the NRA. Straight killing "prohibited customers from selecting the chickens they wanted. Instead, a customer had to place his hand in the chicken coop and select the first chicken he touched. The government argued that many customers could avoid this process so that rabbis could certify the chicken in question as kosher. As an aside… The Schechter brothers were Jewish. They were serving a mainly conservative and orthodox Jewish community. In Yiddish, Schechter meant "slaughter." In the case of poultry, they sold it, which is referred to as "ritual slaughter.

The Question Before the Court

Did Congress unconstitutionally delegate legislative power to the President by allowing him to regulate specific industries without providing guiding standards?

Decision

In a unanimous decision, the Court held for the Schechter Brothers. In a majority opinion written by Charles E. Hughes, the Court stated that the NRA was "without precedent" and was an unconstitutional delegation of legislative authority." The Chief Executive cannot have unbridled control over whatever laws he believes are necessary to achieve a specific goal. The NRA did not establish rules or standards to evaluate industrial activity. This meant Congress failed to provide the essential guidelines for implementing this functional legislative process.

The Court said the NRA allowed the president to write Codes to regulate "unfair competition." The Court found the phrase "unfair competition" too ambiguous to constitute an "intelligible principle" necessary to limit the president's actions in enforcing the NIRA. The president could not have "unfettered discretion."

The Court also held that the Codes violated the Constitution's Commerce Clause. Congress can regulate interstate commerce but not intrastate commerce. Though the Schechter Brothers bought the poultry from out of state, the offense was confined to New York State. The company's activities fell outside of congressional power. This was an in-state situation.

THE DEFEAT OF THE NRA

As expected, the New Dealers were unhappy with the Court's decision. Constitutional issues had the potential to derail a host of New Deal programs. Following his landslide reelection in 1936, FDR pushed back against the Court. At that moment, he was at the height of his political power before Pearl Harbor. He had carried every state but Maine and Vermont. The Congress was overwhelmingly under Democratic control. The Houses were 331 to 89. In the Senate, the numbers were equally astounding, 76 to 16. Given such political power, Roosevelt felt it was time to deal with the Supreme Court.

Specifically, he wanted judicial rulings that didn't undermine his efforts to end the Great Depression. He wanted the Court to rule that his programs did not exceed the government's constitutional authority. In short, he wanted more favorable rulings from the Court, not another "sick chicken" fouling up his agenda. In the simplest of terms, the president had his fill of conservative justices blocking his New Deal legislation.

THE CONSERVATIVE COURT

On February 5, 1937, during a "Fireside Chat," he shocked the nation with a proposal to expand the Court by adding more judges. He felt he could do this based on the Judiciary Act of 1837. This federal statute increased the size of the Supreme Court from seven to nine justices. It also reorganized the circuits of the federal judiciary. Since the Constitution did not define the size of the Supreme Court beyond requiring a Chief Justice and additional associate judges, Roosevelt's legal advisors felt there was precedent for adjusting the Court's size.

What would that mean in practice? The president could nominate one additional judge for every member of the Court over 70 who refused to retire. To entice them to do so, the president included a juicy carrot. The pensions of justices would be increased substantially. Six of the justices were over 70. In theory, the president could appoint up to six justices. The Senate would still have to confirm all nominees. The White House considered this an attempt to reform the court, not to attack it. Either way, nine men in robes were caught in the middle.

On March 9, 1935, FDR spoke directly to the American people. In his ninth Fireside Chat, he challenged the Supreme Court's majority for "reading into the Constitution words and implications that were not there, and which were never intended to be there." That position was soon a matter of public dispute and division. He also said that his legislation was needed to overcome "the Supreme Court's opposition to the New Deal. This, of course, was a purely political charge, partisanship injected into the debate in what was now called Roosevelt's "Court Packing Scheme." With heightened rhetoric, the president said, "the nation had reached a point where it must take action to save the Constitution from the Court, and the Court from itself."

In 1935, the nine justices included:

<u>Conservative Justices Moderate Justices Chief Justice</u>
Pierce Butler (71), Louis Brandeis (80), Charles Evans Hughes (75)

James C. McReynolds (77) Benjamin Cardozo (67)
George Southerland (75), Harlan Stone (64)
Willis van Devanter (77)
Owen Roberts (62)

THE SUPREME COURT - 1937

At first, the public supported the White House's proposal, but only at first. The push back came from all quarters, including Democrats. Later Gallup polls indicated only a slight majority for changing the Court's size.

For many Americans, the Court was sacrosanct. They didn't want political motivations tinkering with it. The American Bar Association opposed the plan. Conservatives came together in opposition. The National Committee to Uphold Constitutional Government was launched in 1937. It was distributed in 15,000,000 letters, challenging the plan. Of that number, 161,000 materials went to lawyers, 68,000 went to business leaders, 137,000 went to the clergy, and 121,000 were sent to doctors.

Support within the party loyalists was divided. Unions and farm blocks had concerns. Was a potentially dangerous precedent being set? The Vice-President, John Vance Garner, opposed it. Henry F. Ashurst, the Democratic Chair of the Judiciary Committee, delayed hearings. His view was "no waste, no worry --- that is the motto of this committee." The untimely death of Majority Leader Joseph T. Robinson complicated things. He was the staunchest Democrat for the proposal. As the legislation moved to the Senate for confirmation, the pushback against the president went viral.

In the Senate, the New Dealers were going against history and tradition. Attorney-General Cummings made an argument for the Administration. His position rested on four points: first, the Court and the judicial system was besieged with the reckless use of injunctions by those who opposed the New Deal; second, injunctions hindered the operation and implementation of New Deal legislation; third, Court was afflicted by the presence of aged and infirm judges who refused to retire; and fourth, there was a need for reform to infuse new blood into the federal court system.

These arguments proved insufficient to sway the Senate. The president's plan died in committee, but not before a scathing critique. The end came in June 1937.

This bill is an invasion of judicial power such as has never before been attempted in this country. It is essential to the continuance of our constitutional democracy that the judiciary be utterly independent of both the executive and legislative branches of the government.

The battle was over. The president had misjudged the American public and the forces arrayed against him. The court-packing scheme was a political disaster. FDR had overreached. The public gave him a very public spanking.

Court Plan Believed Doomed By Van Devanter Resignation And Adverse Committee Vote

Paradoxically, because of his four victorious campaigns, the president was able to name five new justices during his tenure, permitting the "Roosevelt Court" to expand the government's role in the economy and civil rights. The New Deal would live on.

CHAPTER 39 – THE COURT DECIDES

The Supreme Court found itself in an unusual position in the 1930s. On the one hand, the aging jurists were confronted by the Roosevelt Administration to rule favorably on challenges to the New Deal programs. On the other hand, the issues related to racial discrimination and segregation were percolating through the lower courts and in need of adjudication by the Court. In these cases, the question of equal treatment under the law was emphasized in the Fourteenth Amendment. Four instances in particular drew the attention of the Court:

Smith v. Allwright (1944)
Hall v. Kentucky (1938)
Norris v. Alabama (1935)
Murray v. Pearson (1936)

SMITH V. ALLWRIGHT

Lonnie Smith was an African-American dentist in the Fifth Ward in Harris County, Houston, Texas. Smith was a graduate of Maharry Medical School in 1924. He was well-liked in the community, where he provided services to both Blacks and whites. In 1944, he attempted to vote in the primary election as a registered Democrat. He was denied that opportunity. At the time, Texas permitted both political parties to restrict who voted. In the case of the Democratic Party, it could conduct a race-based primary where only whites could participate. At the time, Texas defined a political party as a private entity authorized by the state to determine its requirements and procedures. Succinctly, Texas permitted the political parties to "set their own internal rules." This meant that "white-only primaries were permissible."

That White Supremacy Must Be Maintained in Primaries

Legislators Asked To Consider Only Election Laws

News of the Day in Brief

Charleston

News and Courier

15 April 1944

S.S. Allwright was the chief Harris County election official. Smith sued the county for the right to participate in the Democratic Party primary election. In doing so, he challenged a 1923 state law that authorized political parties to establish internal rules. The case worked through the lower courts until it reached the Supreme Court. The case was argued on January 12, 1944. On April 3, 1944, the Court rendered its decision. The states may not permit or conduct race-based primary elections and must be open to voters of all races." In this 8-to-1 decision, the Texas laws permitting such primary elections were declared unconstitutional. The state could no longer designate and/or delegate its authority over elections to private parties to allow discrimination to be practiced. The Democratic Party could no longer "effectively exclude minority voter participation." Legal disenfranchisement was stopped in Texas and wherever "white-only" primaries existed.

The key question before the Court was whether or not states had the constitutional right to deny voter participation based on party membership. The Texas constitution stated, "Every person qualified by residence in a district or county shall be deemed a qualified voter." Though the Texas Democratic Party was a "voluntary association," it was not protected from State interference if "fair methods and fair expression were not permitted in the nomination of its nominees." Given this, an earlier Texas case was thrown to the wind as was its contention that:

All white citizens of Texas who are qualified to vote under the Constitution and laws of the State shall be eligible for membership in the Democratic Party and as such entitled to participate in its deliberations.

The Supreme Court declared that the Texas Democratic Party was not independent from the state and was free to make policies where state and federal elections were involved. No political party was independent of the State. It could not delegate this authority to a political party. "White-only" primaries were abridging Smith's rights under the Fifteenth Amendment (right to vote) and the Fourteenth Amendment (equal protection under the law). In stating the majority opinion, Associate Judge Stanley Reed said:

A state could not nullify the right to vote by casting its electoral process in a form that permits a private organization to practice racial discrimination in the election.

Lonnie Smith would be able to vote as a member of the Democratic Party.

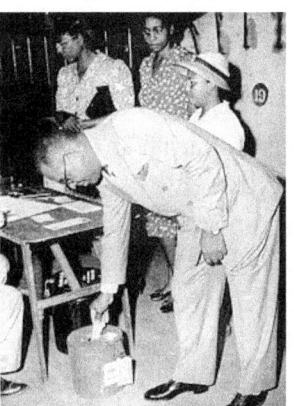

As an aside, Smith's lead attorney was Thurgood Marshall, who worked for the NAACP Legal Defense Fund. Marshall would later become the first African-American justice on the Supreme Court.

THURGOOD MARSHALL

HALE V. KENTUCKY

On August 18, 1936, a murder was committed around 11 pm in Paducah, Kentucky. Joe Hale was arrested for killing W.R. Toon. He was convicted of the murder and sentenced to death in 1936. He was 19 years old at the time. The verdict was appealed. The lower court judgment was confirmed. The NAACP took the case to the Supreme Court. The Court heard the case on March 29, 1938, and reached its decision on April 11, 1938. The Court held that Hale was not provided equal protection under the laws guaranteed to him by the Fourteenth Amendment.

This case involved who sits on a jury. Therefore, it is related to racial discrimination in the selection of juries for criminal trials. The Court held that the State of Kentucky had systematically excluded Blacks from serving on juries.

Hale was convicted in McCracken County, Kentucky. Approximately 48,000 people lived in the country. Over 8,000 were Black. About 6,000 whites were eligible to sit on a jury. Less than 700 Blacks were eligible, and no Black was selected in the trial of Joe Hale. Indeed, no Black had been chosen over the past fifty years. Blacks had been systematically and arbitrarily excluded from the jury lists. No Black had been summoned for service on a grand or petit jury in the county. Nor were the names of any Black placed in the hands of the Sheriff of the County for summoning.

There had been a "long, continuing, unvarying and wholesale exclusion" of Blacks. However, no Black had been excluded because he was not "intelligent, sober, discreet, and an impartial citizen." In a few instances, Blacks served in a federal court at Paducah. The obvious was true. Blacks had been excluded based on color. In a unanimous decision, the Supreme Court held that "the plaintiff's civil rights had been violated." No Black was on the jury that convicted Joe Hale. His conviction was overturned. He was retried in 1938 and was convicted of a lesser crime for which he received a life sentence.

NORRIS V. ALABAMA

The story begins with two dozen young black and white teens "hoboing" on a freight train traveling between Chattanooga and Memphis, Tennessee. Along with them were two young white women. What took place on that train on March 25, 1931, led to an infamous trial known in American jurisprudence's annals as the Scottsboro Boys' trial. It also focused on a judicial system impeding the presence of Blacks on juries. All of the facts in this case reached the US Supreme Court on February 15, 1935. The Court reached a decision that was rendered on April 1, 1935.

Background:

Apparently, a scuffle occurred on the train between the two racial groups. It was not determined who instigated the fight, though the white teens had yelled This is a 'white man's train." The struggle ended when the white teens were forced off the train. Humiliated by this, they went to the local white sheriff, stating they had been attacked. In response, the sheriff deputized a posse and stopped the train at Paint Rock, Alabama. Nine young Black teens were arrested for starting the fight and raping the two women.

THE SCOTTSBORO NINE

Those accused included:

Charles Norris (age 19)   Ollie Montgomery (age 17)
Charlie Weems (age 19   Willie Robertson (age 16)
Andy Wright (age 19)   Roy Wright (age 12)
Eugene Williams (age 13)   Ozie Powell (age 16)
Haywood Patterson (age 18)

Victoria Price (age 17) and Ruby Bates (age 21) were the women involved.

RAPE VICTIMS?

The nine blacks were indicted in early March 1931 in Jackson County, Alabama, for the crime of rape. Word of the arrest and rape spread like wildfire. A lynch mob gathered at the jail in Scottsboro. The mob demanded that the youths be surrendered to them. In response, Sheriff Matt Wann refused to give up his prisoners. He telephoned Governor Benjamin M. Miller, requesting assistance. The governor mobilized the Alabama National Guard to protect the jail. Shortly after, the Sheriff took the defendants to Gadsden, Alabama, under heavy guard. There, the nine Blacks waited for an indictment and a trial.

The trial was conducted with tight security. Some 118 Alabama guardsmen armed with machine guns escorted the prisoners to the courthouse. Access to the courtroom was only by permit. The courthouse seats were for whites. Standing room was only for Blacks. The pace of the trials was fast to avoid violence. The first trial took one and a half days for Charles Norris. The second trial for the remaining youths took one day. As the Supreme Court later said:

The proceedings occurred in a tense, hostile, and excited public sentiment.

Eight of the nine were convicted of rape and sentenced to death. This was in line with the prosecutor's closing statement:

If you don't give these men death sentences, the electric chair might as well be abolished.

As to the defense, the judge ordered the Alabama Bar Association to assist the defendants. Milo Moody, a 69-year-old attorney, was appointed. He hadn't defended a criminal case in over a decade. To assist him, Stephen Roddy was appointed. He was a real estate attorney from Chattanooga and unfamiliar with Alabama law. Technically, the defendants had representation. In a practical sense, the defense could only be called shoddy at best. Things were also complicated by the judge's refusal to change venue.

The medical examiner disputed the charge of rape. He could find no evidence of rape. There was no vaginal tearing to indicate a rape. Initially, the women had said nothing about a rape to the Sheriff. That accusation only came out after cross-examination. There was no evidence of rape beyond the testimony of the women. Some surmised the women were trying to divert attention away from themselves since they were suspected of being prostitutes. If proven, they could be prosecuted for violating the Mann Act by crossing a state line "for immoral purposes."

The Black community was appalled by the decision to execute the young men. They made their feelings known.

The case was appealed and later came before the US Supreme Court. It was one of several cases linked together where the issue of "all-white" juries needed adjudication. In that regard, Norris v. Alabama was the lead case. Clarence Norris claimed that jury selection had systematically excluded Blacks due to racial prejudice. A disproportionate number of Blacks lived in the county compared to the number of Black representatives on juries. In the 8-to-0 decision authored by Charles Evans Hughes, Norris's conviction was overturned since Blacks were unlawfully excluded from the jury.

The prosecution had violated the "equal protection clause" of the Fourteenth Amendment. Essentially, the Court was saying that "racial diversity and proportionality were an expectation in the courtroom." The Court also pointed out that the defendants were denied a fair trial due to ineffective counsel who had no time to really prepare a defense, thereby violating the "due process" clause of the Fourteenth Amendment. It was also determined that Victoria Price and Ruby Bates, the alleged victims, made up their story "out of thin air."

Clarence Norris was not executed, nor was any of the other eight black teens. Norris did, however, spend fifteen years in jail before receiving a pardon from Governor George Wallace in 1976. He lived until 1989. He was the last survivor of the Scottsboro case. As to the others... The Alabama State Legislature passed a resolution recommending a posthumous pardon for all the defendants against whom charges were not dismissed. The legislature also passed a resolution declaring all the Scottsboro boys innocent.

MURRAY V. PEARSON

On January 24, 1935, Donald Gaines Murray sought admission to the University of Maryland School of Law. He was a highly qualified graduate of Amherst University. He would have been the first African-American in the law school if he had been accepted. His application, however, was denied based on race. Gaines' rejection letter said:

The University of Maryland does not admit Negro students, and your application is accordingly rejected.

THE PLANTIFF

The University said it had a duty to follow the "doctrine of separate but equal" enunciated in Plessy v. Ferguson (1890). Therefore, the State of Maryland had to help Murray study elsewhere, including a law school in a different state. The problem was, however, that in the State of Maryland, there was no statutory provision for scholarships or aid to enable a Black to attend a law school outside of Maryland. In response, Murray appealed his case to the University's Board of Regents. The Regents again refused Murray admission to the law school.

On June 26, 1935, a lawsuit was initiated against the State of Maryland and the University of Maryland. The strategy promoted by Thurgood Marshall of the NAACP was to "attack the separate equal doctrine" by using the equal protection clause of the Fourteenth Amendment. It was argued that Maryland had failed to provide separate but equal education for Murray. There was no comparable law school in the state for Blacks. If this were the case, the plaintiff should be allowed to attend the white-only law school. This resulted in the Circuit Court issuing a writ of mandamus ordering Raymond A. Pearson to admit Murray to the law school. Pearson was the president of the University of Maryland.

MARSHALL AND MURRAY

The ruling was immediately appealed to the Maryland Court of Appeals. This Court affirmed the lower court ruling in a unanimous decision. The Court's decision was straightforward:

The State has undertaken the function of education in the law but has omitted students of one race from the only adequate provision made for it, omitting them solely because of their color. If those students are to be offered equal treatment in the performance of the function, they must, at present, be admitted to the one school provided.

Going on the Court said:

The Fourteenth Amendment to the Constitution requires a state to "extend to its citizens of the two races substantially equal treatment in the facilities it provided from the public funds. To single out a specific portion of the people by the arbitrary standard of color and to say that these shall not have the same rights that are possessed by others, denies them the equal protection of the laws.

The case never went to the US Supreme Court. The decision did not outlaw segregation in Maryland, but it did set a precedent. If the state chose to only provide one law school for students, the school had to be available to all races. This ruling was not binding outside of Maryland. Murray graduated in 1938 and went on to practice law in Baltimore.

MITCHELL V. US

Arthur W. Mitchell resided in the state of Illinois. He was a Democrat and the only Black in the House of Representatives. In need of a rest, he decided to take a two-week vacation in Hot Springs, located in Garland County, Arkansas. He purchased a first-class railroad ticket from Chicago's Illinois Central Railroad Company. He began his trip on April 20, 1937. He transferred to the Chicago, Rock Island and Pacific Railroad in Tennessee. He had requested a Pullman sleeper coach. As the train crossed the Mississippi River and entered Arkansas, the conductor, one Albert W. Jones, proceeded to collect fares. He was surprised to find a Black person in the "white-only" section. He directed the Congressman to move to the "black" section.

MITCHELL

The conductor acted under Arkansas's Separate Coach Law of 1891, which covered all 2,063 miles of track within the state. The conductor was obligated to do this by law. He could be fined $25 to $50 if he didn't. Passengers who refused his instructions could be fined from $10 to $200. Initially, the Congressman refused to move. He said he was Arthur W. Mitchell, a US House of Representatives member. In reply, the conductor said:

It doesn't make a damn bit of difference who you are --- as long as you are a nigger you can't ride in this car.

The conductor threatened to stop the train and have Mitchell arrested if he didn't move to the "colored section." To avoid this, the Congressman moved to the "colored" section. His luggage, however, remained in the white section. The train arrived in Little Rock, Arkansas, where the Mayor and the Chamber of Commerce welcomed Mitchell. He never mentioned what had happened.

Once back in Chicago, Mitchell sued the railroad for personal damages in the amount of $50,000. He also filed a complaint with the Interstate Commerce Commission (ICC). He claimed the accommodations for Blacks did not meet the "separate but equal" standard required by the Plessy v. Ferguson decision in 1890.

Mitchell described the Black only section as such:

The car was divided by partitions and partly used for carrying baggage. It was also poorly ventilated, filthy, filled with stench, and odors emitted from the toilet and other filth, which was indescribable.

He pointed out:

The toilet for colored women flushed. That was not always true of the men's toilet. The car was without soap, towels, or running water except for the women's section.

He then noted in his testimony:

By comparison... The white cars were in excellent condition, modern, air-conditioned and equipped with hot and cold running water, soap, and towels, along with flushable toilets for both men and women. Also, first-class passengers had sole use of his only dining and observation car.

Mitchell described the language of the conductor as "too opprobrious and profane," and vulgar to be spread upon the records of the Court.

The ICC dismissed Mitchell's complaint, voting 7 to 5 against him. The ICC said, "The discrimination and prejudice were not unjust or undue." The case next went to the District Court for the Northern District of Illinois. Again, Mitchell's complaint was dismissed. The Court said:

The small number of colored passengers asking for first-class accommodations justified an occasional discrimination against them because of their race.

Mitchell then appealed to the US Supreme Court, where he presented his oral arguments himself. The court rendered its decision on April 28, 1841, four years and seven days after the original incident. Chief Justice Charles Evans Hughes wrote the unanimous opinion for the Court, beginning with an uncontested declaration.

This was manifestly a discrimination against him (Mitchell) in the course of his interstate journey and admittedly that discrimination was based solely upon the fact that he was a Negro.

The Chief Justice then took on the question before the Court:

The question whether this was a discrimination forbidden by the Interstate Commerce Act is not a question of segregation but equality of treatment. The denial to appellant equality of accommodation because of his race would be an invasion of a fundamental right that is guaranteed against state action by the Fourteenth Amendment.

The Court reversed the US District Court's decree and directed that the ICC order be set aside.

As an aside, it wasn't until January 1956 that segregation on interstate transportation ended on America's railroads. It wasn't until 1973 that the Arkansas General Assembly finally repealed the Separate Coach Law of 1891. Mitchell's lawsuit against the railroads led to a settlement. He received $3,750 plus court costs. Because of his legal challenge to upend "separate but equal," he angered many white voters in his congressional district. His political career was over.

CHAPTER 40 – RIOTS

Unfortunately, not all cases concerning justice and fairness were settled in the courts in the 1930s, nor were issues related to civil rights. Equally, no court could end bias and prejudice, along with the emotions of anger, frustration, and hate. No judicial members in black robes could undo how people had been raised and what they thought of others. No learned court ruling could stop rumors and an incident that would explode in the streets. The wisdom of the courts could not prevent a riot.

1935 – New York City

His name was Lino Rivera. He was sixteen years old, Puerto Rican, and black. As the story goes, he stepped into an S.H. Kress "five and dime" store in Harlem. The store, in a mainly Black area on Manhattan Island, catered to folks on a tight budget. It was also known for its reluctance to hire Black clerks. An employee of the store accused the teen of shoplifting a $.10 penknife. Employees in the store threatened to take Rivera into the basement and "beat the hell out of him." He resisted and hit the hand of one of the employees. The manager intervened and called the police. New York's finest arrived and interviewed Rivera, who was soon released. Outside the store across the famed Apollo Theater, a crowd had gathered. A Black woman saw store employees searching the teen. She became hysterical and shouted, "The prisoner was being beaten by his captors." This was not the case. The boy had not been harmed. A few minutes later, an ambulance showed up. That confirmed what the onlookers thought. The ambulance was there to pick up a badly beaten Black youngster. Soon, a rumor spread that the kid was actually dead. The ambulance was there to help the employee with the injured hand. All this led to the "first modern race riot in American history." The date was March 19, 1935.

After releasing Rivera, the police arrested the woman for "disorderly conduct" who had provoked the crowd. The store was quickly closed down, and the crowd was dispersed. To head off future trouble, the police decided to get Rivera to show that he was unharmed. That didn't prove easy at first. He had given the police a false address, and it took time to locate where he lived with his mother. He would appear before the public the next day to ward off any future disturbance.

ALIVE AND WELL

During the night, the Young Liberators planned a demonstration for the next day. However, about 6:00 p.m., rioting broke out. *The New York Times* described the incident:

Roving bands of Negroes, with here and there a sprinkling of white agitators, stoned windows, set fire to several stores, and began looting. By 1:30 a.m. the worst of the rioting was ended, but sporadic outbreaks occurred up until 4:00 a.m.

The next day, a crowd of 10,000 gathered at 235 W. 135th Street, where the Kress store was located. Handbills were distributed that provoked the crowd. One said: CHILD BRUTALLY BEATEN. Another said "the teen was only 12 years old and brutally beaten for taking a piece of hand." At some point, someone threw a brick through the store window. This led to the destruction of the store and adjacent local businesses. To avoid this, some stores put signs saying, COLORED HELP EMPLOYED HERE. The rioting photographs of Rivera were distributed throughout Harlem to prove the boy was alive. The Mayor's Office drew up posters for the same purpose. Before March 20, 1935, over 100 people were injured, and 125 rioters were arrested. Three people died. Approximately $200 million in damage was recorded. Only Black homes and businesses were spared.

The New York papers headlined what had happened.

Order was restored the next day. Mayor Florello LaGuarda set up a multi-racial Commission on Conditions in Harlem. A report entitled A Report on Social and Economic Conditions Responsible for the Outbreak was later submitted to the Mayor. The Mayor chose not to release the report to the general public. Reporters, however, for the *Amsterdam News*, a Black newspaper, gained access to the report, which was eventually published in serial form. Upon reading the Commission's report, a professor at George Mason University coined the phrase, "the first modern race riot." Professor Jeffery Steward defined the characteristics of the riot as: (a) violence against property, not individuals; (b) an absence of violence between racial groups; and (c) a conflict between poorer Blacks and the police.

Though the Mayor suppressed the report, he took positive steps to assist those in Harlem. More Blacks were included in the city government. The city hospital was integrated. Efforts were made to improve sanitation, health care, and police protection in the area. Unfortunately, the Mayor couldn't alleviate the long-term problems of Harlem's residents, mainly racial injustice in all of its odious manifestations. The 1935 riot was but a forerunner to riots in 1943 and 1964.

THE MAYOR

1943 – New York City

It all began at the Braddock Hotel in Harlem on August 1, 1943. Florine Roberts and her son, Robert Bandy, were outside the hotel when they witnessed an altercation between a police officer and a young Black woman. The woman was Marjorie (Margie) Polite. The officer was James Collins. He was stationed in the hotel lobby because the military had designated the area as a "raided premise." It was thought to be a place where prostitution took place, catering to military men. Precisely what happened has been a matter of dispute. One version was that Polite was dissatisfied with her hotel room and raised a very loud fuss. Another view concerned a tip of $1.00 that she had given to the elevator operator, and now she wanted it back. Still another take was that she was drunk and confronted the officer after she left a party. In any event, her actions caught the attention of Officer Collins. According to the official report, she was abusive to the officer. At that point, she was arrested, and things spun out of control.

Bandy, who was in the US Army, witnessed the arrest along with his mother. The mother asked for the young woman's release. Again, the official report stated that Bandy threatened Officer Collins. In the scuffle that followed, Bandy hit the officer and then fled. As he did, he was shot in the shoulder by the police officer. The wound turned out to be superficial. He was taken, however, to Sydenham Hospital for treatment. A small crowd of Blacks followed him to the hospital. A larger crowd of about 3,000 people gathered at the local police precinct: somehow, a rumor got started that Bandy was dead. This precipitated a riot that lasted two days and led to six deaths, hundreds of injured people, and nearly 600 arrests.

Crowds of angry Black citizens congregated at the hospital, the police station, and the hotel. At 10:30 p.m. that night, someone threw a bottle off the roof into the crowd at the hospital. The inflamed crowd dispersed in groups of 50 to 100 people, and the riot was on.

ANOTHER RIOT

Streetlights were broken. White mannequins from stores were stomped on in the streets. Grocery stores were raided for war-scarce items such as coffee, sugar, and liquor. Over 1400 stores were burglarized. Some 4495 windows were broken. The total monetary damage was between $250,000 and $5,000,000, depending on how the damage was calculated. All the characteristics of a riot were present: vandalism, theft, and property destruction. White-owned businesses in particular were damaged. There was little violence outside of Harlem.

Once again, Mayor Fiorello LaGuardia needed to restore order to Harlem. Over 6000 city and military police were called in to end the rioting. Over 8000 National Guard troops were prepared to contain the riot if called upon. Traffic was directed around Harlem to limit the riot area; that is, to keep the violence from expanding beyond the Black neighborhoods and, of course, to avoid conflict between races. All taverns were closed after 2:00 a.m. All of Harlem came under a strict curfew. By August 2nd, the order had been restored, but at a price. It was impossible to stop bloody clashes between Blacks and the police.

CONFRONATIONS | CURFEWS

Once more, the Mayor did what he could to quiet the situation. City workers cleaned up and repaired buildings. Sanitation workers took three days to set things right. Loads of food were brought into Harlem until the expected delivery was possible. That would be until August 6th. The New York City Department of Buildings and Housing boarded all the broken windows. In all cases, a police escort was assigned to all public workers. As in the 1935 riots, the hospitals were organized to care for the injured. By August 4th, traffic was permitted through the area. Taverns were reopened on the 6th.

Again, there was a commission to determine why the riot occurred. The obvious was again noted. There was resentment among the Black residents of Harlem because of the disparity between the avowed values of American democracy and the economic conditions that Blacks were forced to endure. President Roosevelt had announced the Four Freedoms as the goals of the war: freedom from fear and want, and freedom to speak and worship by everyone everywhere in the world, with one exception, it seemed in Harlem. There was resentment against the brutality and discriminatory treatment from the primarily white police department. There was resentment against the segregation of Black and white soldiers in the military. There was resentment against discriminatory practices in civil and private employment. There was resentment against any real effort to reverse the situation.

What did it all add up to? Bandy became a momentary symbol of the failure to treat Blacks fairly. Collins represented the white discrimination and suppression that Blacks endured each day.

1941 - Detroit

Here's a question for you. Have you ever heard the name Isabella Baumfree? Probably not... A few hints... She was an abolitionist before the American Civil War and a civil rights activist after the conflict ended. She also advocated for women's rights and agitated for the Temperance Movement to outlaw liquor. Nothing is ringing a bell. Perhaps a few more clues will help. She was born into slavery in 1787 in Swartekill, New York State. In 1826, she escaped from her enslaver with her daughter. Two years later, she won a court judgment to recover her son. This was the first case in our history where a Black woman won a case against a white man. Once the Civil War commenced, she helped to recruit Black men to join the ranks of the Union Army. She met President Abraham Lincoln during the terrible conflict on Saturday, October 29, 1864. Apparently, she told the president:

Mr. President, when you first took your seat, I feared you would be torn to pieces like Daniel in the den of lions. Then, if the lions did not tear you into pieces, I knew God would save you and has done so, and now I am here to see for myself.

A last clue... She was the first Black woman to have a statue in the Capitol Building. Nothing coming to mind... Time to share... In 1843, she changed her name to Sojourner Truth. Now for the question of the day... How was it possible for this kindly and determined woman of color to cause the Detroit Race Riot of 1943, some 60 years after she died in 1883?

WITH THE PRESIDENT

The Project

Detroit had a problem in 1941. It did not have enough housing for the influx of defense workers, whether Black or white. Ford and General Motors had shifted from producing automobiles to building trucks, jeeps, tanks, and airplanes. Thousands had moved to Detroit for jobs and better pay. The Detroit Housing Commission (DHC) and the US Housing Authority (USHA) proposed a plan to construct 200 units for Black families to alleviate the situation. The project aimed to be located in northeast Detroit, near an existing Black community. It was hoped that the two-story red brick row houses would avoid controversy by being located there. That was not to be. The problem with the *Sojourner Truth Project* was that it was also close to a white community.

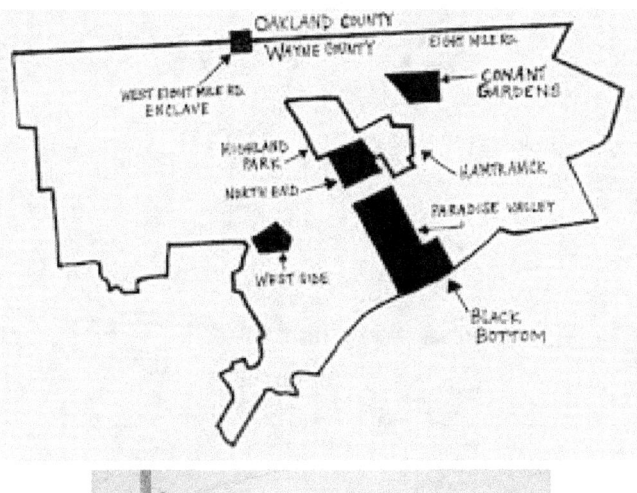

THE SOJOURNER TRUTH PROJECT

The reaction to the project was both immediate and persistent. White residents were outraged that subsidized housing for Blacks was being built. The Mayor's Office was picketed, as were other local and state offices. Congressional representatives were inundated with letters, phone calls, and telegrams. Local housing associations materialized almost out of thin air. The pressure from white homeowners, many of whom were from the South and segregationists, was unceasing.

The DHC and the USHA were caught in the middle. The defense industry needed Black workers, a great many of whom were also from the South, where they were impoverished and oppressed. Things worsened when the Federal Housing Authority (FHA) entered a combustible situation. It declared it would not finance or refinance any new construction in areas adjacent to a Black area. This racist policy incited even more opposition to the project. The DHC and the USHA caved to the white homeowners and their motto: "Rights to Protect, Restrict, and Improve the Neighborhood." The *Sojourner Truth Project* would be designated a housing project for white-only occupancy.

Opposition to this flip-flop was direct and immediate from civil rights activists, many unions, pro-public housing groups, and the Roosevelt Administration. A change in designation was made. Blacks would live in the project.

On February 18, 1942, the first Black families moved into the *Sojourner Truth Project*. Some 1500 state troopers were present to keep the peace. Even with the heavy military presence, hundreds of whites flooded into the area to protest, some violently. Over 200 arrests were made, mainly of white citizens. Their segregationist cry was that they didn't want any "change in the racial patterns of the neighborhood." They threatened to oppose any more projects if some were to be considered. Clearly, the legacy of the project fueled an ongoing anger and resentment that burst forth two years later.

The passions of the moment did not dissipate when Blacks moved into the project. Only an incident was needed for a riot, and it came soon enough.

The Detroit race riot began on June 20, 1943, and continued through June 22nd. Over 6,000 federal troops would be called in to stop the disorder. Some 34 people were killed. Twenty-five were Black. The mainly white Detroit Police Department killed most. Over 400 people were wounded. Of that number, 75% were Black. The extensive property damage reached $2,000,000 or $30,000,000 in today's dollars. Most of the rioting took place in a Black neighborhood called Paradise Valley. It was the poorest area of the city.

The riot was caused mainly by factors such as the migration of over 400,000 people to the city in a short span. In 1941, the city's population was 1,623,452, of whom 150,000 were black. By 1943, Detroit's population reached 2,000,000. Many whites came from agricultural areas, including Appalachia. They brought with them their Southern prejudices and a legacy of Jim Crowism. Defense-related jobs drove the Black migration, leaving behind economic and political oppression. The city's infrastructure was overwhelmed by this influx, including newly arrived immigrants from Eastern Europe. Housing these newly arrived groups was beyond the city's capacity. Blacks were crowded into existing Black areas. One was called Paradise Valley, a 60-block area east of Woodward Avenue. The housing was older and substandard. Landlords exploited the situation. Blacks were forced to pay 2 to 3 times more than families in less dense city areas. The city was a tinderbox of ethnic and racial animosities.

On June 25, 1941, President Roosevelt issued Executive Order 8802. It prohibited racial discrimination in the national defense industries. The order was applied "irregularly." This meant that Blacks were often excluded from skilled jobs and supervisory positions. For example, Ford Motor Company hired Blacks. Ford employed half of all Blacks in the auto industry. Approximately 12% of his workers were Black. The company worked with local Black ministers to identify the potentially best Blacks for jobs. The ministers served as an unofficial screening device to provide the company with reliable long-term workers in labor-intensive jobs. Blacks and whites got along reasonably well. This was not true at the Packard Motor Company. In 1943, the company promoted three Blacks to work on the assembly line next to whites. The company was following Roosevelt's Executive Order. In response, 25,000 workers walked out in a "wildcat strike." The white strikers wanted to control specific jobs. They didn't want to take orders from Blacks. Many whites didn't want to work next to Blacks. White women didn't want to share a bathroom with Blacks. Crudely, they said that Black women "think their fannies are as good as ours."

Tensions were running high in the city. Only an incident was necessary to cause an explosion. Two rumors spread throughout the city in June 1943. The first rumor was that a group of whites had thrown a Black mother and her child into the Detroit River. On June 20th, a rumor spread that Blacks had raped and murdered a white woman on the Belle Isle Bridge. Armed whites invaded Paradise Valley, which, in this instance, did not live up to its name. Everywhere, Blacks were beaten as they got on or off streetcars. Innocent motorists and pedestrians were attacked. Groups of whites set out to kill Blacks. In addition, there was considerable property damage to Black businesses. Blacks did fight back, but generally they were outnumbered and outarmed. Photographs of the day captured the violence.

VIOLENCE

RIOTING

In the aftermath of the riot, both Blacks and whites, as might be expected, blame the other. The white rioters tended to be younger and unemployed. If working, they had semi-skilled positions. They purposely traveled long distances across the city to hunt down Black Paradise Valley. They, as did Blacks, claimed that "one of their own had been attacked unjustly." In some cases, whites entered the city to engage in the violence. The Blacks tended to be older and, in many cases, had lived in Detroit for at least a decade. Since the rioting was concentrated in Black neighborhoods, Black property was disproportionately looted and destroyed. Mayor Jeffries and Governor Harry Kelly asked President Roosevelt to intervene. He responded by invoking the Insurrection Act of 1807. Some 6,000 troops were sent to the city to bring order. A curfew was enforced, and the military now occupied the city's streets. Order was restored.

MARTIAL LAW

The Mayor and most white citizens blamed young Black, unemployed hoodlums for starting the riot. They concluded that other Blacks had entered the city for that purpose. City officials concluded:

Negro hoodlums started it, but the conduct of the police department, by and large, was magnificent.

TROUBLES IN DETROIT

The Kelly Commission agreed. Set up to determine who actually started the riot, this mainly white entity fixed blame on young Blacks, stating that "unattached, uprooted, and unskilled misfits within an otherwise law-abiding Black community were at fault." This view was based primarily on police reports. Few Black rioters were interviewed. Other reports suggested that "Blacks from the South were predisposed to violence." Black leaders were blamed for not heading off the violence. What wasn't included in the report was a history of daily animosity directed at Blacks by the police, along with a lack of minorities in the police force. Discrimination in housing and jobs was not mentioned, nor was the exploitation of Black tenants by landlords in Paradise Valley.

Future Supreme Court Justice Thurgood Marshall was with the NAACP at the time. He challenged the city's handling of the riot and its placement of fault on blacks. He said:

The police unfairly targeted blacks while turning their backs on white atrocities. Eight-give percent of those arrested were black while whites overturned and burned cars in front of the Roxy Theater with impunity as police watched. The weak-kneed policy of the police commissioner coupled with the anti-Negro attitude of many members of the force helped to make a riot inevitable.

James J. McClendon was the Detroit NAACP President. He, too, took issue with the Kelly Report.

We do not condone the acts of hoodlums of our race any more than you condone those who overturned cars, ran down defenseless and enacted other acts of violence on Woodward Avenue. Had more police been stationed on Woodward Avenue rather than concentrated throughout the Negro area, there would not have formed such a gigantic mob of 10,000. It takes no crystal gazer to add the score of Negroes slain by the police or compared the lack of such 'shoot to kill' policy on Woodward Avenue. Where do we go from here?

That was indeed the question before Detroit in 1943, as it would be for future disturbances. Was it possible to avoid the stark headlines of the Detroit Free Press?

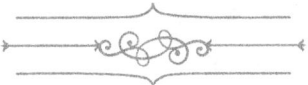

CHAPTER 41 – MISCALCULATION

All presidents take credit for a strong economy and a nation at peace. However, when the economy turns sour or the country feels threatened by outside forces, the DNA of the Chief Executive is to find blame elsewhere than in the White House. President Roosevelt was kin with most politicians who are loath to accept responsibility when things go south. Such was the case in 1937 when the economic gains of the first four years sputtered and sharply declined. That situation is often called "the recession within the Great Depression." The painful events would last 13 months from mid-1937 through most of 1938. With control of Congress and an incumbent in the White House, there was no way the Democrats could absolve themselves of some complicity as the shadows of 1929 hung in the political air.

If nothing else, FDR was a politician who believed in the premises of American capitalism and progressive policies to alleviate distortions in the business cycle. He adhered to a free market and the individual's worth in sorting through his own life, yet was willing to use the power of government to deal with economic disruptions beyond the ability of the average citizen to resolve. Though he was willing to experiment, he was also a pragmatist. Would something work? Would the public support him? Would Congress pass the needed legislation? Always a shrewd calculator of the political risks and benefits, FDR was at heart a cautious leader, always factoring into his decisions the political realities he faced. That, however, didn't mean he couldn't make a miscalculation.

By 1937, the GNP, though not yet as robust as in 1929, was certainly doing better and moving toward a self-sustaining consumer economy. For many in the Administration, " light was at the end of the economic tunnel." As the 1936 presidential election beckoned, the Roosevelt Administration was increasingly concerned about the ongoing federal deficits. The president decided to rein in fiscal policy. Austerity would be the new mantra. He would strive for a balanced budget. He believed the economy was on a "stable recovery path and that further government stimulus programs were unnecessary." Deficit spending to stimulate the economy would be severely reduced; government spending would be decreased by 17%. A balanced budget was now the goal. In retrospect, these actions proved harmful to the economy. By 1938, the government was forced to reverse its policies. Deficits were back in vogue again. The specter of long unemployment lines required a policy change.

A REPEAT OF 1929?

Fiscal policy was altered, and so too was monetary policy. Acting out of concern for rising inflation and to limit banks' risky investments, the Federal Reserve increased reserve requirements for banks. This had the effect of limiting the money supply, increasing interest rates, and discouraging business expansion. As anticipated by the Fed, the economy slowed down.

The Revenue Act of 1937 also occurred at the same time. It increased corporate and personal income taxes while individuals were now contributing to Social Security for the first time. On a macro level, this led to a decrease in disposable income. In short, people had less money to spend. Once more, the net effect was reducing company profitability as sales declined. Consequently, corporate investment and expansion were reduced and sometimes stopped altogether. Invariably, this led to increased unemployment.

The Keynesians in the Roosevelt Administration were alarmed and voiced their sentiment to the president. They felt it was premature to balance the budget and reduce government spending when a consumer-based economy was on the horizon. From their perspective, the budget deficits were insignificant and needed to continue. They pointed out that the deficits had only averaged 3% per year. Succinctly, they felt the economy was not yet out of the woods, and this was the wrong fiscal policy. Concerning monetary policy, the deficit spenders, yeah, "foul." They claimed "cheaper" money was an economic stimulus and was needed. Again, they argued that increased interest rates would hinder progress.

The president and the Fed were not oblivious to criticisms of fiscal deficits. Conservatives howled that the New Deal was too hostile to business, especially in its efforts to rein in monopolies through the threat of antitrust enforcement. They also claimed that the Administration was too friendly to unions and what they called "big labor." Moreover, conservatives pushed back against government intrusion into the private sector, and in many cases claimed the New Dealers were socialists at heart.

To a degree, polls were favorable to conservatives. A Gallop Poll in 1937 asked this question: "Do you think the Roosevelt Administration's attitude toward business was delaying a business recovery?" By a two-to-one margin, the public said yes. However, a Roper Poll in the same year to almost the same question found a different result: 39% said yes; 37% said no. As with all polls, how a question was asked and who was asked affected answers.

The 1937 recession has been called a "recession within a depression." The GNP fell 11%. Unemployment increased from 12.3% in 1937 to 19% by 1939 compared to 25% in 1932. Industrial production declined by almost 30%. The output of durable goods fell through the floor.

Producers reduced expenditures on such goods, and inventories declined. As expected, consumer purchases fell off as joblessness increased, all a sign of decreasing consumer confidence. Personal income fell by 15% and the stock market by 40%. The economy was stagnating. The charts below indicate the decline in the real GNP and industrial production for the years 1937-1938.

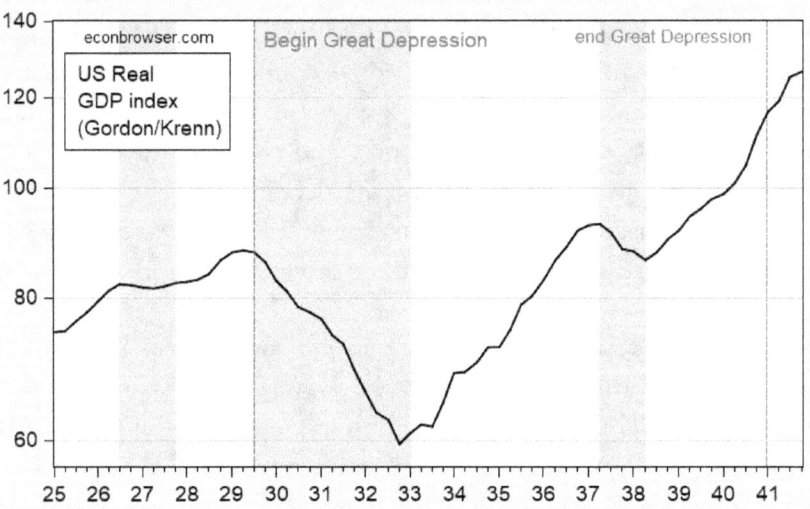

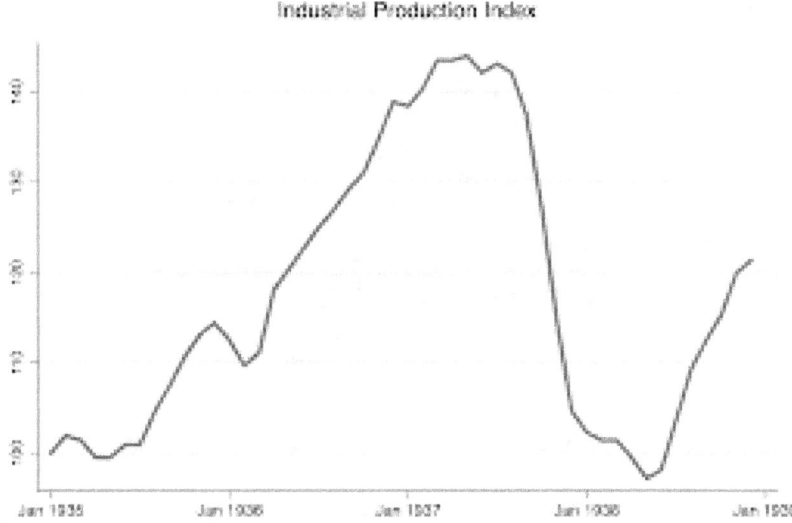

Industrial Production Index

The country was experiencing a "recession within a depression," a most unusual set of circumstances. President Roosevelt was forced to alter his policies, leading to the "Second New Deal. " The White House lobbied for a $5 billion spending program for public works, especially highways and bridges. At the same time, the Fed was pressured to reduce its reserve requirements. Deficit spending was again in the saddle, and the monetary spigots were open. Increasing the money supply and reducing interest rates counteracted the deflationary pressures caused by the recession. Through this action, the Fed encouraged lending and spending while attempting to keep inflation under control. The Keynesians supported the policy shift, not the $5 billion stimulus package. They would have preferred far more.

The reversal in policies pushed back against the recession. The unemployment rate declined. Personal income increased to almost 1929 levels in the aggregate, but not on a per capita basis. Though the farm population fell by 5%, the actual farm output increased by 19% in 1939. But was the consumer-based economy on a sustainable path? That, as always, was the question. What was not in question was FDR's determination to intervene. As he said in a Fireside Chat:

It is up to the government to create an economic upturn by increasing the nation's purchasing power.

ALWAYS THE GREAT FEAR

In pushing Congress for a new stimulus package, the president argued that "big business" was trying to ruin the New Deal by causing a steep economic decline. As the argument went, this would assist the Republicans in the 1938 congressional elections. Roosevelt referred to what he called a "capital strike" by corporate American "economic royalists" and "Sixty Powerful Families" in America. He claimed there was a conspiracy by those who supported monopolies and felt hindered by government regulations and antitrust legislation. The president's views were bolstered by the publication of a book in 1937 entitled *America's 60 Families*. Ferdinand Lundberg, known as an "iconoclastic journalist and writer, wrote the book. His analysis of wealth and class in America led him to the conclusion that, "for purposes of political and economic power," these families worked together in a "plutocratic circle" to influence the economy and the nation's political institutions. He was describing what he called a "cartel of families or individuals that controlled most of the wealth in the United States." By way of example, he charged that William Randolph Hearst had "fascist ambitions, abetted by an unholy alliance of big bankers."

Over a year before the 1937 recession, President Roosevelt accepted the Democratic Party nomination for a second term in Franklin Field, Philadelphia. The date was June 27, 1936. More than 100,000 people had crowded into the stadium on the University of Pennsylvania campus. The evening sky was finally clear of rain, and a "cloud-veiled moon" was in the sky. In his speech, Roosevelt attacked the "economic royalists." His words were direct.

The economic royalists complain that we seek to overthrow America's institutions. They really complain that we strive to take away their power. Our allegiance to American institutions requires the overthrow of this kind of power.

The president provided a short history lesson for those in attendance and the millions listening on the radio.

The fathers of the Republic had achieved political freedom from the eighteenth-century royalists, so it was the function of those who stood with him in this campaign to establish the economic freedom they also sought to establish, which was lost in the industrial and corporate growth of the nineteenth and twentieth centuries.

He then explained the problem facing Americans:

A small group had concentrated into their own hands an almost complete control over other people's property, other people's money, other people's labor --- other people's lives. For too many of us life was no longer free; liberty no longer real; men could no longer follow the pursuit of happiness.

Continuing, he said:

The royalists of the economic order have conceded hat political freedom was the business of Government, but they have maintained that economic slavery was nobody's business. They granted that the Government could protect the citizen's right to vote, but they denied that the Government could do anything to protect the citizen in his right to work and his right to live. Today we stand committed to the proposition that freedom is no half-and-half affair. If the average citizen is guaranteed equality opportunity in the polling place, he must have equal opportunity in the market place.

The president finished his speech, proclaiming:

The brave and clear platform adopted by this Convention, to which I heartily subscribe, sets forth that Government in a modern civilization has certain inescapable obligations to its citizens, among which are protection of the family, and the home, the establishment of a democracy of opportunity and aid to those overtaken by a disaster.

The president's speech was both an explanation and a justification for the New Deal. More than a year later, the "Recession of 1937" challenged the veracity of those polices implemented by the New Dealers. It also provided an opportunity to adjust and evolve in dealing with changing economic conditions. The Roosevelt Administration would not make the same economic miscalculation again. There would be no more recessions within a depression. Acute joblessness would not return under the New Dealers whether the power and influence of the nation's aristocracy was broken remained in dispute.

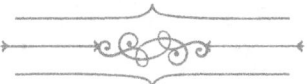

CHAPTER 42 – REARMAMENT

Contemporary historians and economists have questioned whether the New Deal ended the Great Depression. Popular public understanding is that World War II did so, and not the efforts of the Roosevelt Administration. The New Dealers would agree there were still millions out of work in 1940. They would also note that only about 75% of plant capacity was utilized that year. They would also acknowledge that the economy was not self-sustaining at its highest possible level based on consumer demand and domestic peacetime production. Statistically, the country still didn't match the robust numbers 1929, just before the economic collapse. All that was true.

So what did the New Deal accomplish before Pearl Harbor? First and foremost, the Roosevelt Administration provided relief to those most hammered by the loss of jobs. However, in perfect, the Federal Emergency Relief Act of 1932 showed that the federal government would no longer sit on the sidelines while millions were in despair as the American Dream" disappeared before their very eyes. An alphabet of experiments would lead the way, some more successful than others: the PWA, the CWA, the CCC, the AAA, the TVA, the SEC, the NLRA, the FHA, and the NRA. Ultimately, these programs provided relief, a degree of recovery, and generational reform. Here, Social Security, along with the Wagner Act and the Federal Deposit Insurance Corporation, come to mind. Much of this was accomplished through deficit spending and implementing Keynesian economic theories to stimulate the economy. That's where the country stood in 1940, with Europe at war and the Pacific about to boil over.

As to the impact of World War II… Though Nazi Germany, fascist Italy, and Imperial Japan were on the march in the 1930s, American public opinion clung to the notion of neutrality. Americans did not want to go to war. They had had enough of that in France in 1917. That, however, did not mean they wanted to be unprepared for war. With the loss of France and the German invasion of Poland, public attitudes toward isolationism and rearmament changed dramatically. America would have to go on a partial wartime footing.

This change was supported by events in Europe and Asia and carefully worded messages from FDR. Concerning the numerous neutrality laws that hampered assisting Britain and China in almost every manner, the President had to move slowly, never getting too far ahead of public opinion. As he said:

It's terrible to look over your shoulder when you are trying to lead and find no one there.

On another occasion, he said:

My problem is to get the American people to think of conceivable consequences without scaring the American people into think that hey are going to be dragged into war.

By 1940, the president was convinced that:

Hitler was responsible for Europe's drift toward war and might be bent on world domination. He was no longer casually confident of a British and French victory.

Once France fell and England stood alone the president took a more strident stance, telling the American people:

You must master at the outset a simple but unalterable fact in modern foreign relations between nations. When peace had been broken anywhere, the peace of all countries everywhere is in danger.

Mindful of the sacrifices of WWI, millions of Americans preferred staying out of the war engulfing Europe. The president was caught between the isolationists and the interventionists. As late as June 1941, Americans were split on what the nation's foreign policy should be. Most citizens were aware of the paradox facing the White House. Was it possible to aid China in Asia against the Japanese, and Britain in her struggle with Nazi Germany, without being forced into war?

THE ILLUSION OF SECURITY

After France fell to Hitler's troops on June 20, 1940, and before Japan attacked Pearl Harbor on December 7, 1941, the president sent a clear message to the American people that he had first enunciated in 1937.

After all, if Italy and Japan have developed a fighting technique without declaring war, why can't we develop a similar one?

Rearmament was necessary. Doing so meant deficit spending. Billions would be spent. As one historian wrote:

The enormous public works project known as World War II saved the economy and the New Deal by finally providing fiscal stimulus adequate to the economy's needs.

However, here the issue becomes cloudy. There is a vast difference between a command economy directed by the government in wartime and a peacetime economy sustained by consumers, not government military contracts. Almost 10% of the workforce was conscripted into the military at a compensation rate well below normal wages. Over 36% of the GNP was devoted to producing military-related goods. As such, the military had first claim on resources. Inevitably, the production of consumer goods was reduced. That being the case, the wartime economy, though it all but eliminated joblessness, was an economy based on "sacrifice" since normal consumption was severely curtailed. This situation could not be avoided. As stated by one historian:

Meeting the challenges of war required massive government spending, the conversion of existing industries to wartime production, the construction of huge new factories, changes in consumption, and restrictions on many aspects of American life. Government, industry, and labor needed to cooperate. That was the cost of being the "Arsenal of Democracy."

The wartime economy in the United States diverted nearly 40% of the total labor force into military-related employment and the production of mountains of guns and ammunition. Due to the deteriorating military situation in Europe and Asia, the US instituted the Selective Service Act of 1940. It was the country's first peacetime draft. In 1940, 18,633 men were inducted into the armed services. In 1941, the number rose to 921,842. In 1943 and 1944, over 3,000,000 citizens were conscripted. Others enlisted to avoid conscription. All men between the ages of 21 and 35 must register with local draft boards. Ordinarily, these men would have sought jobs in a peacetime domestic economy.

Those not drafted now used scarce resources to make weapons as the country converted to a wartime economy. By way of example… Lingerie factories now make camouflage netting. Baby carriages gave way to field hospital food carts. Lipstick cases became bomb cases. Beer cans have now become hand grenades. Adding machines became automatic pistols, and vacuum cleaners were turned into gas masks. Where General Motors, Ford, and others had made cars, they now produced trucks, jeeps, tanks, personnel carriers, and planes. Everywhere, plants no longer produced consumer goods as they had, and those produced were rationed.

WARTIME PRODUCTION

America had become the "Arsenal of Democracy."

Rationing was imposed, and the public could only buy a small quantity of food and gasoline. Unnecessary personal consumption was curtailed. The "miracle of production" reflected wartime needs, deficit spending, and the unavailability of consumer goods. A common refrain from storeowners to consumers was, "Sorry, but there's a war on." Rationing went into effect in 1943. People were issued ration books. Rationing covered milk, vegetables, eggs, poultry, and meat products, where people were limited to 28 ounces of meat per week. Sugar would be rationed from May 1942 through June 1947. Abiding by the rules was considered everyone's patriotic duty.

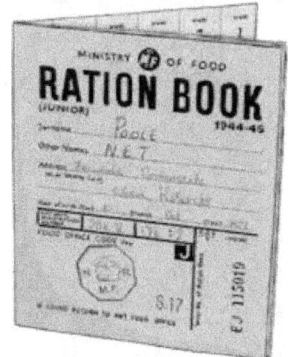

The neutrality grip on the Roosevelt Administration was powerful, pervasive, and supported by an isolationist view held by millions. What was needed was an incident that would shatter America's willingness to avoid war. That incident occurred on December 7, 1941, when the Japanese attacked the American naval base at Pearl Harbor in Hawaii. From that date that will, as FDR said, "live in infamy," the United States entered a global conflict.

Now there were jobs for everyone, men, women, and teens. In 1939, military purchases accounted for only 2% of the GNP. By 1944, it was 40%. Of necessity, this meant work for women and Blacks. Unemployment rose from 14.6% in 1940 to 1.2% in 1944. In that period, the GNP surged. It grew from $91 billion in 1939 to $126 billion in 1941, then to $214 billion by 1945. By 1944-1945, the United States would account for 40% of all war goods produced worldwide. Not counting those in the military, the civilian workforce increased by 8 million to 54 million between 1939 and 1945. National income increased from $73 billion in 1939 to $183 billion in 1945. However, little could be spent on consumer goods. The sale of war bonds increased, as did savings accounts. Those future dollars would be spent once the war ended and pent-up demands needed to be satisfied.

The necessities of war required all Americans to pitch in. Overt racism could no longer prevent military production. That was the reality faced by the New Dealers as the nation converted to a wartime economy.

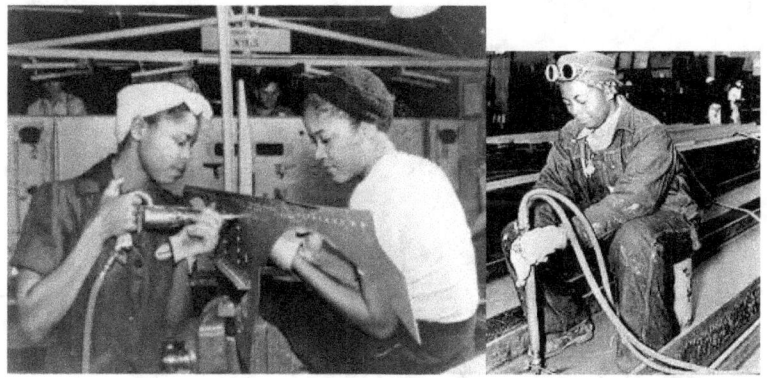

JOBS FOR BLACK WOMEN

IN DEFENCE OF THE COUNTRY

All out production… One example was the shipyards run by Henry J. Kaiser. Using mass production methods perfected by Ford and General Motors, he built Liberty Ships. Initially, it took 365 days to make one seagoing ship, a truck, or a railroad on the ocean. These nondescript ships were necessary to bring the equipment of war across the Atlantic and to the far regions of the Pacific. Ungainly and a prodder at sea, they were one of the keys to winning the war. It only took 92 days, then 62 days to build a Liberty Ship. Kaiser constructed one ship in one day to capture the nation's attention. How did he do it? Different sections of the vessels were built in separate plants. The sections were brought together and then united in a final location in California. It was the assembly line for ships.

A LIBERTY SHIP AND THE VISIONARY

Kaiser noted that many of his workers were women with children. Caring for the kids took priority at times. He remedied that by providing 24-hour childcare centers that included what was later called "early childhood education." Indirectly, the government subsidized the centers. While the moms worked the night shift, the kids slept. In the daytime, trained helpers watched over the little ones. This was especially helpful to economically lower-class families. Kaiser also noticed that his workers took off when they were ill. He responded to this by providing medical clinics to keep his workers healthy. After the war, he envisioned such services for the general public.

Another example was ALCOA, the Aluminum Company of America. Though it had a near monopoly in this necessary airplane product, the federal government chose not to enforce antitrust rules or engage in class warfare by supporting unions, especially anything causing work stoppages. As Secretary of War, Henry L. Stimson said, "I would rather have more sinful aluminum now than good aluminum too late for the war." Washington did, however, help finance a competitor, the Reynolds Aluminum Company. Both companies continue to this day.

The war, of course, had to be paid for. Where bitter battles had been fought over the price of New Deal programs, funds were spent almost without question to prosecute the war. Where the New Dealers had often dueled with corporate leaders, war enforced a truce. The government would direct the war. Corporate America and the private sector would build the sinews of war. "Dollar-a-year men" were business executives sitting on government commissions to help promote policies providing both guns and profits. The government often financed new plants and equipment that businesses leased and purchased after the war at discount prices. There was, however, a wartime tax on excess profits to prevent unseemly profits.

How would the war be financed? Federal expenditures rose from $9 billion to $98 billion between 1939 and 1945. During that period, the government spent $300 billion. That was twice as much as in the entire history of 1789. For three straight years, the government spent $50,000,000,000. Less than 50% of the cost was financed by taxation, even though there was a considerable increase in taxable individual incomes from 4,000,000 in 1939 to 43,000,000 by 1945. To deal with this, a withholding system was introduced by the Revenue Act of 1942, and for the first time in In American history, individual income taxes exceeded corporate taxes. The New Dealers could only look on with envy at this torrent of cash that was generally unavailable to them in the 1930s.

Still, more funds were needed to pay for the war. Borrowing was, of course, the answer. War bonds were issued with a promise by the government to repay the premium with interest in a prescribed period. War bond drives occurred each year of the war. Bonds could be purchased in denominations from $25 to $1,000. Over 85,000,000 Americans would buy $185,000,000,000 in bonds. This partially helped because Americans had money but few consumer goods to purchase. With wage and price controls, surtaxes, and rationing, store windows were bare—cash accumulated. Investing in the war through bond purchases was both patriotic and ultimately profitable.

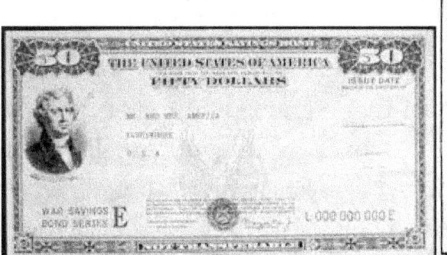
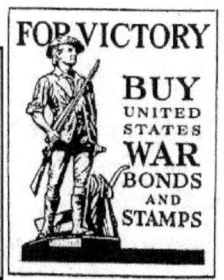

On October 27, 1944, President Roosevelt gave a Navy Day speech. In it he paid homage to America's industrial might and those who made it a powerful force in winning the war. He said:

I need not repeat the figures. The facts speak for themselves. These men could not have been armed and equipped as they are had it not been for the production miracle here at home. The production, which has flowed from the country to all the battlefronts of the world, has been due to the efforts of American business, American labor, and American farmers working together as a patriotic team

We are still left with the question: Did the war end the Great Depression? As a war economy, the answer was yes. There was no question about that. On a macroeconomic level, all the statistics were good (see chart below). Employment was down. Production was up. Personal savings had increased. The problem was that it was a wartime economy, not one based on personal consumption.

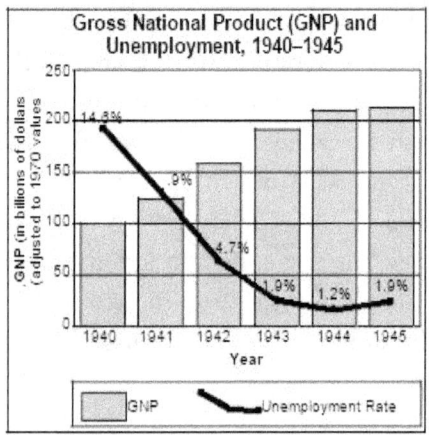

Source: *Historical Statistics of the United States,*
U.S. Bureau of the Census

What would happen when the war ended? What would happen when the government reduced its purchases of military supplies? What would happen when 10,000,000 young men reentered the labor force? What would happen when the war contracts ended? What would happen to female workers when the men went back to work? That question also applied to

Blacks? In summary, would the wartime economy revert to a peacetime, consumer-based economy without slipping back into a depression?

The answer proved a resounding yes. Americans emerged from the war with a pent-up demand for unavailable or severely rationed products. People were ready to buy new cars, appliances, and homes with cash or on credit. Americans were about to go on a spending spree. Initially, demand was greater than supply, and inflation took off. As plants converted to peacetime production, the supply-demand balance came into play. Uniformed men came home to start families, even as they took advantage of the GI Bill that promoted education and home purchases. The conditions were present for sustained postwar growth. Economists generally agree that:

In 1946, civilian output increased about 30%. This was the most glorious single year in the entire history of the US economy. By 1948, real output was on a long-term growth trend.

Unlike Europe and portions of Asia, America emerged from the war unscathed physically. European countries in particular needed to be rebuilt. Cities were in ruin. Industries were bombed into rubble. Agriculture was in disarray. Russian military forces controlled Eastern Europe and a divided Germany. A devastated Western Europe needed to be rebuilt in America's best interests. The Marshall Plan of assistance was the mechanism by which this would be done. American tax dollars would back the plan. Much of the money would be spent in the US for machinery and raw materials across the Atlantic. Agricultural products, the bounty of America's farmers, were shipped to a war-torn Europe. Domestic products marked USA offloaded in British and European ports. American planners understood that a vibrant, robust Western Europe was the best bulwark against Soviet expansion westward. They also recognized that America needed a prosperous Europe to purchase the country's exports. In the Marshall Plan, America merged altruism, vital interests, and pragmatism to heal a weary continent in the first days of what would be called the Cold War. To a degree, this also happened in the Far East. A peaceful, democratic, and rebuilt economy was in America's best interests, whether in Japan or Europe. Named after General George C. Marshall, the effort would distribute 12,4 billion dollars in aid from 1948 to 1952 by the Truman Administration.

As to the question… Did the New Deal end the Great Depression? No. It did, however, help the nation through it. Did a global war end the economic collapse? Yes, as a wartime economy. Did the New Dealers and a world war create the conditions by which a post-war, consumer-based economy could be built and sustained? The answer seems a qualified yes. The chart below supports this conclusion.

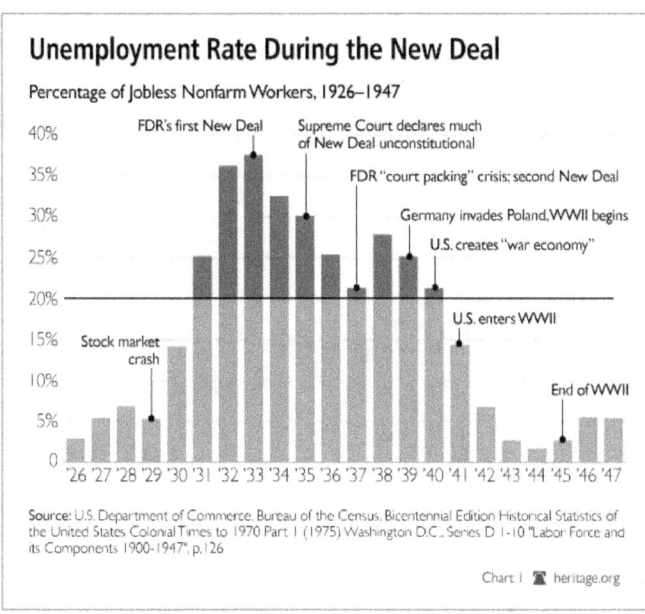

Unemployment Rate During the New Deal

Percentage of Jobless Nonfarm Workers, 1926–1947

FDR's first New Deal

Supreme Court declares much of New Deal unconstitutional

FDR "court packing" crisis; second New Deal

Germany invades Poland, WWII begins

U.S. creates "war economy"

U.S. enters WWII

Stock market crash

End of WWII

'26 '27 '28 '29 '30 '31 '32 '33 '34 '35 '36 '37 '38 '39 '40 '41 '42 '43 '44 '45 '46 '47

Source: U.S. Department of Commerce, Bureau of the Census, Bicentennial Edition Historical Statistics of the United States Colonial Times to 1970 Part 1 (1975) Washington D.C., Series D 1-10 "Labor Force and its Components 1900-1947", p.126

Chart 1 | heritage.org

Untouched by bombing raids and tanks crashing through her streets, the country was physically almost immune to the horrors of devastated Europe and Asia. It would end the war as the world's most productive and wealthiest economy. The country was on the brink of a self-sustaining, consumer-driven economy far exceeding even the most expansive goals of the New Dealers.

CHAPTER 43 – MARIAN

On Easter Sunday, April 9, 1939, over 70,000 people gathered in the mall before the Lincoln Memorial on a chilly day. The clouds hung low, announcing it would be a blustery day for those in attendance and, of course, for the heralded singer they had come to hear. Included in the unsegregated audience were two Supreme Court Justices, three members of the Roosevelt cabinet, and four senators. NBC would broadcast nationwide what they were about to hear.

A platform had been built on low-level steps in front of the memorial. The singer stood on the makeshift platform directly in front of the "great emancipator." Those who sat in front and stood could see the seated martyred president and the most famous American singer, Marian Anderson, at a glance.

MARIAN ANDERSON

Initially, she wanted to sing at the Constitutional Hall in Washington, D.C. The Daughters of the American Revolution (DAR) owned the building. The governing board of the DAR denied Anderson's wish to use the facility. Sarah Corbin Robert made the announcement. The most famous singer on two continents would have to find another venue. This had nothing to do with her artistic skills or political views. The DAR had a white-only policy, and Anderson was a Black woman. She wasn't allowed to use Constitutional Hall because there was a white-artist only clause printed in every contract issued by the DAR. Only white entertainers could appear on their stage, very much like the capital's Constitutional Hall, where Black audiences were segregated to a small section of the balcony away from whites. Washington, D.C., was a Jim Crow city, though also the heart of the American experiment in democracy. Those in attendance were aware of this curious paradox. In public accommodations such as schools and parks, segregation ruled, as it did unofficially with housing. Only in Black theaters was there a degree of integration. The statues of Jefferson, Madison, and Washington hovered over a city deeply entrenched in the notion of "separate but equal." The town lacked "home rule." The local government was still controlled by the US, under the sway of Southern politicians.

There was immediate pushback against the DAR. The most formidable critique came from Eleanor Roosevelt. Outraged by what took place, the president's wife issued a scathing statement of resignation from the DAR. She did so in her weekly newspaper column, *My Day*, which was read by millions:

They have taken this action, which has been widely criticized in the press. To remain as a member implies approval of that action, and therefore I am resigning. I am in complete disagreement with the attitude taken in refusing Constitutional Hall to a great artist… You had an opportunity to lead in an enlightened way and it seems to me that your organization has failed.

In a forceful letter to the DAR the First Lady stated her view.

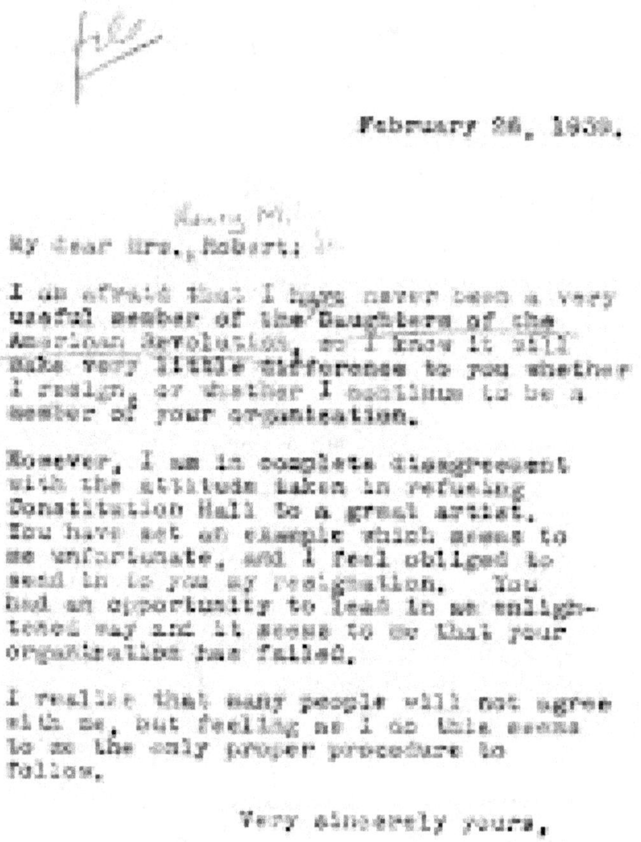

February 26, 1939.

My dear Mrs. Robert:

I am afraid that I have never been a very
useful member of the Daughters of the
American Revolution, so I know it will
make very little difference to you whether
I resign, or whether I continue to be a
member of your organization.

However, I am in complete disagreement
with the attitude taken in refusing
Constitution Hall to a great artist.
You have set an example which seems to
me unfortunate, and I feel obliged to
send in to you my resignation. You
had an opportunity to lead in an enlightened way and it seems to me that your
organization has failed.

I realize that many people will not agree
with me, but feeling as I do this seems
to me the only proper procedure to
follow.

Very sincerely yours,

The *Philadelphia Tribune* had a harsh review of the DAR. It stated:

A group of tottering old ladies, who don't know the difference between patriotism and putridism, have compelled the gracious First Lady to apologize for their national rudeness.

The *Richmond Times-Dispatch* wrote:

In these days of racial intolerance so crudely expressed in the Third Reich, an action such as the DAR's ban... seems all the more deplorable.

THE TWO FIRST LADIES

The Lincoln Memorial was chosen because of its unusual history. The memorial was dedicated on May 30, 1922, during the presidency of Warren G. Harding. On a blazing hot day, many gathered for the ceremony. Those Blacks invited for the dedication found themselves roped off from whites. Shelby Davidson, the president of the Washington D.C. NAACP, wrote that:

Platform seats reserved for whites were in chairs and within distance of the speakers that might be called reasonably, considering the crowd, while back of those seats were those reserved for colored, roped off from those occupied by whites, and placed about a block away from the Memorial in the grass and weeds with rough-hewn benches with no backs or supports.

At the dedication, Dr. Robert Russa Moton was asked to speak. He was the principal of Tuskegee Institute in Alabama. As a Black man, he was considered a "safe speaker" who would emphasize Lincoln's legacy without advocating for the end of "separate but equal." In speaking on behalf of American Blacks, he said:

Today, in this inspiring presence, is raised a symbol of gratitude for all who are blest by the sacrifice (Lincoln's death). But in all our vast country there are none more reverent that the 12,000,000 black Americans who, with their fellow countrymen of every race, pay devout homage to him who was for them, more truly than for any group, the author of their freedom. There is no question that Abraham Lincoln died to save the Union. The calm and greatness of Abraham Lincoln lies in this, that amid doubt and distrust, against the counsel of chosen advisers, in the hour of the Nation's utter peril, he put his trust in God and spoke the word that gave freedom to a race and vindicated the honor of a Nation conceived in liberty and dedicated to the proposition that all men are created equal.

He went on to say in his closing words:

Twelve million black Americans share in the rejoicing this day. As yet, no other name so warms the heart or stirs the depths of their gratitude as that of Abraham Lincoln. To him above all others we owe the privilege of sharing as fellow citizens in the consecration of this spot and the dedication of this shrine. In the name of Lincoln 12,000,000 black Americans pledge to the Nation their continued loyalty and their unreserved cooperation in every effort to realize in deeds the lofty principles established by his martyrdom.

ROBERT MOTON AT THE SHRINE

Before giving his speech, Moton received a Western Union Telegram from William H. Taft. It was dated May 23, 1922, only a week before the dedication. Though respectful and considerate, the note was also a directive to avoid specific subjects in the name of national harmony. All that was a polite way of saying Moton's remarks were open to scrutiny and censorship. Moton understood the implied message. You may speak, but only within certain limits. The telegram stated:

Shall have to ask you to cut five hundred words, and suggest that in making the cut, you give more unity and symmetry by emphasizing tribute and lessening appeal. I am sure you wish to avoid any insinuation of an attempt to make the occasion one for propaganda. Our personal relations make me feel that you will understand my motive in the suggestion.

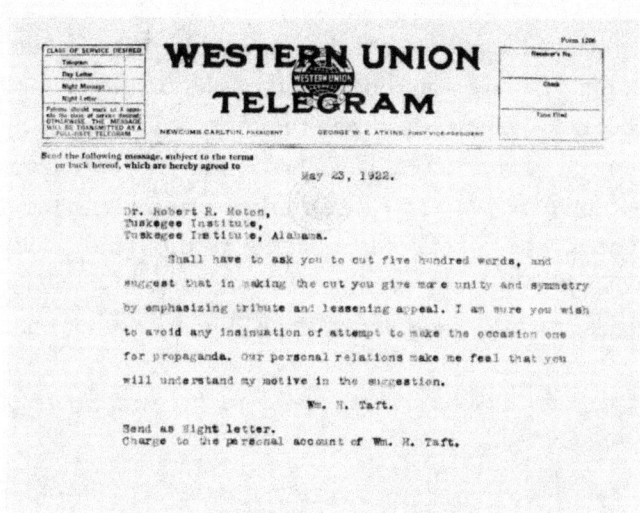

As to the Lincoln Memorial... Sol Hurok was Marian Anderson's personal secretary. He met with Harold I. Ickes, the Secretary of the Interior. Apparently, they discussed the DAR situation and the need for a venue. Hurok pointed out that the Washington, D.C. Board of Education refused Anderson. What could be done? Out of this meeting, a suggestion was made. An open-air concert on the steps of the Lincoln Memorial. It would be open to everyone.

Harold Ickes introduced Marian Anderson to the assembled crowd on that fabled Easter Sunday. He said to the desegregated crowd, which stretched all the way from the Lincoln Memorial to the Washington Monument:

In this great auditorium under the sky, all of us are free. Genius, like justice, is blind. Genius draws no color lines.

As Ices spoke, an announcer for the NBC Blue Network stated the obvious to millions of radio listeners.

Marian Anderson is singing this public concert at the Lincoln Memorial because she was unable to get an auditorium to accommodate the trenmendous audicence that wishes to hear her.

As millions listened on the radio, Marian Anderson began to sing. As one reporter said, 'She closed her eyes. Her voice poured out, soft, vast, and enveloping." As fate would have it, the sun burst forth for a moment. Whatever her nervousness, she began the concert with a stirring rendition of My Country, 'Tis *of Thee*. Her choice was a deeply patriotic song, sometimes known as *America*. Alone on the platform with her pianist and under the gaze of the fallen president and with thousands looking on, she sang, her voice forceful and sweet, a rich contralto. Many who heard her, whether Black or white, wept. Later, she would say of that opening song:

I could not run away from this situation. If I had anything to offer, I would have to do it now.

And so she sang ...

As she sang, a few in the audience noticed a tiny change in the lyrics; that was on the third line: instead of singing "of thee I sing," she sang "to thee we sing." This was a small change with significant meaning. Her change turned the singular into the plural and united in her mind all Americans, Black and white.

My country, 'tis of Thee,	*My country, 'tis of Thee*
Sweet Land of Liberty	*Sweet Land of Liberty*
Of thee I sing;	**To thee we sing;**
Land where my fathers died,	

Land of the pilgrims' pride,
From every mountain side
  Let freedom ring.
My native country, thee,
Land of the noble free,
  Thy name I love;
I love they rocks and rills,
The woods and templed hills,
My heart with rapture thrills,
  Like that above.

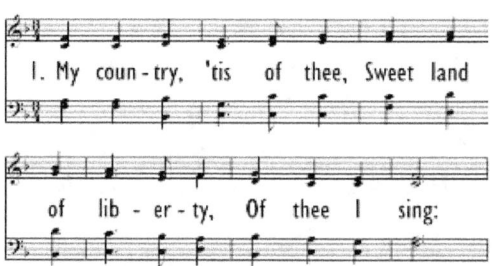

As to why she made the change…

We cannot live alone. And the thing that made this moment possible for you and for me, has been brought about by many people whom we will never know.

We implied community and embraced group responsibility. Though she was never a civil rights activist, she believed prejudice would disappear if she performed and behaved with dignity. Thus, the we…

Later, she would say of the "we" change and of her singing:

When I sing, I don't wasn't them to see that my face is black. I don't want them to see that my face is white. I want them to see my soul. And that is colorless.

A few years later, Anderson received a public apology from the DAR:

The National Daughters of the American Revolution deeply regret it did not give Marian Anderson the opportunity to perform her 1939 Easter Concert at Constitutional Hall, but today we join all Americans in grateful recognition that her historic performance on the steps of the Lincoln Memorial was a pivotal point in the struggle for racial equality. Ms. Anderson's legendary concet will always be remembered as a milestone in the Civil Rights movement. The beauty of her voice, amplfied by her courage and grace, brought attention to the eloquence of the many voices urging our nation to overcome prejudice and intolerace. It sparked change not just in the DAR but in all of America.

The apology closed by saying:

The Daughters of the American Revolution celebrates the life, the talent, and the legacy of Marian Anderson. America is a better place because of her dreams and her sacrifices. As a nation, we can be grateful that she opened so many doors for those who follow, and, as an organization, the DAR is genuinely pleased to tribute to her...

THE BEAUTIFUL VOICE

The *New York Times* recounted the event (see next page). What was written was almost poetic, inspiring, and a permanent footnote in the nation's effort to treat all citizens with dignity and respect. In that sense, it reflected the vision of the New Deal to move beyond the Great Depression and the legacy of "Jumping Jim Crow." That effort continues to this day.

FDR

Marian Anderson Sings for 75,000 at Lincoln Memorial

WASHINGTON, April 10 (UP).—Marian Anderson, Negro contralto who was barred from two Washington auditoriums because of her race, sang to more than 75,000 persons yesterday in a free, open-air concert beneath the statue of Abraham Lincoln. The halls from which she was barred seat 4000 and 1000 persons.

The throng jammed the mall between the shrine of the Great Emancipator and the Washington Monument. It was broadcast to millions of others. No broadcast had been planned for the concert canceled when she was unable to get a hall.

Miss Anderson almost wept when she thanked the audience for its applause. She had been introduced by Secretary of Interior Harold L. Ickes, who arranged the concert on the steps of the Lincoln Memorial after the Daughters of the American Revolution and the city School Board had refused to let her hire their auditoriums.

All Are Free

"In this great auditorium under the sky, all of us are free," Ickes said. "When God gave us this wonderful outdoors and the sun, the moon and the stars, he made no distinction of race or creed or color . . ."

Ickes, apparently referring to the DAR and the School Board, said that "there are those, even in this great capital of our democratic republic, who are either too timid or too indifferent" to follow the principles of racial tolerance of Lincoln and Thomas Jefferson."

Miss Anderson was greeted by Associate Justice Hugo Black of the Supreme Court, Senate Majority Leader Alben W. Barkley, D., Ky., Secretary of the Treasury Henry Morgenthau, Assistant Secretary of the Interior Oscar L. Chapman, Sens. Robert Wagner, D., N. Y.; Arthur Capper, R., Kan.; Joseph Guffy, D., Pa.; and Robert Taft, R., Ohio, and many congressmen. Chief Justice Charles Evans Hughes and Mrs. Franklin D. Roosevelt had been among her sponsors but they were not present.

She sang "America," an operatic aria, and a group of Negro spirituals, including "Nobody Knows the Trouble I've Seen."

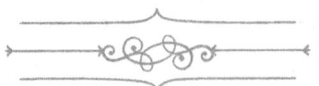

CHAPTER 44 – JUDGMENT

How should we judge FDR and the New Deal regarding their impact on Blacks in America? The question should be approached with caution. It is important to note what an earlier Roosevelt said:

We must remember not to judge any pubic servant by any one act, and especially should we beware of attacking the men who are merely the occasions and not the cause of disaster.

President Theodore Roosevelt

FDR had ambitious goals. Deal with the Great Depression and reconstruct the American economy. In doing this, he had many supporters. It is also true that he had many political enemies. On the left, he was attacked by liberals and radicals for not "providing enough relief and for maintaining the capitalistic system." On the right, conservatives claimed his policies were "socialism in disguise, and that an interfering activist government was destroying a proud history of self-reliance." Ultimately, the New Dealers tempered their most progressive positions in line with the president's understanding of prevailing public attitudes. That meant compromise and a center-left position. In doing so, the White House practiced the "art of the possible." That meant preserving the free-market system. There would be no nationalization of industry. The Social Security System's safety net "paled by comparison with European countries." The Roosevelt Administration helped the nation muddle through a horrendous economic period.

As to race… At the extremes, two possibilities clamor for our attention. First, there is the view that the New Deal treated all Americans justly and fairly. That was, of course, not the case. The second view is diametrically different. The New Deal consciously implemented patently racist policies. Again, that does not seem to be true. Between these extreme positions is a theme, possibly closer to the truth. The New Deal policies often fell short of promoting genuine racial equality and civil rights for all citizens. This position explains both the aspirations of the New Dealers and the limitations they faced in a society resistant to changes in race relations. Most Americans in the 1930s opposed desegregation in public education, housing, and the workplace.

We should recall what the Roosevelt Administration was up against in three words: The Great Depression. As has been shown, it is far too simplistic to view the stock market crash as the cause of the worst economic calamity in American history. A healthy economy should have handled the contraction in the business cycle. That, as it turned out, was not the case. There were too many long-term underlying causes that exacerbated the situation. Record corporate profits had led to overexpansion and a glut of goods in the marketplace. Wages did not keep up with this increasingly large surplus. Consumers couldn't continue to fuel further expansion, nor could they consume what was being produced. The frenzy on Wall Street propelled a widening distribution of wealth. The wealthiest one percent of Americans owned over a third of all American assets—this concentration of wealth limited economic growth. The rich could only consume so much. The middle class, by comparison, was stretched to the limit and was deeply in debt. Purchasing automobiles and household appliances had contributed to that situation. The nation's banks operated without the FDIC. This created a climate of panic when the industry faltered due to loans used for stock market speculation and other risky ventures. In rural America, farmers were harassed by surpluses and low prices, leading to foreclosures and evictions from the land. Additionally, the high tariff restricted exports and contributed to the economic slide.

The Roosevelt Administration had to contend with these realities, manifested most blatantly by the granite wall of the Solid South, whatever his personal feelings concerning Blacks. President Roosevelt needed Congressional support for his programs, and the votes of millions when running for reelection. That meant he had to practice the oldest rule of American politics, "the art of the possible." He had to compromise. At the margins, he could do what was possible. As perceived by Blacks, that, of course, was always too little.

The Social Security Act initially excluded domestic workers, tenant farmers, and sharecroppers. Exclusionary policies appeared again with the Tennessee Valley Authority and the Agricultural Act when federal payments were paid to landowners for land taken out of production, but not to Blacks who worked the land. While the Wagner Act encouraged the rise of unions, it did not require such organizations to be integrated. The drafting of Blacks into the military services did not end racism in the ranks. Always, it seemed, there was an "exception" when it came to Blacks and equality of treatment. And then there was the ongoing question of lynching. The president's position was the result of a careful political calculation.

If I came out for the anti-lynching bill now, they would block every bill I ask Congress to pass to keep America from collapsing. I just can't take that risk.

The New Dealers faced America's entrenched racial order, the result of at least 200 years of white dominance on the North American continent. They were not able to overcome this reality. In an aspirational sense, they could only deal with it at the margins, incrementally only doing what was possible.

Though the Roosevelt Administration attempted to provide equal pay through relief programs and a minimum wage, it always ran into the "exception rule." As one supporter of the Southern wage prejudice position stated:

In view of the cheaper living conditions among the Negroes, they are done no injustice by such differentials. Comparatively they can receive the same improvement in conditions by a small wage increase that a significant increase would bring to white labor.

The New Deal catered to the majority white population. There was no question about that. However, that didn't mean Blacks wouldn't benefit from what the New Dealers wrought. One historian put it this way:

Blacks were not the intended citizens for these programs, but they did benefit from them, such as labor laws that encouraged unions and defined minimum wages and safety factors on the job.

Roosevelt's reluctance to speak out against lynching, the poll tax, and the oppression of Blacks in the South colored his time in office before World War II. Paradoxically, the war provided the circumstances permitting the president to speak out more forcibly about race. Executive Order 8802 was issued in June 1941. It stated that:

The federal government would not discriminate against any worker regardless of race, color, creed, or national origin in the federal government or defense-related administration.

That position was tested in January 1942. The captain of a US merchant ship refused to take on 25 Black sailors. The president's immediate response was quick and unequivocal:

Questions of race, creed, and color have no place in determining who are to man our ships. The sole qualification for a worker in the maritime industry, as well as any other industry, should be his loyalty and his professional or technical ability and training.

Roosevelt expanded on this view, saying on a later date:

In some communities employers dislike to employ women... In others they are reluctant to hire Negroes. In still others, older men are not wanted. We can no longer afford to indulge such prejudices and practices.

Though President Roosevelt and his New Dealers were a motley group of diverse backgrounds and points of view, they were united in their rejection of laissez-faire orthodoxy concerning the Great Depression. The business cycle was not sacred, nor was the notion of some "invisible hand" self-correcting a depression. For the New Dealers. The government's responsibilities went far beyond a balanced budget and an aversion to deficit spending. The federal government was obligated to provide for a strong national defense. That was an accepted national responsibility, as was the need to provide a legal and financial structure in which the private sector could thrive. For the New Dealers, it was, however, the obligation of the elected officials to also rescue and reform the weakened economy and the onerous unemployment that stalked the land. In this, they were in the tradition of American progressive thinking. They were animated by a moral impulse to improve the lives of all Americans through government action. That included Blacks.

Again, the question: was the New Deal a "bad deal" for Blacks? Perhaps the question should be turned around. Was the New Deal as good as it might have been for Blacks? To a degree, Blacks in America answered the question at the polls. In 1928 they voted for Herbert Hoover and the Republican Party of Lincoln and emancipation. In response to the economic collapse in 1929, they began shifting to FDR in the 1932 presidential election. In 1936, the political shift was complete. Blacks overwhelmingly voted for the president in the election. This continued in 1940 and 1944, when FDR broke tradition and won two more terms. Why was there a revamping of political allegiance? Perhaps the simplest explanation is this. Despite its faults, the New Deal legislation did assist Blacks, providing them with greater opportunities than in the past, and a sense of hope for the future. In this, Blacks were kin with President Roosevelt as he spoke quietly to all Americans during one Fireside Chat:

The test of our progress is not whether we add more to the abundance of those who have much; it is whether we provide enough for those who have too little.

The Black sociologist and civil rights activist W.E.B. Du Bois stated the case for the realization of this goal, pointing out:

The American Negro has a longing to attain self-conscious manhood. He would not Africanize America, for America has too much to teach the world and Africa. He would not breach his Negro soul in a flood of white Americanism, for he knows that Negro blood has a message for the world. He simply wishes to make it possible for a man to be a Negro and an American, without being cursed and spit upon by his fellows, without having the Door of Opportunity closed roughly in his face.

FDR and the New Dealers encouraged that hope for all Americans, though this was always an elusive outcome of their efforts. Still, FDR and his administration did what was politically possible when America was challenged first by economic calamity, and then by a global war. As FDR often pointed out, the New Deal was more than "buildings and elected officials." It was aspirational in almost every sense. It sought to create a better America out of the economic chaos of the Great Depression and the sacrifices of World War II. That unceasing task challenges not only all presidents but also the public. As President Roosevelt said:

Let us never forget that government is ourselves and not an alien power over us. The ultimate rulers of a democracy are not President and the senators and congressmen and government officials, but the voters of the country.